West Point 1915

WEST POINT
1915
Eisenhower, Bradley, and the Class the Stars Fell On

MICHAEL E. HASKEW

ZENITH PRESS

First published in 2014 by Zenith press, an imprint of Quarto Publishing Group USA Inc.,
400 First Avenue North, Suite 400, Minneapolis, MN 55401 USA

The information in this book is true and complete to the best of our knowledge. All
recommendations are made without any guarantee on the part of the author or Publisher, who
also disclaims any liability incurred in connection with the use of this data or specific details.

We recognize, further, that some words, model names, and designations mentioned herein
are the property of the trademark holder. We use them for identification purposes only. This
is not an official publication.

Zenith Press titles are also available at discounts in bulk quantity for industrial or sales-
promotional use. For details write to Special Sales Manager at Quarto Publishing Group
USA Inc., 400 First Avenue North, Suite 400, Minneapolis, MN 55401 USA.

To find out more about our books, visit us online at www.zenithpress.com.

ISBN: 978-0-7603-4652-5

Library of Congress Cataloging-in-Publication Data

Haskew, Michael E.

  West Point 1915 : Eisenhower, Bradley, and the class the stars fell on / Michael Haskew.
    pages cm

  Includes bibliographical references and index.

  ISBN 978-0-7603-4652-5 (hbk.)

  1. United States Military Academy. Class of 1915--History. 2. United States Military Academy.
Class of 1915--Biography. 3. Generals--United States--Biography. 4. Eisenhower, Dwight D.
(Dwight David), 1890-1969. 5. Bradley, Omar Nelson, 1893-1981. 6. United States. Army--
Officers--Biography. I. Title. II. Title: Eisenhower, Bradley, and the class the stars fell on.

  U410.N11915 .H47 2014

  355.0092'273--dc23

                            2014020177

Acquisitions Editor: Elizabeth Demers   Design Manager: James Kegley
Project Manager: Madeleine Vasaly   Layout: Helena Shimizu

On the front cover: The cadets of the class of 1915 pose on the steps of Christ Lutheran
Church on May 3, 1915, in a photograph by William H. Tipton.

On the frontis: The West Point Cadet Chapel, designed by architectural firm Cram,
Goodhue, and Ferguson. *Library of Congress*

Printed in the United States of America

10 9 8 7 6 5 4 3 2 1

Dedication

To my wife, Elena, an inspiration for more than thirty years

Contents

ACKNOWLEDGMENTS

When I initially proposed the idea for this book, the enthusiasm for it was overwhelming. It has become a reality because of the encouragement, assistance, and continuing support of a number of people. These include my editor, Elizabeth Demers, and the editorial and production groups of Quarto Publishing Group, who have done outstanding work. Thanks to Marilee Meyer of the West Point Association of Graduates; Suzanne Christoff; Casey Madrick; Elaine McConnell and Laura Mosher of the United States Military Academy Library; Paul Barron and Cara Sonnier of the George C. Marshall Foundation; Samantha Kenner and Kathy Struss of the Dwight D. Eisenhower Presidential Library and Museum; Susan Bonser of the Gettysburg Foundation; and Sandra Hornung of the Cameron County, Pennsylvania, Historical Society for research assistance. For their unflagging enthusiasm, heartfelt thanks to dear friends and colleagues Roy Morris Jr., Flint Whitlock, B. Paul Hatcher, Richard Lee, Butch Lunsford, Al Hoke, and Rod and Diane Adams. Special thanks to Maj. Gen. William B. Raines Jr., US Army (ret.), West Point Class of 1968, and Lt. Col. Sherman L. Fleek, US Army (ret.), United States Military Academy Command Historian, for their assistance, and to Greg Henry for technical contributions. Finally, thanks to my children, Amanda, Adam, and Allie, for believing in their dad and to Emmett, Winston, and Matilda, the best four-legged friends a man could have.

Michael E. Haskew
Chattanooga, Tennessee May 2014

INTRODUCTION

The content of the handwritten note was almost too terrible to contemplate. Just hours earlier, Gen. Dwight D. Eisenhower, supreme commander of the Allied Expeditionary Force, had set in motion Operation Overlord, the invasion of Nazi-occupied Europe. Victory in World War II hung in the balance.

Meant for release to the public only in the event of failure, the note read: "Our landings in the Cherbourg-Havre area have failed to gain a satisfactory foothold and I have withdrawn the troops. My decision to attack at this time and place was based upon the best information available. The troops, the Air and the Navy did all that bravery and devotion to duty could do. If any blame or fault attaches to the attempt it is mine alone."

On the morning of June 6, 1944, more than 150,000 men, five thousand ships, and eight thousand aircraft were committed to the invasion of Western Europe. However, the decision to commence the largest amphibious operation in military history lay squarely on the shoulders of one man. In the most favorable circumstances, the responsibility for sending thousands into harm's way was daunting. The present situation was anything but ideal.

For Dwight D. Eisenhower, preparation to shoulder the burden of command had begun more than thirty years earlier on the plain at West Point. A graduate of the class of 1915, he went on to serve two terms as president of the United States, carrying with him the lessons and experiences of four years as a cadet.

Although Eisenhower is indeed the most celebrated of the 164 young officers who graduated from West Point in June 1915, he was, in fact, one of fifty-nine who reached the rank of brigadier general or higher—the most in any West Point graduating class. The group has become known as the "Class the Stars Fell On."

Classmate Omar N. Bradley was present during the preparations for Operation Overlord and during the arduous trek toward victory in Europe. Bradley initially commanded the 82nd and 28th Infantry Divisions, followed by II Corps, First Army during the Normandy campaign, and eventually 12th Army Group during the Allied drive into Germany. Bradley gained fame by leading more than 1.2 million troops in combat, more than any other American general in history. His care and concern for the common soldier led to his nickname, "the GI's General."

Still other members of the class of 1915 are worthy of much more than relegating their stories to the darkened recesses of history. Their contributions to the military, sacrifices on the battlefield, forays into business and industry, and development of the modern infrastructure of the United States are significant.

Eisenhower and Bradley achieved five-star General of the Army rank. Two graduates of the West Point class of 1915 reached four-star general rank. James Van Fleet was wounded in France during World War I, led the 4th and 90th Infantry Divisions and III Corps in World War II, and later commanded the US Eighth Army during the Korean War. General Joseph T. McNarney was responsible for the reorganization of the US Army command structure in the 1930s under Chief of Staff Gen. George C. Marshall, served on the Roberts Commission that investigated the preparedness of commanders in Hawaii prior to the Pearl Harbor attack, and served as military governor of occupied Germany after World War II.

Other senior World War II–era leaders from the class of 1915 included Lt. Gen. George Stratemeyer, elevated to command the US Army Air Forces in the China-Burma-India Theater in 1943; Lt. Gen. Hubert Harmon, who commanded the Sixth and 13th Air Forces, led the effort to establish the US Air Force Academy and served as its first superintendent; and Lt. Gen. Henry Aurand, who served as director of Defense Aid, sending Lend-Lease war materiel to Great Britain and the Soviet Union.

Lieutenant General John W. Leonard commanded the 9th Armored Division during its drive into Germany and the capture of the bridge across the Rhine River at Remagen, while Lt. Gen. Stafford Irwin led the 5th Infantry Division in Western Europe. Lieutenant General Joseph Swing commanded the 11th Airborne Division during operations in the Philippines, Maj. Gen. Charles W. Ryder commanded the 34th Division in North Africa and Italy, and Maj. Gen. Leland Hobbs led the 30th Infantry Division in Normandy.

Major General Luis R. Esteves was born in Aguadilla, Puerto Rico, the son of a former Spanish army officer and a mother of German and Dutch descent. Esteves graduated 97th in the class of 1915 but was nearly barred from receiving his commission in the US Army. At the time, the people of Puerto Rico were not US citizens. Therefore, it was believed that Esteves was ineligible for a commission in the Regular Army. However, he did receive his second lieutenant's bars following research by the US War Department that revealed the commissioning of several foreign-born individuals during the Revolutionary War, including the Marquis de Lafayette and Baron von Steuben.

Esteves tutored Eisenhower in Spanish because ability in a second language was required of all cadets at West Point. He was the first Puerto Rican graduate of the US Military Academy and is remembered today as the father of the Puerto Rican National Guard. Two years after his graduation, Congress passed the Jones Act, granting US citizenship to all Puerto Ricans.

Major General John Bragdon graduated fifth in the class and served as assistant chief of Military Construction and deputy chief of engineers for the army before returning to civilian life as a construction engineer and executive. He accepted the position as special advisor for public works planning to President Eisenhower and later served as a member of the Civil Aeronautics Board. One of his major contributions was the implementation of the Federal Aid Highway Act of 1956, which facilitated the construction of the US interstate highway system.

Perhaps the member of the class of 1915 with the greatest name recognition at the time of graduation was Louis A. Merillat Jr., an All-American football player for West Point's Army Black Knights in both 1913 and 1914. Merillat graduated ninety-third and reached the rank of major during World War I. He was severely wounded during an air attack at Avocourt, France, on October 5, 1918, but he returned to play a season in 1925 with the Canton Bulldogs of the National Football League.

Merillat also became something of a soldier of fortune, joining the French Foreign Legion before training units of the Chinese army and then working with the Iranian military. When World War II broke out, he returned to the United States, reenlisted in the army, and commanded its installations in Miami Beach, Florida, with the rank of colonel.

During World War I, a number of young officers from the class of 1915 served in France. Four received the Distinguished Service Cross and several the French Croix de Guerre with Palm for heroism. Van Fleet received two Silver Stars. By 1920, a total of eleven classmates had died, two of whom were killed in action during the war. Twelve had resigned their commissions or retired. Two had been disabled as a result of service.

On June 10, 1940, only eighteen months prior to US entry into World War II, fifty-eight members of the class gathered at West Point for their twenty-fifth reunion. After a quarter century, twenty-three members had died, while thirty-two had resigned or been discharged. Many of those who remained were destined to play key roles in the global conflict.

On June 5, 1944, the weather in Western Europe was atrocious, the worst for the English Channel in early June in half a century. High winds, rough seas, and heavy rains had already necessitated a postponement of the invasion for twenty-four hours. A second delay was anathema. At 4:15 a.m., Eisenhower gathered his subordinate commanders. A window of opportunity—thirty-six hours of decent, but far from perfect, weather—would allow just enough time. The senior commander flashed his characteristic grin and said, "OK, we'll go."

The hastily scrawled note was later tucked away, unneeded and nearly forgotten. Sometime afterward, Eisenhower presented it to a junior officer as a keepsake.

While it may be true that the advent of World War II provided a catalyst for promotion, recognition, and senior command, it must also be acknowledged that many of the young officers of the class of 1915 rose to the occasion time after time and became the mature, battle-hardened war leaders of 1945 and beyond. Eisenhower's own rise to senior military command was remarkably swift, primarily due to his ability to forge cooperative efforts among groups of officers with varied backgrounds. It was a skill that would serve him well as a leader in coalition warfare.

Eisenhower assumed the role of supreme Allied commander in January 1944. Only two years earlier, he had been a relatively unknown lieutenant colonel serving as chief of staff to Lt. Gen. Walter Krueger and the Third Army. In a photo with Krueger and other members of his staff, he was identified as "Lt. Col. D.D. Ersenbeing."

During their West Point days, the future supreme Allied commander had also seen the potential for greatness in others. Writing the commentary for Bradley's entry in the 1915 *Howitzer*, the Academy yearbook, he noted that Bradley's most prominent characteristic was "getting there," and continued, "if he keeps up the clip he's started, some of us will some day be bragging to our grandchildren that 'sure, General Bradley was a classmate of mine.'"

After World War II, Bradley became the second member of the class of 1915 to achieve five-star General of the Army rank and headed the Veterans Administration (VA). He served as chief of staff of the US Army from 1948 to 1949 and then as the first chairman of the Joint Chiefs of Staff from 1949 to 1953. When Bradley died in 1981, *Time* magazine noted that in 1943 he had been a fifty-year-old career soldier who had never seen combat. However, that situation changed rapidly and he became "a tireless infantry leader who seemed to be everywhere at once. Dressed in a grimy old trench coat, his fatigues stuffed into his boots . . ."

Bradley once addressed a group of soldiers training for D-Day and said to them, in his plain-spoken Missouri monotone, "Fellows like me have been in this a long time, and you know we wouldn't be arranging this unless we were fairly sure it would work."

The prominent roles played by Eisenhower and Bradley in the course of modern events are well documented. However, the comprehensive service record of the West Point class of 1915 is unsurpassed in American history. The magnitude of its collective contribution to victory during World War II, the shaping of the postwar world, and the making of modern America is virtually immeasurable. Its stories are heroic and tragic, familiar and obscure, while offering glimpses of the lives of a generation of military and civilian leaders.

The "Class the Stars Fell On" is remarkable not only because of its moment in history, but also because of its intensely human experience.

PART I

From the Mountains to the Prairies

CHAPTER ONE

Cross-Section of America

The West Shore Railroad special chugged along the banks of the Hudson River. The run from Weehawken, New Jersey, through New York City and Albany, and finally west to Buffalo, was routine. This morning, however, the train was scheduled to stop at West Point, where many of its passengers would gather up their belongings and step off the train into a new life.

In June 1911, the United States Military Academy was in its 109th year. For more than a century, young men had come there to learn the arts of military command and bearing. The curriculum consisted of such courses as civil and military engineering, ordnance and science of gunnery, law, Spanish, drill regulations (Hippology), natural and experimental philosophy, chemistry-mineralogy-geology, drawing, and drill regulations (cavalry and artillery).

The academic experience at the Academy had changed little since Sylvanus Thayer, a career US Army officer who served as superintendent from 1817 to 1833 and came to be known as the "Father of West Point," had emphasized engineering and thus elevated the institution to one of the foremost colleges for that discipline in America. Steeped in tradition, West Point had produced officers for the US Army since 1802, when its first class, consisting of two young lieutenants, had graduated. It had endured a horrific civil war that had ended less than half a century earlier as its progeny held the highest of command responsibilities in both the Union and Confederate armies. It had borne the ebb and flow of financial shortfall, the wax and wane of political indifference, and the decline of its rudimentary facilities.

Still, West Point maintained a command presence as imposing as its spit and polish graduates. Its stern, gray edifice was a fortress guarding tradition and seemed to whisper the motto of "Duty, Honor, Country" that would be ingrained in the psyche of every second lieutenant who left its hallowed grounds with a commission in the United States Army.

Although the sun was not yet full in the sky, the heat weighed on the shoulders of the young men who spilled from the train onto the platform, milling around. They sized up one another, they stared at the dark Gothic fortress that crowned a nearby hill, and then they began the dusty walk up the steep dirt road toward the top of that hill and the wide plain that featured a spectacular view of the Hudson River Valley below.

The young men of the West Point class of 1915 left their civilian lives along that road. Few if any of these men, most of them in their late teens, grasped the magnitude of the journey they were beginning. By the time all 287 of them arrived, they were the largest plebe class to have entered the Academy. By graduation, their ranks had thinned to 164, the largest number of graduates in Academy history up to that point. The attrition rate of more than 40 percent is mute testimony to the rigors of life at West Point.

Among those who persevered, stood the tests, and reached graduation day in 1915 were soldiers whose careers would shape the military and political future of the United States and indeed the world for more than half a century. It included soldiers who would die young and soldiers who would leave varied legacies for better or worse. These were the soldiers of the Class the Stars Fell On. Fifty-nine of those who received commissions on June 12, 1915, would earn at least the rank of brigadier general, an unprecedented number in American history.

They came to West Point from forty-six states and territories, the Panama Canal Zone, and the Philippine Islands. They hailed from big cities, small towns, the mountains, and the prairies, each with their own motivation and heretofore limited perspective on the world. They were rich and poor, privileged, and working class.

One of the prospective plebes trudging up the hill that day was Dwight David Eisenhower of Abilene, Kansas. Taller than most of the others, and slightly older at twenty, the thoughtful new cadet had been lured eastward by a free education, paid for by the American taxpayer. He learned soon enough that that education was anything but free.

Muscular, with light blond hair and blue eyes, Dwight was born the third of seven sons on October 14, 1890, in Denison, Texas, to David and Ida Eisenhower. His father had moved the family south from Dickinson County, Kansas, to take a job cleaning locomotives for the Cotton Belt Railroad. With their roots in Pennsylvania, the Eisenhowers had come to the prairie in the 1870s in search of cheap farmland. Before Dwight's second birthday, the family returned to Abilene, Kansas, where David went to work at the Belle Springs Creamery.

As Dwight grew up in Abilene, he was fascinated by stories of the city's history. Only a few decades earlier, the town that had sprung to life along the Chisholm Trail bustled with the cattle drives, saloons, and bravado of the Old West. The boy's imagination conjured images of cowboys, lawmen, and adventurers. It was to be a lifelong interest. He also developed into a fine football player.

The seven Eisenhower brothers managed to complete their high school educations, and Dwight worked for two years in the Belle Springs Creamery. The story goes that he flipped a coin with his brother Edgar, the winner heading to college and the loser holding on with a night engineer's position at the creamery and sending money to the other. Edgar set out for the University of Michigan.[1]

Dwight worked long hours at the creamery, and on occasion his friend Everett "Swede" Hazlett Jr., whose father owned a local gas lighting store, would stop by to play cards or pass time in conversation. Years later, Eisenhower acknowledged that it was Swede who first planted the seeds of a service academy education in his mind. The two cooked up an ambitious agenda. Both would apply to the US Naval Academy at Annapolis, Maryland; the US Military Academy at West Point, New York, would be a second option.

Hazlett secured his appointment to Annapolis and served with the US Navy until a heart attack cut his career short in 1939. Recalled to active duty during World War II, he taught at the Naval Academy and then supervised the naval reserve officers training program at the University of North Carolina. Eisenhower and Swede Hazlett maintained a lifelong friendship until Hazlett died of cancer in 1958.

For Dwight, the road to West Point was something of a test in itself. He wrote a letter to Congressman Roland R. Rees, who replied that he had no appointments available. Rees did advise that Dwight contact Senator Joseph L. Bristow, who was authorized to make one appointment to each academy for 1911. The enterprising young man from the wrong side of the Abilene tracks knew no people of political influence; however, he solicited the support of prominent citizens and the town newspaper editors, asking for letters of recommendation.[2]

Senator Bristow was slow to respond to a letter from Eisenhower written in August 1910. Two weeks later, the impatient young man from Abilene took up his pen again.

On September 3, 1910, Dwight wrote the senator in forthright, plain-spoken language:

> Dear Sir: sometime ago I wrote to you applying for an appointment to West Point or Annapolis. As yet, I have heard nothing definite from you about the matter, but I noticed in the daily papers that you would soon give a competitive examination for these appointments.
>
> Now, if you find it impossible to give me an appointment outright, to one of these places, would I have the right to enter this competitive examination?
>
> If so, will you please explain the conditions to be met in entering this examination, and the studies to be covered. Trusting to hear from you at your earliest convenience, I am, Respectfully yours, Dwight Eisenhower, Abilene, Kansas.[3]

Within the month, Eisenhower was sitting with seven other candidates in the Office of the Superintendent of Public Instruction in the state capital of Topeka, taking Senator Bristow's examination. When asked his preference, Dwight replied that either Annapolis or West Point would be acceptable—in effect, he thought, doubling his chances for an appointment. Weeks of hard work, burning the midnight oil at the creamery with the help of Swede Hazlett, brought results.

When the scores were tallied, only George Pulsifer Jr. (who received an at-large appointment to the class of 1915, was wounded in World War I, and achieved the rank of major), scored higher. Pulsifer, however, had specified his preference for West Point, elevating Eisenhower to the top of the Annapolis list and placing him second for West Point. Bristow asked a close advisor, Phil

Heath, to review all eight applications, and Heath placed Eisenhower ahead of Pulsifer for the West Point slot. Bristow chose not to appoint Eisenhower to Annapolis, naming him to the US Military Academy instead.

Eisenhower and Hazlett were disappointed that they would not be class-mates, but fortuitously Eisenhower was spared an even greater disappointment. Having turned twenty in October 1910, he was actually too old to gain admission to Annapolis. He was also required to submit a letter to Bristow certifying his age in years and months and the length of his residency in the state of Kansas.

Eisenhower replied to Bristow the day after receiving the senator's letter of appointment. On October 25, 1910, he wrote, "Your letter of the 24th instant has just been received. I wish to thank you sincerely for the favor you have shown me in appointing me to West Point.

"In regard to the information desired; I am just nineteen years and eleven days of age, and have been a resident of Abilene, Kans. for eighteen years. Thanking you again, I am very truly yours, Dwight Eisenhower."

Curiously, Eisenhower's twentieth birthday had passed eleven days earlier. In his August 1910 letter to Bristow, he had also stated that he would be "nineteen years of age this fall." This was either a second inadvertent misstatement of his age or a deliberate attempt to ensure that there would be no confusion as to his eligibility for admission to West Point.[4]

In January 1911, the four-day West Point entrance examination took place in St. Louis, Missouri, at Jefferson Barracks on the edge of the city. Eisenhower had never been so far from home. He took the train to St. Louis, decided to see the sights, and got lost. Well after dark on his first night in the city, he snuck back into his assigned lodging. His scores on the academic and physical examinations were good enough to place him in the middle of the group of Academy hopefuls. Five months later, he boarded the train in Abilene for the long trek to West Point, with a first stop in Kansas City and then a short visit with Edgar in Michigan before making the journey's final leg to the Academy.

When they reached the plateau above the train station, the new arrivals gained their first taste of military life. A long row of tables, each with a cadet behind it, stretched in front of the administration building. Stepping into the forming lines, each plebe was required to sign a form tersely stating that the individual agreed to serve eight years in the US Army from the date of his acceptance into the service. When asked whether or not they used tobacco, some cadets responded, "No, sir."

In 1903, just after the observance of the Academy's centennial, a program of renovation and construction had begun. The immense riding hall and heating plant were completed in 1909, and the Old Cadet Chapel, built in 1836, was dismantled and moved to the cemetery while a new chapel was being constructed. To the east, the unfinished academic building, with its rock-faced granite walls and limestone decoration, was rising a short distance from the cliffs.

The new arrivals had little time to take notice. In a well-choreographed and somewhat harrowing procession, they were hustled away to surrender their cash to the treasurer, as no cadet was allowed to carry currency. A cursory physical followed, and then the cadets were assigned to one of six hundred-man companies. The tallest went either to A or F Company, with the shorter cadets, or runts, in B, C, D, and E Companies. Companies A and F, known as flankers, marched on either end of the Cadet Corps formation. Classification by height maintained symmetry of uniforms and equipment in the ranks. Standing slightly taller than five feet ten inches, Eisenhower was in F Company.

From there, baggage went to storage—not to be seen again for nearly two summers, at which point the new cadets would first be eligible for leave. Some shuffled off to barracks that fronted a quadrangle, where they met their roommates for the first time and saw their new quarters.

Others double-timed to the barber shop for a regulation short haircut and then scrambled to the cadet store for their mattresses, sheets, and blankets. Then came the issue of uniforms, gray flannel trousers and tunics with assorted other garments.[5]

All the while, the upper classmen and yearlings—second-year cadets who had recently been on the receiving end of merciless hazing themselves—meted out loud orders along with liberal amounts of harassment. It was only the beginning. Since the 1850s, the hazing of new arrivals at West Point had risen to an art form. Tradition demanded that plebes endure the rigors of "Beast Barracks," a wave of hazing that stripped away any arrogance or overconfidence, and along with it any vestige of civilian consciousness that lingered. The new arrivals were "Beasts," referred to regularly as the "scum of the earth."

By 5:00 p.m. on that whirlwind first day, the Beasts assembled in their somewhat ragged ranks. They stood at attention on the parade ground as the Corps passed in review. The sight was daunting.

Then, they swore the oath of allegiance:

> I do solemnly swear that I will support the Constitution of the United States and bear true allegiance to the national government; that I will maintain and defend the sovereignty of the United States paramount to any and all allegiance, sovereignty, or fealty I may owe to any state, county or country whatsoever, and that I will at all times obey the legal orders of my superior officers and the rules and articles governing the armies of the United States.

Fourteen members of the class of 1915 were known as "Augustines." These young men had gained appointments to West Point during the late spring of 1911 and officially entered the Academy on August 1, fully six weeks behind those who had arrived in June. The Augustines had generally gained admission due to an act of the US Congress that changed the guidelines for appointments to the service academies. Previously, legislators had been allowed only one appointment to West Point every four years. The change provided for an appointment every three years.

Among these Augustines was eighteen-year-old Omar Nelson Bradley of Moberly, Missouri. Born February 12, 1893, on a farm in rural Clark County, Omar was the son of John Smith and Sarah Elizabeth Bradley. John worked as a schoolteacher, often walking several miles a day to and from home to teach in one-room schoolhouses around the town of Higbee, usually with his son in attendance. Omar, an excellent student, remembered his father as an outstanding marksman and hunter who taught him not only to love books and learning but also to appreciate the outdoors and sports—particularly baseball.

In January 1908, John Bradley died of pneumonia at the age of forty-one. Omar was a few days shy of his fifteenth birthday. Within months, his mother, known as Bessie, decided to relocate to Moberly, about fifteen miles from Higbee. Omar attended the local high school and delivered the newspaper, the *Moberly Democrat*, to earn a little money to supplement his mother's income as a seamstress along with the rent she received from taking in boarders.

After graduating from high school in the spring of 1910, Omar remained concerned for his mother's financial welfare. He worked for the Wabash

Railroad in the supply department and as a boiler repairman, hoping to save enough money during the course of a year to enroll at the University of Missouri in Columbia. He intended to continue working, finding another job in Columbia while pursuing a law degree. By the end of the year, however, his mother had remarried. The path to Columbia seemed wide open.

Abruptly, however, the young man's plan took a major detour.

During a conversation, John Cruson, the Sunday school superintendent at Central Christian Church, where the Bradleys worshipped, suggested that Omar seek an appointment to West Point instead. When Omar responded that he could not possibly afford such an educational opportunity, Cruson explained that the expenses were paid by the government.

"He put me straight," Bradley remembered years later. "He told me that not only was West Point free, but that the cadets were paid a small monthly salary while there. He went on to explain how one got an appointment through one's congressman, competing against other candidates."[6]

When Omar wrote to Congressman William M. Rucker requesting an appointment, he was informed that Rucker's only allowed appointee was then in his third year at West Point. If Bradley still wanted to seek an appointment, he would have to wait a year to compete for it. Then came the congressional action that allowed Rucker to fill an opening at the Military Academy for the autumn of 1911.

On June 27, Bradley received a letter from Congressman Rucker. It contained both the proverbial good news and bad news. The letter informed Omar that another appointment was indeed available. However, Congressman Rucker lived in Keytesville, Missouri, about thirty miles from Moberly, and his first choice for the appointment was a boy from Keytesville named Dempsey Anderson. If Bradley so chose, he could be the alternate appointee.

The entrance examinations for the August appointment were to be given during the first week of July at Jefferson Barracks on the outskirts of St. Louis. Omar would have only eight days to prepare. Nevertheless, he made the most of the time available, studying late into the night for a week after long days working in the Wabash Railroad boiler repair facilities.

Although he considered the opportunity a long shot, Bradley asked the Wabash Railroad for time off and a free train pass from Moberly to St. Louis. Somewhat surprised that he was granted both, he set off for Jefferson Barracks, met Dempsey Anderson, and learned that his direct competition was not only a year older but had been preparing for the examination for the previous year.

Seven months earlier, Dwight Eisenhower had come to Jefferson Barracks to compete for a coveted appointment. Now it was Bradley's turn. Although he considered mathematics his strong suit, Omar struggled mightily with the four-hour algebra section. In order for the test to even be counted, two-thirds of the questions had to be answered.

Despondent and with far fewer than the required number of questions completed, Bradley decided to turn in his test paper. As he approached the proctor, he noticed that the man was devoting his full attention to reading a book. Not wishing to disturb the officer, Omar returned to his seat and gave it another try, eventually completing enough of the examination to make it count.

"Then, almost magically, the theorems started to come to me. I fell to work eagerly," he remembered. "At the end of the four hours, I thought I had completed a bit more than the necessary 67 percent, but not by much."[7]

Heartened by his intellectual rally, Bradley stayed three more days and completed the battery of examinations. Still, he could not bring himself to believe that he stood a reasonable chance of entering West Point. When a telegram arrived on July 27, he was amazed to learn that the appointment was his and that he was to report to West Point before noon on August 1. Thinking some kind of error had occurred, he telephoned Dempsey Anderson, who confirmed that he had also received a telegram, informing the former favorite that he had failed the examinations.

Even after a congratulatory letter from Congressman Rucker arrived, Bradley offered to decline the appointment in favor of Anderson. However, Dempsey would have none of it and responded that the long shot from Moberly had won the appointment fair and square.

Meanwhile, time was growing short. Bradley hastily packed some personal belongings and clothing and shipped them to West Point in a steamer trunk. He carried a single change of clothes in a small suitcase as he hurried to the Moberly station on July 30, and he boarded the Wabash train bound for Highland Falls, New York. He spent the following night in the town's hotel before reporting as required to the gate of the US Military Academy.[8]

From the beginning, the Augustines, it seemed, were somewhat second class. They had missed the hell of Beast Barracks and the incessant hazing that the June entrants had experienced, and so they received their own rugged reception. Nevertheless, they made up for lost time as best they could. Their entry regimen was similar to that of their predecessors, filling out forms and rushing from one location to another. Bradley gave up the hundred dollars he had scraped together. At just under six feet tall, he was assigned to A Company.

Dwight Eisenhower and Omar Bradley had come to West Point from America's heartland in search of an education and possibly a career. In some ways, they were typical of the mainstream cadet population with its majority of white, Protestant descendants of European immigrants. Certainly their introduction to life at West Point was representative of the collective experience.

In other ways, they would eventually set themselves apart, becoming two of the greatest soldiers in American history, the products of humble upbringing, molded and shaped by the Spartan life of the Academy and the US Army, and then rising to the challenge of command and political leadership during two world wars and the uneasy peace of the Cold War. They became the most exceptional among a class of exceptional men.

However, in the summer of 1911 all of this lay in the future. As the class of 1915 began its journey, its ranks included individuals who reveled in the rigid, uncompromising, and cloistered life of West Point. Others merely accepted it, bearing up to its tremendous challenges and highest expectations. Still others fell away.

The specter of war loomed in Europe. Unrest and violence gripped neighboring Mexico and the southwest frontier of the United States. Four years at West Point would instill the highest qualities and refine the mettle of men who accepted the probability that they would face the sternest of tests. While some of their stories have been lost to time, others remain, still capable of stirring admiration.

CHAPTER TWO

Both Humble and Highly Placed

While it is true enough that the young men who came to West Point in the late spring of 1911 were from varied backgrounds, it is something of a stretch to assert that the Cadet Corps of the United States Military Academy and, in turn, the Officer Corps of the United States Army represented the true socioeconomic spectrum of America.

Demographically, the makeup of the Cadet Corps in the early years of the twentieth century was similar to that of the general officers of the army—predominantly white, Protestant, of upper-middle or upper class origin.[9] Although Henry Ossian Flipper, the first black West Point graduate, had received his commission in 1877, there were no black cadets when the class of 1915 arrived at West Point, no female cadets, few Hispanics, and a relative handful of Catholics. During Dwight Eisenhower's plebe year, there were three Jews, none of whom would graduate.[10]

Sixteen members of the class of 1915 were legacies, and three were third-generation graduates. Fathers and grandfathers, several of whom had held significant command responsibilities in the army and served during the Civil War, the Spanish-American War, and the Philippine Insurrection, had set high standards for the next generation. A number of these elder officers would reach their professional zenith during World War I while their sons were beginning their own careers as junior officers.

In contrast, Eisenhower had come to West Point to obtain a free college education and to play football. Omar Bradley had similar motivation. Regardless of why these young men had chosen West Point, pedigree seems to have had relatively little to do with their success or failure once there.

When James Alward Van Fleet arrived at West Point, he had traveled from rural Florida, a country boy who thrived in the outdoors, played football, and delivered the salutatory address at his high school graduation. Hunting, fishing, and the common chores of a subsistence household consumed his days. At nineteen, he was already hardened to the challenges of simply getting along.

Born on March 19, 1892, in Coytesville, New Jersey, James was the seventh and youngest child of William and Medora Schofield Van Fleet. William was one of those entrepreneurial individuals who always believed he was on the verge of tremendous success. Nearly sixty years of age when James was born, William had been moderately successful in Chicago with investments in real estate, a theater, and even a zoo but had lost everything in the Great Fire of 1871. Later forays into railroads and mining also failed.

The Van Fleet family, like the Eisenhowers and Bradleys, was poor. William struggled to support his wife and children, and in 1893 he moved them to Florida for the second time. James grew up in the town of Bartow, where his father ran a newsstand adjacent to the local post office.[11]

Medora Van Fleet was the niece of Gen. John M. Schofield, a prominent Union officer during the Civil War who had graduated seventh in the West Point class of 1853. Schofield was a recipient of the Medal of Honor and served as commanding general of the US Army (the senior post in the service prior to the creation of Army chief of staff) and secretary of war. Although James was certainly aware of his great uncle's service record, his appointment to the US Military Academy appears to have come about through his father's relationship with congressman S. M. Sparkman, a former business associate.

Apparently, William and Medora Van Fleet agreed that their son should attend West Point. Perhaps the prospect of a free college education and a potential career were motivating factors. The parents considered sending James to a preparatory school, but they faced the reality that they were financially unable to do so. Professor R. B. Huffaker of the Summerlin Institute, where James had attended secondary school, helped him prepare for the West Point entrance examinations, which he passed.[12]

Two months shy of his eighteenth birthday when he arrived on the plain at the Academy, Joseph Taggart McNarney was nearly three years younger than his classmate Dwight Eisenhower. Born on August 28, 1893, Joseph was the second of four children of James Pollard and Helen Taggart McNarney of Emporium, Pennsylvania. James was a prominent lawyer and was active in local civic organizations. As the Cameron County district attorney, he won the conviction of one Ora O'Dell, who was on trial for the murder of his wife. O'Dell was sentenced to death and hanged on June 2, 1908.

Helen Taggart McNarney headed the local temperance union, and the few photographs of her that remain depict a prim and proper woman, dressed in a long, dark skirt and blouse or shirtwaist with a high neck and long sleeves thoroughly buttoned. Joseph's paternal grandfather, Thomas McNarney, had worked as a post office clerk in Cameron County for thirty years until his death in 1898.

Historians in Emporium today describe "General Joe" as a private man, and relatively little detail of his youth has survived. A photo taken circa 1901 shows the boy standing among a group of children, each of them dressed in Native American costume. When the photo was reproduced in the local newspaper in August 1945, the caption read, "The General Is Still A 'Good Indian,'" noting that as a boy, McNarney insisted that the other children acknowledge him as a warrior chief.

Joe also became a member of the Boys' Brigade, an interdenominational Christian organization based in Scotland that had spread to the United States in the late nineteenth century, particularly in major cities of the Northeast, the Midwest, and California. The Boys' Brigade, which continues to flourish around the world today, includes military-style drill and a basic rank hierarchy. Joe rose to the rank of sergeant.

A 1910 graduate of Emporium High School, Joe was in the class behind his older sister, Jean. In the autumn of 1907, the two hosted a "conversation party" in honor of their cousin, Elsie Leiter, who was visiting from Williamsport. The *Cameron County Press* reported on the event, one of several times Joe would be mentioned in the paper:

About sixty guests were present. The porches and lawns were beautifully decorated with Japanese lanterns. Each guest was supplied with a card, upon which were arranged ten topics of conversation. The young men chose a partner for each topic and at a given signal the young ladies were lead [*sic*] to one of many seats or cozy corners arranged about the yard and porches and conversed upon the subject. At the end of ten minutes the signal was given and partners were exchanged and the next subject discussed until the end of the programe [*sic*]. During an intermission refreshments were served. The singing of many popular songs added to the enjoyment of the occasion, and all expressed themselves as having passed a very pleasant evening.[13]

Joe's uncle, Lt. Col. Frank T. McNarney, had been a sergeant with the 10th US Infantry Regiment and seen action near Santiago during the Spanish-American War. He later served as an officer in the 7th Cavalry Regiment, famed for its epic last stand with Gen. George Custer at the Little Bighorn. In a letter dated July 6, 1898, which was reproduced in the *Cameron County Press* two weeks later, Frank McNarey wrote:

By good luck I am still without a scratch. We opened the ball July 1st and for nearly half of the day we were under a deadly hail of every-thing and from all sides, and we couldn't see a thing. We were actually in a slaughter pen, but we kept on the go, till we did sight the Spaniards then we forced them back almost into the city. The American loss was about 1,200 killed and wounded, but we gained ground and captured positions which seemed almost impregnable. The Spaniards are not the weaklings and cowards the papers make them out to be. . . .[14]

It is plausible that young Joe may have chosen West Point because he was influenced by his uncle's recollections of military service. In early August 1910, the same newspaper observed that Joe was "a thorough scholar, as well as an exemplary young man. We have not the least fear but that he will pass the examination with high honors. It is an honor to the efficiency of Emporium High School that they teach every course required by the West Point examining board and two languages more than Uncle Sam requires."

The newspaper further noted that Joe was headed for a "training acad-emy" to study in preparation to take the West Point entrance examinations after receiving a coveted appointment to the Academy from Republican Charles F. Barclay, congressman for Pennsylvania's 21st District. In con-clusion, the writer crowed, "Cameron County has never in its history been favored with an appointment to West Point."

Several months later, Joe passed the entrance exams, and when he left home for the Academy on June 12, 1911, the *Cameron County Press* celebrated, "The best wishes of Joe's many friends go with him, and the day will come when Emporium will be proud of her soldier boy. Joe has the 'real stuff' in him and is sure to make good."[15]

The admission ordeal of Hubert R. Harmon is perhaps unique in the history of the Academy. The youngest of five children, Hubert was born to Millard Fillmore and Madeline Kendig Harmon in Chester, Pennsylvania, on April 3, 1892. His father, named for the former president of the United States, had graduated from the Academy in 1880, attained the rank of colonel, and served as commandant of cadets at the Pennsylvania Military Academy, now Widener University, in Chester.

Hubert was said to have initially favored the US Naval Academy at Annapolis, Maryland, but he ultimately decided to apply to West Point. In preparation, he attended Polytechnic Preparatory School in Brooklyn, New York, for two years. Family ties were likely a strong influence on his decision for West Point, and when he arrived there in the summer of 1910, two older brothers, Kenneth and Millard, were already well on their way toward graduation and commissioning in the US Army.

Barely a week into the rigors of training and acclimating to his West Point regimen, Hubert's situation took a bizarre turn. He was abruptly summoned to the office of the superintendent, Col. Hugh Scott. The superintendent supposedly held a roster of cadets in his hand and asked Hubert whether the other two cadets named Harmon were any relation. With some degree of pride, Plebe Harmon answered that the two were indeed his brothers.

Scott informed Hubert that American taxpayers would certainly not be getting their money's worth by paying for the education of three brothers from the same family. Since Kenneth and Millard were already enrolled at West Point, Hubert would have to leave.

Stunned by the turn of events, Hubert went home. His father was infuriated and contacted officials in Washington, D.C., and in the highest echelons of the army, but to no avail. It seemed that the military career of the youngest Harmon was over before it had begun.

Sometime later, Hubert's father and mother left the United States for the Philippines, and a Brooklyn boarding house became Hubert's new home. Although the rest of the story may be somewhat apocryphal, Hubert Harmon's luck began to change. The landlady, a kindly Irish woman, lent a sympathetic ear to her boarder's tale. Her husband was well connected in New York–area politics, she told Hubert, and it might do some good to relate the unfortunate circumstance to him.

As the story was passed down in the Harmon family, Hubert joined the man in his living room that very night. A series of introductions followed, and over drinks the local ward boss reassured the young man that things would work out. In June 1911, Hubert arrived at West Point for the second time. With Colonel Scott assigned to other duty and older brother Kenneth a recent graduate, there were no more complications for Hubert.[16]

Alexander Pennington Cronkhite, appointed from the 15th Congressional District of New York, was the son of Maj. Gen. Adelbert Cronkhite, an 1882 graduate who was soon to render noble service during the Great War as commander of the 80th Infantry Division during the 1918 Meuse-Argonne Offensive. Cronkhite's maternal grandfather was Brig. Gen. Alexander Cummings McWhorter Pennington Jr., an 1860 graduate who served with the 2nd US Artillery and the 3rd New Jersey Cavalry during the Civil War. Pennington was commended for bravery at Cedar Creek, Beverly Ford, and Gettysburg. He later served during the Spanish-American War and commanded all fortifications along the east coast of the United States from Connecticut to Maine. The young Cronkhite's paternal grandfather, Lt. Col. Henry McLean Cronkhite, served as a surgeon with the 26th New York Infantry during the Civil War.

New Yorker John French Conklin was the son of Col. John Conklin Jr., an 1884 Academy graduate who served with the artillery in the Philippines. Major General John Lincoln Clem, famed as the "Drummer Boy of Chickamauga" during the Civil War, was a maternal uncle. Conklin's maternal grandfather, Gen. William H. French, graduated from West Point in 1837 and rose to command the 1st US Artillery on the eve of the Civil War. As a brigadier general, French led Union brigades at Seven Pines, Gaines's Mill, and Malvern Hill during the Seven Days Battles. He commanded the Third Division, II Corps, Army of the Potomac, at the Battle of Antietam, heavily engaging Confederate troops holding a sunken road that later became known as Bloody Lane.

French later commanded the III Corps but fell from grace with Gen. George G. Meade, commander of the Army of the Potomac, who asserted that French had failed to move with initiative against the Confederates during the Mine Run Campaign in the autumn of 1863. His career in the field army ended in the spring of 1864, and he reverted to his prewar rank of colonel. After the war, he commanded coastal fortifications on both the East and West Coasts.

From an old-line Virginia family, William Frazer Tompkins of Richmond had no doubt heard stories of his grandfather's military career. Colonel Christopher Quarles Tompkins had earned a degree from the College of William and Mary by the age of seventeen and then graduated from West Point in 1836. As a lieutenant of artillery, he fought in skirmishes at Locha-Hatchee and Fort Lauderdale during the Seminole Wars of the mid-1830s, participated in an expedition to California in 1846–1847, and served on garrison duty at Monterey during the Mexican War.

With the outbreak of the Civil War, Christopher Quarles Tompkins became a colonel in the Confederate 22nd Virginia Infantry Regiment. The 22nd Virginia fought at Scary Creek and Carnifex Ferry in 1861, and by the following year Colonel Tompkins was reported to have left the service of the Confederate Army. Another notable colonel of the 22nd Virginia, killed in action at Winchester in 1864, was George S. Patton Sr., the grandfather of Gen. George S. Patton Jr., the latter being the 1909 West Point graduate who gained lasting fame leading the US Third Army in Europe during World War II.

Douglas Hamilton Gillette of Philadelphia shared a common thread with classmate John Conklin: his father had also graduated from West Point in 1884. Cassius Erie Gillette attained the rank of major and spent twenty-two years in the army commanding fortifications and surveying along the Georgia, Florida, Rhode Island, and California coastlines. He commanded a battalion of engineers and served as an instructor at the Army School of Engineering. When he resigned his commission in 1906 to accept the post of superintendent of the Philadelphia water filtration plant, the *New York Times* took note of the event.[17]

By the time Stafford LeRoy Irwin entered West Point, his family name was already well known in military circles. In 1856, his grandfather, Brig. Gen. Bernard J. D. Irwin, accepted an appointment to the army as an assistant surgeon. For heroism during the Apache Wars, he was awarded the Medal of Honor, although belatedly. The action took place in February 1861, but the medal was not established until the following year; however, the general's heroism was remembered, and he received the honor thirty-three years later, on January 21, 1894. Bernard Irwin spent thirty-eight years in the military, serving with the Union Army during the Civil War, some of that time as a prisoner of the Confederates. After the war, he served as senior medical officer at several posts, including West Point from 1873 to 1878.

Stafford Irwin's father, Maj. Gen. George LeRoy Irwin, graduated from the Academy in 1889 and served during the Spanish-American War, the Philippine Insurrection, and the occupation of Cuba from 1906 to 1909. During World War I, he would command the 57th Field Artillery Brigade, 32nd Infantry Division. He was commended for his conduct during the Second Battle of the Marne, the Oise-Aisne Offensive, and the Meuse-Argonne Offensive.

Pearson Menoher, an at-large appointee from Virginia, was named after his mother, Nannie Wilhelmina Pearson Menoher. His grandfather was a veteran of the Union Army during the Civil War, and his father, Maj. Gen. Charles T. Menoher, graduated from West Point in 1886.

An original member of the Army General Staff, Charles served during the Spanish-American War and became provost marshal during the occupation of Cuba. He completed three tours of duty in the Philippines. During World War I, he commanded the 5th Field Artillery Regiment and the famed 42nd Infantry Division, known popularly as the Rainbow Division. He rendered distinguished service during the Champagne-Marne, Saint-Mihiel, and Meuse-Argonne Offensives. Charles later served as the first chief of the Air Service, which was separated from the Signal Corps as its own line component of the army in June 1920. He then became embroiled in a famous controversy with his assistant, Gen. Billy Mitchell, over the future role of airpower. Relieved at his own request in October 1921, Charles commanded the Hawaii Department and then the IX Corps in San Francisco. He retired in 1926 after forty years of service. Pearson's younger brother Darrow and half-brother William also attended the Academy.

William Pierce Evans, a member of the West Point Class of 1878, served most of his army career in the Philippines and commanded the 19th Infantry Battalion in operations against insurgents in the spring of 1901. Following an extended illness, he returned to the United States, serving with the War Department in Washington, D.C., and as a lieutenant colonel with the 11th Infantry Regiment. His son, Vernon, received an at-large appointment as a resident of the nation's capital.

James Basevi Ord was born in Mexico and received his appointment from California. His father, Capt. James Thompson Ord, died in 1905 at the age of forty-one, and his interment control form at Arlington National

Cemetery lists the "Puerto Rican Regiment" as his service organization, a reference to the forerunner of the modern 65th Infantry Regiment that was authorized by Congress in 1899 after the Spanish-American War. Young James's grandfather, Maj. Gen. Edward Otho Cresap Ord, was an 1839 graduate of West Point. He fought in the Seminole Wars and was seriously wounded in Corinth, Mississippi, during the Civil War.

Major General Ord commanded the left wing of the Union Army of the Tennessee under Gen. Ulysses S. Grant and the XIII Army Corps at Vicksburg. He was wounded a second time during the siege of Petersburg and, following his recovery, participated in the campaign that resulted in the fall of the Confederate capital of Richmond. During the weeks before Robert E. Lee surrendered the Confederate Army of Northern Virginia at Appomattox, Ord's skillful handling of his command was instrumental in bringing about the final victory.

John Ellis Rossell was the son of Alabama-born Brig. Gen. William Trent Rossell, an 1873 West Point graduate who served in various engineering roles around the United States. The brigadier general was a member of the Mississippi River Commission and chief of engineers, retiring in 1913 only to be recalled four years later with US entry into World War I. After forty-two years of service, he retired a second time in 1918 and died the following year.

Sidney Carroll Graves, an at-large appointee from Washington, D.C., was the son of Maj. Gen. William S. Graves, an 1889 West Point graduate. General Graves served during the Spanish-American War and distinguished himself in combat while commanding an infantry company at Caloocan during the Philippine Insurrection. He briefly led the 8th Infantry Division during World War I and was subsequently ordered to command the American Expeditionary Force in Siberia during the Russian Civil War. From the autumn of 1918 until the withdrawal of his command in April 1920, General Graves capably fulfilled his primary mission to safeguard Allied supply lines along the Trans-Siberian Railway and avoided entanglements with Russian military factions and troops of other countries. He later served as a juror during the court-martial of General Billy Mitchell and commanded US troops in the Panama Canal Zone.

Henry McElderry Pendleton, another Washington, D.C., resident appointed to the Academy at-large, was the son of Colonel Edwin Palmer Pendleton, an 1879 Academy graduate who commanded the 29th Infantry

Regiment and served extensively in the Philippines. Donald Angus Davison, appointed from the 5th District of Illinois, was the son of 1885 Academy graduate Lorenzo Paul Davison. The elder Davison served in China, Puerto Rico, and the Philippines, attained the rank of major, and retired due to physical disability in 1904. Recalled to the service with US entry into World War I, he died in the Philippines in 1917.

Oscar Andruss Straub, appointed from the 29th District of Pennsylvania, was the son of Oscar Itin Straub, an 1887 graduate of West Point who served in the Coast and Field Artillery. The younger Straub's maternal grandfather, Gen. Elias Van Arsdale Andruss, was an 1864 graduate and veteran of the Civil War.

Brigadier General William Preble Hall graduated from West Point in 1868 and earned the Medal of Honor at White River, Colorado, on October 20, 1879. Hall rescued another officer who had been surrounded by as many as thirty-five Native Americans. He was a champion marksman with both revolver and carbine and went on to serve in Puerto Rico during the Spanish-American War and as adjutant general of the US Army. His son, Blackburn Hall, was appointed to the Academy from the 14th District of Missouri.

A senatorial appointee from Delaware, John Ross Mendenhall was the son of Clarence Miles Mendenhall, who attended West Point with a recommendation from Gen. William T. Sherman, famed for his campaign through Georgia and the March to the Sea during the Civil War. Apparently, Clarence resigned from the Academy in 1881, never served in the army, and pursued a career in civil engineering. John Ross Mendenhall was the grandson of Col. John Mendenhall, an 1851 Academy graduate. During the 1850s, Colonel Mendenhall saw action in the Seminole Wars and was involved in several skirmishes while on frontier duty at Fort Leavenworth, Kansas, and in the Dakota Territory.

Colonel Mendenhall was an innovative artillery commander during the Civil War, advocating the formation of an artillery reserve capable of massing fire in support of any area threatened by enemy penetration. He earned praise for the support his guns provided at Shiloh, and during the Battle of Murfreesboro his cannon shattered a Confederate infantry attack to seal the Union victory. At war's end, he was commander of the artillery reserve of the Department of the Cumberland. He later occupied posts in several states and was commander of the Department of Alaska. He died in 1892 while serving as colonel of the 2nd Artillery Regiment.

A member of a prominent South Carolina family, Edmund DeTreville Ellis traced his connection to the Academy to a distant cousin, Col. Richard DeTreville, a member of the Class of 1823. Born on James Island, near Charleston, Ellis received his appointment to the Academy from Sen. Benjamin Tillman. He was already a college graduate, having entered the University of South Carolina at the age of sixteen in 1906 and earning a bachelor's degree in civil engineering.

When the Panic of 1907 hit the country, the stock market fell to half its value of the previous year. Money got tight, and Ellis financed the remainder of his South Carolina education by handling the laundry service for fellow students at ten cents a load for pickup and delivery. In the winter, he sold coal to students to heat their dormitory rooms.

At its inception, the West Point class of 1915 was historic, establishing a precedent with one of its number. Luis Raul Esteves was the first Puerto Rican to enroll and graduate from the US Military Academy. Under the terms of the Treaty of Paris that ended the Spanish-American War, Spain ceded Puerto Rico to the United States in 1899. Raul's father, Francisco Esteves Soriano, had served in the Spanish military but considered being governed by the Americans an improvement over Spanish dominion.

Raul's father urged him to pursue a military career. However, his mother, an immigrant of Dutch and German extraction, favored the engineering profession with study in the United States—even though the family did not possess the financial wherewithal to fund a college education for him. Subsequently, the young man read a newspaper article announcing competitive examinations for West Point admission. Here was an opportunity to study in the United States, obtain a degree, and enter military service. Without his parents' knowledge, Esteves sat for the examination and won an appointment. When he arrived at West Point in June 1911, he possessed only a working knowledge of the English language. In the regimented environment of the Academy, the ability to cope with such a barrier made his achievement even more remarkable.

Wealthy, dirt poor, or scion of a military family—searching for an education, identity, or career—the young men who came to West Point in June 1911 would soon discover that the rigors of the classroom and the army's physical demands on its future officers played no favorites. Before them lay promise—and trial.

PART II

On Point

CHAPTER THREE

The Army and the Academy

In the summer of 1911, a film crew employed by Thomas A. Edison Inc. arrived at West Point. As motion pictures were a new and innovative form of entertainment, the crew's equipment, entourage, and presence on the plain must have created something of a stir, even at an institution known for its staid and sober atmosphere.

On that sunny day over a century ago, the rattling 16mm camera recorded a fleeting, flickering glimpse of life at the US Military Academy. The short subject opens with a wide shot, panning the grounds of the Academy and pausing briefly to take in the stately buildings, manicured lawns, and shrubs. Cadets in uniform complete their calisthenics, drill, and line up for inspection in front of their barracks. They march in close formation while spectators, most of them young ladies, take in the precision performance from benches along the perimeter of the field. The marching band, though silent to the viewer, is in fine form. A small child darts onto the parade ground but is quickly retrieved by a woman, with the tramping band only steps away.[18]

Originally copyrighted by Edison on October 24, 1911, and titled *A Day at West Point Military Academy, New York*, the brief film was later re-edited, given a new title—*Captains of Tomorrow*—and paired with a second

Edison production, *He Couldn't Get Up in the Morning*. The split-reel film tandem was then copyrighted again, on July 14, 1917, just as the United States entered World War I. Undoubtedly, numerous members of the class of 1915 are present in the film, and when the brief documentary was released the second time to heighten patriotic fervor across the land, a number of them were girding for war in Europe.

The presence of Edison's crew at the Academy represents the rapid advance of technology, the immediacy of communication, and the broadening worldview of the US Army in the development of its young officers in the early twentieth century. The Wright Brothers had flown at Kitty Hawk less than a decade earlier. Ford Motor Company had introduced the Model T in 1908. The telephone, patented in 1876, was used widely. And while the pace of rural electrification was slow, wires festooned the urban centers as companies competed to provide power. As for the military, the airplane, machine gun, tank, and submarine were propelling the art of killing to new heights of efficiency, while lethal poison gas blinded and suffocated indiscriminately.

On March 31, 1911, Congress approved its first pledge of monetary support for the army's fledgling Signal Corps aviation service, appropriating $125,000 for the purchase of five Curtiss and Wright aircraft. A single plane had been purchased from the Wright Brothers directly by the Signal Corps two years earlier, and the congressional action validated a slowly but surely evolving perspective on the nature of future wars. The dash and adventure of a pilot's service appealed to significant numbers of West Point cadets, and several members of the class of 1915 were to assume major roles in the development of Army airpower.[19]

The world was changing, and West Point was compelled, albeit at its own pace, to contemplate change as well. For now, though, the long shadow of Sylvanus Thayer continued to shape virtually every facet of the cadet experience.

Thayer had refocused the Academy curriculum from the classical and liberal arts foundation that had characterized higher education in early to mid-nineteenth century America. He had instituted the cloistered regimen that allowed only one furlough during a cadet's four years at West Point, ten weeks after satisfactory completion of the second year. Christmas leave was given only to cadets who managed to excel in their studies and steer clear of trouble. Thayer's doctrine for shaping young officers forbade them to hold personal cash or to receive such from an outside source. In something of a Darwinian survival of the fittest, he had also advocated separating those who excelled at their studies from those who lagged behind in academic pursuits.[20]

Aside from the military arts, classroom time was primarily consumed with mathematics, chemistry, physics, engineering, and the knowledge that would be required of a soldier. The top graduates typically were placed in the Corps of Engineers, while the Cavalry and Coast Artillery awaited those further down the academic chain, followed by the lowest echelon, whose graduates were earmarked for the Infantry. During the 1911–1912 academic year and into the foreseeable future, the vast majority of instructors, as they had been for generations, were army officers who taught the same curriculum they had been taught, and much of the instruction was mind-numbing rote memorization.

The *Annual Report of the Superintendent United States Military Academy* for the period of September 1, 1911, through August 31, 1912 (the plebe year for the class of 1915), lists a total strength of 1,314. Among these were 113 commissioned officers, 6 civilian instructors, 541 Academy cadets, 652 enlisted army and Academy personnel, and 2 foreign cadets. *The Official Register of the Officers and Cadets of the United States Military Academy* for 1912 lists the civilian instructors as engaged in foreign languages, fencing, and military gymnastics.

The twin pillars of honor and tradition pervaded West Point, and cadets of the day adhered to their then-unwritten honor code, which simply stated, "A cadet will not lie, cheat, or steal." It was expected that West Point cadets and officers of the US Army would conduct themselves as gentlemen. The code itself was not formally set down in writing until 1922, when Superintendent Douglas MacArthur, a 1903 graduate, formed the Cadet Honor Committee to deal with possible infractions. Until that time, interpretation of the honor code was straightforward. An officer's word was considered his inviolate bond. To be found guilty of an infraction of the code meant certain dismissal. Allegations of certain offenses such as theft were handled according to standard military regulations.

In its modern form, the honor code ends with the phrase, ". . . or tolerate those who do." This tenet relates directly to the obligation of the cadet to report honor code infractions within a reasonable period of time or risk dismissal for failure to do so. While cadets of the era followed suit with that understanding, the code itself did not specifically reflect this admonition until 1970.

More than thirty years after his graduation, Eisenhower, serving as chief of staff of the army at the time, wrote to Gen. Maxwell Taylor:

> Since your visit to my office a few days back I have had West Point very much on my mind. . . . I think that everyone familiar with West Point would instantly agree that the one thing that has set it aside from every other school in the world is the fact that for a great number of years it has not only had an "honor" system, but that the system has actually worked. . . . We have succeeded early in a cadet's career in instilling in him a respect amounting to veneration for the honor system. The honor system, as a feature of West Point, seems to grow in importance with the graduate as the years recede until it becomes something that he is almost reluctant to talk about—it occupies in his mind a position akin to the virtue of his mother or his sister.[21]

Tradition hardly needed to be defined. It spoke to every officer, every cadet, every civilian, and every visitor who set foot there. After the Academy had been in existence for little more than a century, the fraternity of West Point graduates numbered only slightly more than five thousand. Their names resonated with the history of the nation: President James K. Polk; Mexican War hero and President of the Confederacy Jefferson Davis; Union general and president Ulysses S. Grant; and Gens. Robert E. Lee, Thomas J. "Stonewall" Jackson, J. E. B. Stuart, George G. Meade, George B. McClellan, and William T. Sherman were alumni. General George Armstrong Custer, who had made a name for himself at the Battle of Gettysburg and lost his life at the Little Bighorn, was the "goat," or bottom graduate, of the Class of 1861.

For the Cadet Corps, the uniform, the regimen, and the fortress on the Hudson River—possession of which Gen. George Washington believed held the key to an American victory in the Revolutionary War—were constant reminders of their charge. Those who had come from military families already had at least some notion of the heritage they had accepted and pledged to propagate. The others quickly discovered the essence of their commitment. They also learned that for every task or challenge, there was a West Point way to determine the solution. Deviating from the West Point path was strongly discouraged. By the time the class of 1915 graduated, there was a clear understanding of and appreciation for the methods they had encountered and endured. And in a changing world, their West Point education clearly helped them make decisions on the battlefield as well as in the halls of government.

The West Point campus that was to become so familiar to the class of 1915 was spread atop the natural palisades of the Hudson River Valley. On the west side of the campus, the forty-six-star flag flew until 1912, when the territories of New Mexico and Arizona were admitted to the Union, resulting in the addition of two stars and a national emblem that would remain unchanged until the end of future President Eisenhower's second term in office with the admission of Alaska and Hawaii in 1959. Beyond the flagpole were the two oldest buildings on campus, the homes of the commandant of cadets and the Academy superintendent, built in 1820. Since August 1910, Maj. Gen. Thomas H. Barry had held both posts.

The colossal construction program that was well underway at West Point in 1911 is accompanied by a bit of irony. The *Superintendent's Report* for 1912, which incorporated the annual review of the Inspector General's Office conducted during the third week of June that year by Brig. Gen. George F. Chase, indicates that when the class of 1915 arrived on campus, the new riding hall was 78 percent complete, and that by December 14, 1911, it was deemed finished with the exception of marble and slate work and the setting of plumbing fixtures.

Intended for training and drill in horsemanship, the building was impressive, but the cost of construction had exceeded its budget. In five short years, tanks were crawling and snorting across European battlefields, the horse cavalry was becoming symbolic of a bygone military era, and the riding hall itself was an anachronism that later found renewed life as Thayer Hall, an academic building.

Nevertheless, at the time of its construction, the immense riding hall was a source of pride. Robert C. Richardson, a lieutenant of the 23rd Infantry Regiment who served as a member of the English faculty at the Academy during the period, described the building as "splendidly impressive with its broad flat buttresses . . . the lower level of the galleries being reached by a flight of steps that cling to the steep retaining wall of the road. The great arena is 150 by 600 feet and is covered by a cantilever roof, so that when the eye first encounters this interior, a sensation of its vastness holds the spectator in its grip.

"The roof is mostly of glass," Richardson continued, "so as to afford a maximum of light, and the floor is covered with tanbark to make more endurable any sudden and unexpected descent from the back of a capricious beast. The building is steam-heated and electric lighted, for during winter months, equitation drills extend into the late afternoon."

By drawing curtains, the great hall could be divided into three smaller halls for the conduct of classes; it included stalls for a hundred horses. It was large enough for the Academy's artillery battery to drill indoors as well. Officers and cadets sharpened their polo skills. Every Wednesday and Saturday afternoon, cadets played one another or entertained civilian teams from the surrounding area. Along the west wall and the north and south ends of the hall, balconies accommodated the large number of spectators who gathered for major events.[22]

Occupying a hillside farther west, the Cadet Chapel, dedicated in 1910, combined Gothic architecture and the stone strength of a medieval fortress, its flanks and tower soaring skyward. To the north, the majestic Hudson River flowed while Storm King Mountain and Constitution Island lay in the distance. On the south side sat the gymnasium, destined for the wrecking ball in 1924 to make way for Washington Hall; the Cadet Barracks, also known as Old Central; the West Academic Building, later named in honor of Gen. John J. Pershing of World War I fame; and Grant Hall, the cadet mess.

The East Academic Building, slated for completion in 1913 and later named Bartlett Hall, was 26 percent complete according to the 1912 *Superintendent's Report*, and work was progressing on the first and second floor walls of the main structure. The contract for construction of the building had been signed in the summer of 1911, and the total cost, including contractor's profit, was slightly less than $397,000, excluding the expense of the "chemical laboratory and map room." Debris from the construction project was used to fill in Execution Hollow, a large depression on the main parade ground near Trophy Point, where the Battle Monument, the largest column of polished granite in the Western Hemisphere, had been erected in 1897 by a group of Civil War veterans.

Adjacent to the riding hall was the old library, which was later torn down prior to the construction of a new library building on the same site. Moving to the east, the Officers' Mess, Cullum Hall, and Lincoln Hall, which once served as quarters for bachelor officers, had been constructed within the last decade or so. Kosciuszko's Monument at Clinton Parapet was still without its crowning figure of the Polish officer who had designed the defenses of West Point during the Revolutionary War. It would come two years later.

Around the circle, where today sit cannon from the Revolutionary War and links of the Great Chain that once barred ships from passing along the Hudson, stood the West Point Hotel, where Gen. Douglas MacArthur's mother had taken up residence during her son's cadet tenure. In 1911, the lessee who had operated the hotel vacated the premises on the expiration of the lease, and a new five-year agreement was signed with Mrs. Emilie Logan at an annual rental rate of $100. A word of explanation followed in the 1912 *Superintendent's Report*:

> This was the best arrangement that could be made owing to the condition of the old building and the fact that no guarantee could be given as to length of time the old hotel would be permitted to remain standing and occupied. . . . A new modern hotel of sufficient size to accommodate the friends and relatives of cadets is an urgent necessity. The present building is old, inadequate and lacking in all modern conveniences and should be replaced as soon as funds can be made available for the purpose.[23]

Awed by the splendor of the campus, even in the midst of one of the greatest construction and renovation programs in Academy history, Lieutenant Richardson seemed almost breathless in his description of the sight. "In the little plaza at the junction of the Power House and Riding Hall, the road winds and passes under the mediaeval arch of the Post Headquarters, or Administration Building. At this point, the bulk and dignity of the buildings are stupendous, and admiringly we stand, imprisoned, it would seem, in a quadrangle of Middle Age fortresses, whose sternness and solemnity seem symbolic of discipline and strength."[24]

The grounds themselves needed sprucing up, and General Chase noted that a portion of the area of Execution Hollow that had been filled in was graded and seeded with grass. Sidewalk and road construction, as well as general landscaping, were also in order. General Chase further observed that a "large amount of cleaning up work has been done. Small stables in rear of officers' quarters, chicken-houses and other unsightly temporary shacks have been removed and the places cleaned up."

Despite the commitment to improving the Academy grounds and facilities and the progress that had been made, the inspector general related that a grand total of twenty-two projects, already identified in prior reports, remained to be undertaken. Among these were the construction or renovation of the new and existing officers' mess and quarters, the West Academic Building, the engineer barracks, the children's schoolhouse, the South Gate Guardhouse, the army service barracks, the laundry, and the post exchange. The estimated cost of the remaining tasks at hand was $3 million, and a detailed report was already circulating in Washington, D.C., on the desk of the secretary of war.

While West Point was in the midst of this physical renovation, the United States Army faced the challenge of maintaining a global presence a decade after the victory of US land and naval forces in the Spanish-American War. The conflict lasted less than four months, and the decisive triumph over Spain, a traditional European power, heralded the emergence of the United States as a player on the world stage. Fewer than four hundred American military personnel had been killed in action during the war, and total casualties were just over four thousand. Nearly 2,600 of the dead had perished due to non-battlefield related illness. The 1898 Treaty of Paris made the Philippines, Guam, and Puerto Rico American possessions and put Cuba under the control of the US (temporarily).

For thirteen years, the army had fought against a strong insurgency in the Philippines, and at various times American troops were deployed along the southwestern border of the United States and in China, Mexico, Cuba, Puerto Rico, Panama, Hawaii, and Alaska. The US armed forces were adapting to the responsibilities commensurate with protecting national interests that had become suddenly global in nature.

Mobilizing the relatively large number of troops necessary to prosecute the Spanish-American War had proven problematic, and subsequently Secretary of War Elihu Root initiated a number of reforms in the army. With the Militia Act of 1903, popularly known as the Dick Act after its principal advocate, Representative Charles Dick of Ohio, Congress specified that state militias would serve as the country's National Guard and required it to both conform to an organizational structure and employ equipment similar to that of the Regular Army. At the height of the Spanish-American War in 1898–1899, the strength of the US Army had reached nearly 275,000. By 1911, with a greater reliance on its capability to mobilize reserve elements, its ranks had been reduced to 83,675.[25]

Through the years, further legislation, reorganization, and continuing global obligations would cause the army's numbers to rise and fall, particularly in the context of the national emergencies brought about by two world wars. The continuing presence of a core professional force and its cadre of trained, experienced officers, such as those minted at West Point, remained vital in the execution of its mission.

In the early years of the twentieth century, the highest echelons of army command were dealing with a myriad of issues right down to the rifle the common infantryman carried. Adopted as standard issue in 1892, the Norwegian-designed bolt-action Krag-Jorgensen rifle had performed poorly against the Spanish infantry, which carried the German Mauser rifle. In response, the army replaced the Krag-Jorgensen with the Springfield Model 1903, in many ways a virtual copy of the Mauser design. The Springfield 1903 came with problems of its own, and after Mauser filed suit, the US government eventually paid a $3 million settlement for patent infringement.

On August 4, 1911, Adm. Heihachirō Tōgō of the Imperial Japanese Navy arrived in New York. Tōgō was the hero of the great naval battle that had been fought at Tsushima six years earlier, during which his warships had devastated the Russian Baltic Fleet. Tōgō's skillful command of the Japanese naval contingent at Tsushima had made him an international celebrity, and more important, hastened his country's victory in the Russo-Japanese War of 1904–1905. In similar fashion to the American victory in the Spanish-American War, the defeat of Czarist Russia had established Japan as a world power; it had become the first Asian nation to defeat a traditional European power in a modern war.

While the two nations shared a common recent emergence among the nations of the world, they were already approaching a collision course. Japanese influence and primacy in Asia could not be denied; however, US interests in the Pacific were steadily growing.

Tōgō had sailed to New York aboard the Cunard liner *Lusitania*, destined four years later to be torpedoed by the German submarine *U-20* off Ireland's Old Head of Kinsale, resulting in the deaths of more than a hundred Americans and pushing the United States closer to entering World War I. The admiral was en route to Washington, D.C., where his itinerary included a private meeting and dinner with President William Howard Taft and stops at George Washington's Mount Vernon home and the US Naval Academy at Annapolis. Returning to New York via Baltimore and Philadelphia, he was to visit the Navy Yard, the Metropolitan Museum of Art, and West Point before traveling on to Boston and Buffalo.

Reluctant to be interviewed, Tōgō greeted reporters near the docks in lower Manhattan as he arrived just after midnight. Eight days later, the admiral, whom the *New York Times* described as a "dapper little man, not much more than 5 feet tall, with the kindest and most modest appearance imaginable," came to the US Military Academy. Both Tōgō and Major General Barry were resplendent in their white uniforms as they posed for photographers in the summer heat while officers and their wives beamed in the background. Tōgō stood only shoulder high to the West Point superintendent.[26]

A representative of the Inspector General's Office performed his annual review from August 7 to 14 and wrote in his 1911 report:

> I was present at the Academy the day of Admiral Tōgō's arrival. I had visited the corps the night before in camp eight to ten miles from the post. They broke camp, marched into the post in the morning; they were formed to receive the Admiral at 10:30 a.m. On account of delay in his arrival they were kept under arms until after twelve o'clock.
>
> A review followed in the afternoon, in quick and double time, reception to the Admiral which the First Class attended in the afternoon, a dress parade and passing in review by the companies in the evening. It seemed to me a very severe test on the physical endurance of these young men, but I observed them at a regular hop that night and the strain seemed not to have affected them, showing that their physical condition is excellent.

The officer further stated that he had observed the instruction of the plebes of the fourth class in their drills, setting up, dancing, swimming, and artillery instruction, and found that every aspect proceeded satisfactorily. While the majority of the class had been at the Academy since mid-June—only seven weeks—some, including Omar Bradley, had just arrived on August 1.

As Tōgō observed the cadets passing in review and accepted the military honors rendered, none of those present could see the future. However, the Pacific rivalry between Japan and the United States was already beginning to simmer. Thirty years later, the officers of the West Point class of 1915 would find themselves on the brink of war. Undoubtedly, some of them would remember that sunny day on the plain when they saluted the eminent Japanese admiral.

CHAPTER FOUR

Life at West Point

During three weeks of Beast Barracks, the new arrivals' day began with reveille and the pounding of drums at 5:20 a.m. Quickly clambering down iron stairs to the walkway below, they stood at attention for ten minutes, waiting for their cadet officers to appear. The tardy were summarily hustled to their places in the ranks, dogged by yearling corporals. The Beasts had not yet earned the title of plebe. That would come if and when they survived initial indoctrination.

By 5:50, room inspection was underway. Then came breakfast, followed by the repetitive instruction of basic drill intermingled with a healthy dose of physical conditioning. The cadets learned and repeated the proper ways of saluting, marching, facing, and how to carry a nine-pound rifle. The Beasts were sometimes made to march with their weapons for such prolonged periods that they would remember the fatigue in their shoulders for the rest of their lives.

Those who made mistakes received quick correction from a stern, noncommissioned officer cadet, who regularly addressed the infractor as "Mr. Ducrot," "Mr. Dumbguard," or "Mr. Duflickit." Those who were slower to catch on to the finer points of marching were relegated to the "Awkward Squad," and Dwight Eisenhower was one of those unfortunate enough to receive such intensified additional instruction.

"Military drill was a problem," he later recalled. "Although my physical condition was excellent, and I had handled guns all my life, I had no training in marching. To keep in step with the music of the band was more than difficult, and the instructors constantly barked at us to get our shoulders back, our heads up, and *get in step*. For days I was assigned to the Awkward Squad until I could co-ordinate my feet with the beat."[27]

For the residents of Beast Barracks, forty-five-minute periods of midday physical exercise were meant to be done in unison, both while marching and standing in ranks. These were punctuated by frequent short rests, no longer than a minute in duration. The new cadets spent the afternoons learning the components of the rifle, its disassembly, and its cleaning, then putting it back together under the watchful eye of an instructor.

All the while, any unfortunate Beast caught slouching was forcefully reminded of the art of bracing, or posture, by a cadet officer. Shoulders back. Head up. Chin in. Stomach tight. Forward lean on the hips.

Every aspect of the cadet's life was rigidly controlled. Uniforms cost $160, and those who were unable to foot the bill in full were allowed to do so over time, a portion of their $50 monthly pay deducted to retire the debt. The government further allotted each cadet one ration per day at an estimated cost of forty cents, making the total annual compensation of a West Point cadet $746. The cadet received credit for his monthly stipend, and expenses were charged to the ledger.

To provide for the expense of his first officer's uniforms and equipment and to allow the future lieutenant to graduate from West Point debt free, an additional $14 went to the "equipment fund" each month, accumulating to $704 during the course of four years. English instructor Lieutenant Richardson reasoned:

> This provision is a very wise and beneficial one to the cadet, for he enters the Service free from the terrifying load of debt. Formerly the Equipment Fund was turned over to the graduating cadet, without any restriction whatsoever. The consequence was that the largest part of it was spent in New York a few days after graduation, and the young officer was in debt for his uniform for many months thereafter. He started his career with a millstone around his neck, to which weight a few added that of a wife. As one experienced officer remarked, "The ladies are all right, but do not marry until you are out of debt, else every time you take a drink in the Club, you will feel as if you are swallowing the baby's socks."[28]

Physical deportment and good manners were instilled in the cadets as well. An individual's conduct at mealtime was choreographed to the last detail. Lieutenant Richardson related:

> Once in the mess hall, the new cadet is allowed to eat all he wishes without interference. At the meal, however, he must comply with the instructions for the position of a cadet at table in the mess hall.
>
> This position shall be wholly without constraint. While eating the body shall be erect on the hips, inclining slightly forward, elbows off the table. When not eating he will sit at ease in his chair, erect or leaning back as he desires. His forearms may be kept in his lap, or his hand or hands may rest easily upon the table. At no time in the mess hall shall he tilt his chair back or elevate his feet, or turn his chair away from the table. Whenever a cadet is spoken to in the mess hall, he will look at the person speaking to him.[29]

Although the Cadet Corps was relatively small, preparing the meals was a continuous undertaking. The food was plentiful and served by uniformed waiters:

> One of the most important and difficult duties of the Treasurer is catering to eight hundred ravenous young appetites. To be a successful Mess officer for this large number requires much study, especially in this age of the high cost of supplies. The food provided is excellent in quality and well prepared. In general it is plain and wholesome, just what one would expect at a military school, but the menu is sufficiently varied so as to please even the fastidious. Southern palates are not forced to long for fried chicken nor Eastern palates for oysters. To make the New Englander feel quite at home periodic boiled dinners gladden their gastronomic lives. Then, too, ice cream, since the installation of an electric freezer, has become as common as the proteids.[30]

In 1901, the time-honored ritual of hazing had drawn a complaint from a former cadet's parents and prompted a congressional investigation. As a result, the superintendent was instructed to curtail the practice. Still, tradition lingered, and the most common forms of the supposedly curbed harassment included extended periods of performing a strenuous exercise called an eagle in which the offender was stripped to the waist and made to execute a type of deep knee bend with his arms extended. At times, the offender was required to complete up to 150 repetitions. Plebes also endured such discomfort as an occasional spoonful of Tabasco sauce on the tongue.

For all its criticism, Beast Barracks served its purpose. The cadet who struggled through it was indoctrinated. Lieutenant Richardson wrote:

> All sense of his own importance, if he ever had any, has oozed away rapidly. Like Bob Acres [a popular fictional character featured in Richard Brinsley Sheridan's play *The Rivals*], it sneaked out of the ends of his fingers the first few days, and he realizes what a very small fish he is in this new pond. He rapidly acquires a most receptive mood in which he absorbs the most important lesson that a sailor must learn, OBEDIENCE. The officers and cadets in charge of him demand unhesitating and instant compliance with their orders. To this end the new cadets are made to execute every order at a run, not to harass them as they sometimes think, but to form the habit of immediate obedience. This trait is the foundation of discipline, toward the inculcation of which in the new cadet, an excellent beginning is made in "Beast Barracks."[31]

When Beast Barracks concluded, the surviving plebes joined the remainder of the Corps in camp, a collection of tents that housed six companies of cadets located in the northeast corner of the plain. They drilled, exercised, marched, and saluted until September. Those who were not proficient swimmers received additional instruction at the gymnasium pool.

Every morning, plebes marched across the parade field, carrying the appropriate shoes for dance instruction. Once they reached Cullum Hall, they quickly donned their shoes and lined up along a wall. First, they learned to waltz. Then came the two-step, followed by the most popular dance of the day, the foxtrot.

The two arduous months of camp ended with an elaborate farcical funeral for some unfortunate rat or mouse that the plebes had managed to trap. If they failed to collect a rodent, a reasonably sized grasshopper would do the trick. The plebes were required to assume an appropriately "mournful" attitude, some carrying buckets in the procession to catch their copious tears. Others played musical instruments in a mock dirge while the deceased was borne to its final resting place. The bereaved wore underwear with dress jackets worn backwards and buttoned in the rear, or other ridiculous costumes.

At the end of camp, the cadets returned to their quarters, and the academic year began in earnest. The day started with reveille at 6:00 a.m., then outdoor roll call by company. Breakfast was at 6:30, followed by time for cadets to get their rooms in order. Classes met from 8:00 until lunchtime at noon, resumed at 1:00 p.m., and concluded at 4:00. Cadets took advantage of free time to study or engage in athletics until dinner was served at 6:00 p.m. After, two hours remained to study or take care of other responsibilities, such as shining shoes or brass. At 8:00 p.m., the familiar wail of taps drifted across the plain.

Getting accustomed to the West Point routine took time for those who had virtually no prior knowledge of military life. Cadets committed errors of omission and of commission, simply falling into demerits and punishment or earning them by knowingly flaunting the rules. Eisenhower wrote:

> In the first days, when I knew as little as possible about the Army, General Orders had been read and among other instructions we were required to salute all officers. Ten days later, I was double-timing down the street when I heard a band coming. But before it turned the corner I encountered the most decorated fellow I had ever seen. I hesitated just a second, then snapped to attention and presented arms but he did not return the salute. I did it again and a third time. Realizing that he was not going to return my salute, I made inquiries later and was somewhat mortified to learn I had been saluting not an officer but a drum major.[32]

The affable Eisenhower soon became popular among his fellow cadets and was known as "Ike," a nickname he had heard for years in Kansas that his mother detested. He found plenty of mischief and always took great delight in it. During his plebe year, Eisenhower and fellow cadet Layson Atkins of California, known to the Corps as Tommy, were called to account for an infraction. Corporal E. E. Adler ordered the two plebes to report to his room at the end of the day in "full dress coats." Eisenhower remembered:

> Tommy suggested that we obey the literal language of the order. . . . The full-dress coat is a cutaway with long tails in the back, and tailored straight across the waist in front. At the appointed time, each of us donned a full-dress coat and with no other stitch of

clothing, marched into the Corporal's room. We saluted and said
solemnly, "Sir, Cadets Eisenhower and Atkins report as ordered."

The sound that Corporal Adler let out was the cry of a cougar.
While his roommate, a rather easygoing man named [L. T.] Byrne,
became convulsed with laughter, the Corporal was transformed
into a picture of outraged dignity.

The two unruly plebes were made to report later in full uniforms, including their
rifles, and were braced against the barracks wall until, remembered Eisenhower,
"we left our bodily outlines on it in perspiration. But afterward, we and the other
plebes had a lot of laughs—quiet ones—out of Adler's temporary discomfiture."[33]

Smoking in his quarters, along with a general disregard for the rank and
privilege that upper classmen had assumed, resulted in a litany of violations
and an accompanying mountain of demerits for Eisenhower. Each month,
a cadet could absorb a maximum of nine demerits without punishment.
However, those who received ten or more were regularly detailed to walk
them off, one hour per demerit, marching while carrying a rifle. Eisenhower
did his share of walking. He was also confined to quarters. Eventually, several cadets he knew well were reassigned to different companies to break up
a troublemaking group that enjoyed gambling and carousing.

Classmate Charles C. Herrick, himself as much of a free spirit as the
Academy would allow, remembered a particularly risky venture that
Eisenhower and others tried:

One of the worst offenses at the Point was to get caught off the res-
ervation. But somehow it never worried Ike and some of the others.
They'd sneak out the lavatory windows, and past the sentry post and
off they'd go up the Hudson in a rented boat to Newburgh for coffee
and sandwiches. Imagine, they'd travel 30 miles—15 there and 15
back—just for chow. If any of those guys had been caught, they'd
have been thrown right out of the academy.[34]

Nicknamed "Dad," Herrick was an Illinois appointee. He ranked 150th in
conduct for his tenure at West Point. The goat of the class of 1915, graduating with an overall class rank of 164, he served as an officer of the 30th
Infantry Division during World War I and was discharged from the army in
1922. Returning to active duty with the outbreak of World War II, he was a

member of the War Department General Staff from 1942 to 1943. He worked as an investment banker, retired with the rank of colonel in 1951, and lived for years in Oakland, California, where he led the local civil defense organization, was the chief executive of the Veterans Administration Hospital, and served as Oakland's US postmaster. He died at the age of eighty-three in 1974.

A sampling of the offenses recorded on Eisenhower's permanent record during his four years at West Point include "late at chapel; late to target formation 7:05; absent at 8 a.m. drill formation; room in disorder afternoon inspection; Sunday overshoes not arranged as prescribed at retreat; tarnished brasses at inspection; chair not against table at 8 a.m. inspection; shelves of clothespress dusty, and dirty washbasin at retreat inspection."

Although Eisenhower stood a somewhat respectable thirty-ninth in conduct despite the forty-three demerits he tallied at the end of his plebe year, his comparative position rapidly deteriorated. Following his second year, he stood sixty-sixth in conduct with ninety-six demerits. As an upperclassman in 1914, he ranked 105th with sixty-eight demerits. As a member of the first class, he garnered one hundred demerits and ranked 125th in conduct for the year. On a cumulative basis, his record placed him ninety-fifth in conduct in the class of 1915.

On more than one occasion during his presidency, that less than stellar disciplinary record was brought to Eisenhower's attention. He thought that it might well be a good example of exuberant and miscreant youth failing to foretell the full measure of a man's future. Historians have speculated that Dwight Eisenhower's rough-and-tumble upbringing as a middle child on the Kansas prairie helped him get through the four challenging years of West Point. His work experience and his relatively advanced age upon entrance— close to twenty-one—were further advantages that others did not share.

Beast Barracks roommates were assigned alphabetically, and Eisenhower's was a fellow Kansan by the name of John Henry Dykes. Despite their shared origins, this young man had experienced quite a different childhood, including money and family connections. He had just turned seventeen when he came to the Academy, and the harshness of Beast Barracks seemed more than he could bear. To make matters worse, he told Eisenhower through tears that his hometown had turned out en masse and a band had performed a musical sendoff as he departed on the train for West Point. Returning home a failure would no doubt be excruciating.

Through the years, Dykes has been described as a ne'er-do-well who did not have the right stuff for West Point. Years later, when Eisenhower recalled the experience, he politely declined to name him. In his book *At Ease: Stories I Tell to Friends*, the aging former president said, "My crude efforts at bucking him up were no help. At the first examinations during our plebe year, he left the Academy. I liked him and I still think it was only his youth and sheltered existence that defeated him in his chances for a military career."[35]

Dykes, from Lebanon, Kansas, was the son of a doctor whose family was friendly with influential Kansas Republican Charles Curtis, later elected to the US Senate and vice president in the administration of President Herbert Hoover. Dykes remembered that Eisenhower encouraged him, saying, "It won't always be like this."

Apparently, the cruelest blow came when Dykes was found deficient in mathematics and English after the first round of examinations. On January 9, 1912, he was discharged. Thirty-one years later, in December 1942, Eisenhower was named supreme commander of the Allied Expeditionary Force, tasked with leading the preparation and execution of the D-Day invasion of Nazi-occupied Europe on June 6, 1944, and the subsequent Allied offensive that doomed the Third Reich. When Dykes, then living in Enid, Oklahoma, heard the news, he wrote to Eisenhower, "This will lead to the presidency in 10 to 15 years." To that, Eisenhower responded, "I don't think so, but I appreciate your kindness."

Dykes's son Delmar later remembered a seminal event in his father's life:

> In 1952 Dad and three or four men from Enid drove up to Abilene to see Eisenhower launch his campaign. Dad hadn't seen Eisenhower since 1911, and naturally he was wondering if he'd be recognized. Eisenhower spoke to several people in the crowd, then looked at John Dykes, and without a second's hesitation he flashed the famous grin and said, "Hi, Johnnie." Returning to Enid that night, Dad was a very happy man.[36]

When Beast Barracks transitioned to camp, Eisenhower acquired a new roommate, coincidentally another Kansan. Paul A. Hodgson was from Wichita, and like Eisenhower he was an exceptional athlete. The two shared a close friendship during their four years at West Point and throughout the rest of their lives. P. A. Hodgson was much more concerned with academics than Eisenhower. He ranked consistently in the top twenty-five in the class and graduated eighteenth.

Still, when it came to generating a little excitement, Hodgson found himself along for the ride and suffering the consequences on more than one occasion. Then, just ten weeks before graduation, P. A. failed to notice that two cadets were absent when he checked rooms in his barracks at taps. Found guilty of neglect of duty, he was busted from lieutenant to private.

Hodgson told *Collier's* magazine in 1955 that his roommate could be a "sly one about minor duties about the room. We were supposed to take turns opening the windows at night and closing them first thing in the morning. But Ike dressed so fast that he could linger in bed—and I, a slower dresser, always had to get out of my warm bed onto the cold floor and close the windows. I was always very careful about cleaning my part of the room whereas Ike was very nonchalant. But somehow I always got the demerits."[37]

One of many lessons that Dwight Eisenhower learned at West Point was the value of human dignity. As a yearling, he admitted to doing his part in ensuring that plebes knew their place at the Academy, and one of several routine questions that might be asked of an offending underclassman was, "Mister, what is your PCS?" The initials stood for "previous condition of servitude," and the question translated as "What did you do before coming to West Point?"

When one plebe on an obvious errand came rushing down a sidewalk and failed to yield the right of way, he ran smack into Eisenhower, who responded with the characteristic yearling look of disdain followed by a coarse bellow: "Mr. Dumbguard, what is your PCS? You look like a barber."

When the plebe got to his feet, he replied, "I was a barber, sir."

Remembering that the moment was far from his finest, Eisenhower recalled:

I didn't have enough sense to apologize to him and make a joke of the whole thing. I just turned my head and went to my tent where my roommate, P. A. Hodgson, was sitting. I looked at him and said, "P. A., I'm never going to crawl another plebe as long as I live. As a matter of fact, they'll have to run over and knock me out of the company street before I'll make any attempt again. I've just done something that was stupid and unforgivable. I managed to make a man ashamed of the work he did to earn a living."

And never again, during the remaining three years at the U.S.M.A., did I take it upon myself to crawl a plebe.[38]

Academically, Eisenhower maintained a generally average performance in the upper half of his class. As a plebe, he ranked fifty-seventh overall with a strong standing of tenth in English, thirtieth in practical military engineering (surveying), thirty-ninth in history, and a weak 112th in math. His yearling rank dropped to eighty-first, and he finished ninety-seventh in math, seventy-ninth in French, seventy-eighth in drawing, and seventieth in military hygiene. His high performance was in drill regulations infantry at sixteenth. During his third year—or cow year, as it was called—Eisenhower's best academic finish was in chemistry-mineralogy-geology, and he ended the year ranked sixty-second in the class. As a first class cadet, his best showing was twenty-seventh in hippology. Coupled with the well-known 125th standing in conduct, he graduated the Academy sixty-first in his class.

Omar Bradley reveled in the rigid life at West Point. The boy from Moberly who had lost his father at a tender age found the structure, emphasis on athletics, and opportunity for education exhilarating. However, he also believed that the late arriving "Augustines" were always considered inferior to the other members of the class of 1915. They had, after all, escaped the three harrowing weeks of Beast Barracks. Bradley saw the situation as simply one more obstacle to overcome.

Bradley embraced the discipline that West Point proffered, and he learned quickly to steer clear of trouble. During his first month in barracks, "Brad" received sixteen demerits for offenses such as knocking his hat off with his own rifle twice and sitting at the dinner table with his collar improperly askew. In contrast to Eisenhower, Bradley ranked twenty-ninth in conduct on graduation day in June 1915.

Bradley was soft-spoken and devoted to baseball, and he later regretted that he had not pursued his studies with greater zeal. "Academically, we cadets were grouped into twelve-man sections numbered 1 to 28 according to our grades," he wrote. "The top men were in Section 1; those with the worst grades ("goats") in 28. Based on my test scores at Jefferson Barracks, I started off near the bottom: Section 24 in math, Section 27 in English and history. However, by dint of hard study, I moved up throughout the year and by June my overall class standing was 49. Had it not been for English—my toughest course—I would have stood even higher. . . . Unfortunately my athletic activities during my four years at West Point had a pronounced impact on my grades and academic class standing."[39]

Despite his concentration on athletics, Bradley managed to remain in the upper third of his class during all four years at West Point. Following his plebe year, with a ranking of 160th in English, he slipped to fifty-third in his class as a yearling with low ratings of 113th in drawing, 109th in French, and 106th in military hygiene. During his cow year, he improved to forty-third overall. Despite a strong showing of ninth in cavalry and artillery drill regulations, he was plagued by a low ranking of 118th in Spanish. During his first class year, Bradley's foreign language woes climaxed at 127th in Spanish, while his highest rating was sixth in conduct, followed by fiftieth in civil and military engineering. His cumulative performance placed him forty-fourth in the graduating order of the class of 1915.

Bradley also found something of a challenge with his roommate—or "wife," in cadet slang. He remembered:

> The roommate assigned to me turned out to be a trial. He was Benjamin W. Mills, a lackadaisical Southerner, born in Georgia and raised in Florida. He was not too bright and seldom applied himself seriously to his studies. Against all rules, he smoked and continued to smoke throughout his four years at West Point. Had I not spent countless hours coaching him in math and science, Bennie Mills would not have made it through the first year.[40]

Benjamin Willis Mills, an Augustine appointed from the 3rd District of Florida, graduated 160th—fifth from the bottom of the class of 1915. Initially a lieutenant with the 9th Infantry Regiment, he transferred within the year to the Signal Corps, stationed in San Diego, California, and became a student aviation officer, one of the army's first. He subsequently returned to the Infantry, rose to the rank of colonel, and served as director of the Army Board for the Promotion of Rifle Practice, retiring in the summer of 1939.

During World War II, Mills returned to active duty. Unsuccessful in obtaining an assignment abroad, he retired in 1945 while mourning the loss of a son, Benjamin Willis Mills Jr., a 1941 graduate of the Citadel who was killed in action in Belgium in the autumn of 1944. His brother, Maj. Gen. Robert H. Mills, served as chief of the US Army Dental Corps from 1942 to 1946. Benjamin Mills died of a heart attack in Washington, D.C., on February 6, 1947.

James Van Fleet was a country boy from Florida, and though he was not alone in his rural upbringing, he sometimes felt out of place among a Corps of high achievers. He was experienced in handling a rifle, rated expert all four of his years at West Point, and had no difficulty with the physical requirements of the Academy. He recognized, however, that he had never developed good study habits, and the fact that he had always read slowly and needed to pronounce each word out loud to assist comprehension further compounded his academic challenges. At times, particularly during his plebe year, Van Fleet came close to being overwhelmed. A letter from his father no doubt helped buoy the young man's spirit:

> Stick with it! Persevere . . . plug along. . . . Be ever watchful, studious, and work hard. Banish from your heart all unhappy memories. After the first year, you will have it easier. When one task is finished, jump in another. Don't hesitate, and do not falter. Don't waver, don't wait, keep on going. Merit begets confidence; confidence begets enthusiasm; enthusiasm conquers the world. You have got the ability to win, and all you need is confidence. My dear son, if you want knowledge, you must toil and work hard for it.[41]

A quiet young man, Van, as he came to be known, shied away from social activities, particularly those formal occasions that called for refinement and grace on the dance floor. Others tended to consider him a loner, short on conversation, and somewhat abrupt. His entry in the 1915 *Howitzer*, West Point's yearbook, stated, "Perhaps this reticent attitude has kept some of us from knowing him as well as we should. . . ."[42]

Although Van Fleet raised his academic standing from 115th at the end of his plebe year to a lofty 48th as a yearling, his frustrations in the classroom continued. By the time his cow year concluded, he had free-fallen to 78th overall, ranking particularly low in Spanish and drill regulations. His best showing that year was in drawing, as he ranked 35th. He graduated from the Academy ranked ninety-second overall, with his highest standing in practical military engineering (surveying) at 25th.

For the highest future achievers of the class of 1915, advancement in rank came slowly at the Academy. Eisenhower managed to make corporal after his plebe year but was busted back to private for a second infraction of dancing too enthusiastically at one of the frequent campus hops. He later made sergeant and finally color sergeant in F Company.

Bradley, believing his Augustine status had impeded his advance in rank, wore a clean sleeve for three years before rapid promotion to sergeant, first sergeant, and lieutenant in F Company. Van Fleet concluded his West Point tenure as a sergeant, while Joseph McNarney wore a clean sleeve— remaining a private all four years—as he quietly earned an expert rifleman's badge and graduated 41st in the class.

Hubert Harmon was another clean sleeve in the class of 1915. He graduated 103rd and received low marks in most of his curriculum with the exception of drawing. The family connection stayed with Hubert, and when it was discovered that his older brother Millard was a recent graduate, an exceptional hazing experience was revived. Millard had proven himself adept at crawling on all fours and reciting a little poem, "Doodle bug, doodle bug, your house is on fire!" Logically, upper classmen remembered Millard as "Doodle" and decided to see whether the extraordinary ability to call doodle bugs was a family trait. Hubert was on his hands and knees frequently, crawling across sidewalks in search of the elusive doodle bugs. He earned the nickname "Little Doodle." Although Millard was later known as "Miff," the nickname stuck with Hubert, and he was known to fellow officers and friends as Doodle for the rest of his career.[43]

There were social diversions at West Point to be sure. The frequent hops allowed the cadets to mix with young ladies from the surrounding area, while musical performances and parade exhibitions brought visitors, both military and civilian, to the campus regularly. Each year, the Dialectic Society produced the Hundredth Night stage performance. Held in February, it was so named because it was held one hundred days before the beginning of June Week, when a series of events culminated with graduation.

On February 19, 1915, several cadets of the first class led the afternoon matinee and evening performances of *The Grand Strategy*, playing to packed houses. The three-act musical comedy was written by James Ord with lyrics by John Harris, and Edward McGuire sang "I'm the Guy" to the delight of the crowds. Ord, George Peabody, and Douglas Gillette danced, as the *New York Times* described the next day, a "combination, foxtrot, rag, hesitation feature."

For Eisenhower, Bradley, and Van Fleet, the athletic experience at West Point shaped their careers as surely as drill, classroom effort, or any other aspect of cadet life. Eisenhower made no secret of the fact that playing varsity football and baseball were prime motivations in his decision to apply to the Academy. Bradley came from Missouri with a strong arm and a talent for baseball, and Van Fleet knew the hard knocks of the football field so well that an injury during his last year of high school prevented his trying out for the football team as a plebe, a disappointment that would eventually be swallowed up in triumph.

A fellow cadet remembered Eisenhower's soaring confidence as the time for varsity football tryouts approached in the fall of 1911. Ike had played tackle, halfback, and quarterback at Abilene High School when he returned to class to study for the competitive West Point examinations, and at 160 pounds he was bigger than most adversaries he encountered on the field.

That situation changed at West Point. Though Eisenhower was tough, he was considered fairly lightweight and failed to make the varsity football team as a plebe. He was beside himself with disappointment, and when P. A. Hodgson did make the squad, Eisenhower redoubled his efforts to make the team in 1912. He played for the Cullum Hall team, a junior varsity squad that competed with local high schools. He made the varsity baseball team, but the coach—hard-drinking Samuel Strang Nicklin, a journeyman major leaguer who had helped the New York Giants win the 1905 World Series—attempted to change his hitting style. Eisenhower did not play in a single game.

By the fall of 1912, Eisenhower's weight was up to 174 pounds. He had worked hard on speed and agility. When he stood out during a scrimmage against a football team made up of active-duty soldiers, the varsity coaches took note. The team's head coach, Capt. Ernest Graves, had Ike's worn-out equipment switched for better gear.

Eisenhower sat on the bench during the first game against Stevens Institute, but he earned a start against Rutgers in a 19–0 win the following week. Newspaper reporters took note of the young Kansan who also played linebacker on defense. After a 6–0 loss to a powerhouse Yale team, his break-out game occurred on October 26 against Colgate. Graves put Eisenhower in the game late in the fourth quarter, and he scored the touchdown that turned the contest around. Army won 18–7, and the *New York Tribune* reported, "The work of Eisenhower brought joy to the Army rooters."[44]

The Carlisle Indian School football team, coached by the famed Glenn "Pop" Warner, visited Army on November 9, 1912, and Eisenhower had earned the start playing both ways, halfback on offense and linebacker on defense. The star of the Carlisle team was Jim Thorpe, already a legend-ary athlete. A Native American of the Sac and Fox tribe, Thorpe had won gold medals in both the pentathlon and decathlon during the 1912 Summer Olympics four months earlier. He is recognized by many as the finest athlete of the first half of the twentieth century.

Early in the game, Eisenhower ran well up the middle. Quarterback Vernon Prichard handed off tackle to halfback Leland Hobbs, who scored the touchdown that proved to be the lone bright spot for Army that day.

Stopping the All-American Thorpe proved impossible for the Army defense in a 27–6 loss, but Eisenhower and his fellow linebacker and classmate Charles Benedict once hit the star running back with a high-low combination so hard that Carlisle called timeout. After Thorpe gathered himself, the Carlisle offense was at it again. When Eisenhower and Benedict came at him another time, Thorpe stopped short and the two defenders slammed into one another. The Army linebackers were so shaken up that neither returned to the game.

The *New York Sun* reported, "Army had a rattling good back in Eisenhower, who was the best man to carry the ball in the Indian game," and forty years later Thorpe was asked if he remembered that 1912 game at Army. His response was a guttural "Good linebacker."[45]

In a 1961 speech, Eisenhower reflected on Thorpe and his athletic prowess. "Here and there," he commented, "there are some people who are supremely endowed. My memory goes back to Jim Thorpe. He never prac-ticed in his life, and he could do anything better than any other football player I ever saw."[46]

Eisenhower's football career, though full of promise amid speculation that he might in fact receive All-American honors, was short-lived. Two weeks after the Carlisle game, Army met Tufts University. Teammates remembered some fine running early in the 15–6 victory, but then it hap-pened: as he pushed forward to maintain momentum, Eisenhower felt his knee twist, and then something ripped. He stayed in the game for a few more plays, but then went to the ground and had to be helped from the field.

That afternoon, Eisenhower was in the West Point dispensary. Five days later, he was released. A November 26 article in the *New York Sun* noted, "Eisenhower is limping, but it is hardly likely that he will be kept out of practice. He is one of the Army's strongest offensive backs and a terrific line smasher."[47]

The story appeared four days before the annual showdown with Navy. That same day, Eisenhower was in the Riding Hall practicing dangerous monkey drills, a routine in which the rider mounts and dismounts the horse while at a full gallop. He later remembered that the doctors issued no prohibition against physical activity, and the impetuosity of a young man wanting to get back to normal activity is understandable. In the middle of the drill, he crumpled to the ground.

During four agonizing days in the infirmary, the doctors worked on the seriously injured knee. Clearly, Eisenhower's football days were over. He watched Army lose 6–0 to Navy, and Coach Graves howled, "Here I come up with the best line plunger and linebacker I've ever seen at West Point and he busts his knee in the Riding Hall."[48]

It was a bitter blow. Eisenhower, however, could not stay away from the football field, and became a cheerleader. He also coached the Cullum Hall team, honing his leadership and team-building skills further. The junior varsity squad performed well, but nothing took the place of actual competition. Efforts to strengthen the knee were unsuccessful. Through the years, a number of former Tufts players apologized to Eisenhower for inflicting the terrible injury—so many that he openly speculated as to just how many men Tufts had had on the field during the game.

"In those days, West Point was sports oriented to a feverish degree," Bradley remembered. "The most esteemed cadets in the society were star athletes. . . . There were marvelous advantages to being on varsity athletic squads. We plebes were 'recognized' by the upper classmen. We did not have to say 'sir' each time we spoke to them and we were spared hazing on the athletic fields and at mealtimes. We sat at a special training table in the dining hall where discipline was loose, almost nonexistent."[49]

In the spring of 1912, Bradley made the varsity baseball team. Although he failed to make the varsity football team that fall, he played on the Cullum Hall team. He played left field on the 1913 Army baseball team and was particularly proud of its 16–6 record and a close 2–1 win over Navy. Weighing nearly 180 pounds, Bradley made the varsity football team as backup center in 1913 and played in one game. The 1914 baseball team finished 10–5, and Bradley gained another letter in left field.

The 1914 football team went undefeated at 9–0, and the defense gave up just twenty points all season. Bradley played in five games. Again playing left field for the 1915 baseball team, Bradley remembered that the 18–3 Cadets were considered by many to be the best baseball squad in the history of the Academy.

He later wrote:

> I have never regretted my sports obsession for a moment. It is almost trite to observe that in organized team sports one learns the important art of group cooperation in goal achievement. No extracurricular endeavor I know of could better prepare a soldier for the battlefield. West Point sports also gave me an excellent opportunity to take the measure of many men who would serve with, or under, me in World War II. It is noteworthy, I think, that all the men on our 1914 baseball team who remained in the Army went on to become generals.[50]

In 1913, the Army football team completed an 8–1 record with the passing combination of quarterback Prichard and All-American end Louis Merillat becoming a sensation. Headlines touted "Louis to Merillat" and predicted an unbeaten campaign. Prichard snatched victory from near certain defeat against Colgate, ripping a seventy-yard touchdown run with ten seconds left in the game to seal a 7–6 win. Army had not beaten Navy since 1905, but Merillat caught two touchdown passes from Prichard and ran sixty yards for a third in a 22–9 victory. Center John McEwan, halfback Hobbs, and halfback and punter Hodgson were standouts.

The most memorable game of the 1913 season, however, was the 35–13 home loss to Notre Dame on November 1. The day before the game, the *New York Times* reported, "The Army hopes to defeat Notre Dame by a decisive score to-morrow and thus secure confidence to themselves and their supporters."[51]

The outcome was quite different. The forward pass had emerged as a new offensive dimension, both to enliven the game and to reduce the number of serious injuries players were incurring. The Fighting Irish unveiled an aerial attack that day that raised the forward pass to new heights, changed the future of college football, and contributed to the growing stature of a young receiver named Knute Rockne. Notre Dame quarterback Gus Dorais completed 14 of 17 passes for 243 yards and two touchdowns.

The 1914 football season was historic for Army, which finished 9–0 and captured the collegiate national championship. In quick succession, the cadets vanquished Stevens Tech, Rutgers, Colgate, Holy Cross, and Villanova. They exacted a measure of revenge for the embarrassing 1913 loss to Notre Dame with a 20–7 victory over the Fighting Irish as Hodgson rushed for two touchdowns. A 28–0 shutout of Maine set up the closest game of the season, a 13–7 win over Springfield on November 21 as a number of starters were rested or played sparingly in preparation for the showdown with Navy the following week.

The winning streak was not without cost. Hodgson was slowed with an ankle injury. McEwan nursed a banged-up shoulder and a deep leg bruise. Prichard battled tonsillitis. With Hodgson out of the Springfield game, Van Fleet started in the Army backfield and scored a touchdown. His performance was impressive and secured another start against Navy.

Although he did not play football at the Academy until his first class year, Van Fleet was an outstanding athlete. He made the varsity when coach Charles Daly took note of his speed and hard-hitting play on both offense and defense during scrimmages. During one practice, he carried the ball at full speed through a gap and collided head-on with Bradley, who was playing defense. For the rest of his life, Van Fleet carried a scar on the left side of his face.[52]

Before an estimated thirty thousand spectators at Franklin Field in Philadelphia, Van Fleet played the entire game against Navy in a 20–0 victory, calling the signals for the Cadet defense that held the Midshipmen scoreless and running well on offense. Prichard threw to Merillat for a touchdown, Hodgson scored despite two fumbles, and Benedict crossed the goal line a third time for Army. Van Fleet received the game ball and kept the zero from the Navy side of the scoreboard as a remembrance.[53]

In addition to Eisenhower, Bradley, Van Fleet, and Prichard, other cadets of the class of 1915 also excelled in athletics. John MacTaggart starred on the basketball team. Hobbs played baseball, basketball, and football and was a member of the track and field team, as was Hodgson, who set high jump and broad jump records. Merillat, the celebrated football All-American, played with the Canton Bulldogs of the fledgling National Football League in the 1920s.

One of the finest athletes in West Point history, Alexander M. "Babe" Weyand entered the Academy as a member of the class of 1915. However, a deficiency in French forced him back a year to the class of 1916. An All-American tackle, Weyand lettered in football for five seasons and was the captain of the 1916 team that went undefeated at 9–0 and won the national championship.

Weyand was also the Cadet Corps heavyweight wrestling champion for three years and competed in wrestling as a member of the US team during the 1920 Olympics. As for his military career, he was wounded and decorated for bravery during World War I, but hearing loss precluded a combat command during World War II; he served as the army's first provost marshal general in London. He became a noted author, particularly on sports-related topics, and was elected to the College Football Hall of Fame in 1974. He died in 1982.

The importance of athletics at West Point cannot be overemphasized. Eisenhower shared the sentiment that Bradley expressed in an autumn 1945 letter to Gen. Maxwell Taylor: "It has often been likened to war," he said of football, "the razzle-dazzle passes to the Air Force, the end sweeps to racing armored columns and the busting through the middle to the bone-shattering Infantry attacks. . . . The analogy is a good one in so far as each contest required guts, brains, physical power, skillful teamwork, and heart. . . ."[54]

Reflecting on his tenure as supreme Allied commander during World War II, Eisenhower wrote of his football days at West Point, "Thirty years afterward, I found myself in the midst of war. I had occasion to be on the lookout for natural leaders. Athletes take a certain amount of kidding, especially from those who think it is always brawn versus brains. But I noted . . . how well ex-footballers seemed to have leadership qualifications and it wasn't sentiment that made it seem so."[55]

PART III

World War I

CHAPTER FIVE

Embryonic Careers

At 9:55 a.m. on June 12, 1915, the Corps of Cadets formed and, accompanied by the West Point band, marched to the Battle Monument, where a sizable crowd of dignitaries and family members had gathered on this warm, sunny morning. The ceremonies opened with a prayer. Then Secretary of War Lindley M. Garrison stepped to the rostrum and spoke of tradition and duty.

As their names were called, the cadets received their diplomas in order of class ranking. They swore an oath to defend the Constitution of the United States. A review followed, and then it was over. Their four years of labor, sacrifice, and learning the military arts were at an end, and 164 new second lieutenants joined the ranks of the US Army. A month earlier, the *New York Times* had reported that the number of graduating officers was actually greater than the 105 second lieutenant slots available on active duty.[56]

The Saturday morning ceremonies were the culmination of a week of activities at West Point, beginning with a graduation sermon and proceeding through infantry, cavalry, and field artillery demonstrations, class reunions, a cadet hop, athletic events, and parades. The *New York Sun* noted that this was the largest graduating class in Academy history to date and that more than 240 young men had originally reported as plebes in 1911.

"Eighty-four delinquents have left. This is a large percentage of 'failure' for a class at West Point," the *Sun* reported.[57]

The newspaper related that two cadets, William E. R. Covell of the District of Columbia and Edwin R. Kimble of Galveston, Texas, were vying for the title of honor graduate. It also reported that Luis R. Esteves of Puerto Rico and Anastacio Quevedo Ver of the Philippines were members of the class from the United States' "insular possessions," and that Robert B. Lorch of Kentucky was the oldest cadet to graduate, at twenty-six years and five months of age. The youngest graduate was Clyde R. Eisenschmidt of Oklahoma, who came to the Academy on June 14, 1911, and was required to remain there at his own expense until his seventeenth birthday on July 30, when he could be formally admitted in accordance to regulations. On June 8, Thomas Larkin of Washington won the final physical tests and was named the strong man of the Corps.

Following the lengthy commencement ceremonies, the newly graduated officers boarded a train for New York City to enjoy a performance of the Broadway musical *Chin Chin* and a celebratory dinner at the Hotel Astor.

As the festivities subsided, the bloodletting of World War I neared the end of its first year. Closer to home, revolution and civil war had wracked Mexico for some time, and the unrest threatened the southwestern border of the United States. On October 19, 1915, the United States formally recognized the government of Mexican President Venustiano Carranza, incurring the wrath of revolutionary Francisco "Pancho" Villa in the process.

Villa responded with several bloody attacks against Americans. On January 10, 1916, his guerrillas raided a train in the Mexican province of Chihuahua and summarily executed seventeen US citizens. Two months later, more than 1,500 of Villa's men crossed the border and attacked the town of Columbus, New Mexico. A detachment of the US 13th Cavalry Regiment was camped nearby, and in the ensuing gun battle eighteen Americans, eight of them soldiers, died. Eight more were wounded. Sixty-seven of Villa's gunmen were shot dead.

President Woodrow Wilson took action, dispatching Gen. John J. Pershing and a force of infantry, cavalry, artillery, and even airmen and planes in pursuit of Villa. Pershing crossed the border into Mexico on March 15, 1916, and played a frustrating game of cat and mouse with Villa for the next eleventh months. Finally, on the eve of US entry into World War I, the Punitive Expedition was withdrawn.

Pershing's force had failed in its primary mission, the capture of Villa, due in part to the fact that both the US and Mexican governments placed restrictions on their movements. Rules of engagement were limited in a similar manner to that experienced by American commanders in Vietnam a half century later. Villa outwitted the Americans on several occasions and never committed his forces to a decisive battle. Tensions between the US and Mexican governments heightened, and there was talk of war. The two sides exchanged fire on more than one occasion, but the threat of open conflict eventually abated. In failure, the Punitive Expedition nevertheless provided valuable experience for young officers in the field, including several members of the class of 1915.

While Pershing was chasing Villa, the German government sent a bizarre communiqué to the government of Mexico. Known as the Zimmermann Telegram, its text invited Mexico to enter World War I on the side of Germany and Austria-Hungary by declaring war on the United States. In exchange, when victory was won, the territory comprising Texas, New Mexico, and Arizona, lost to the United States decades earlier, would be restored to Mexico.

Although the Mexican government declined the offer, the content of the Zimmermann Telegram was leaked to the US government by British intelligence. Along with the German resumption of unrestricted submarine warfare in the Atlantic, the diplomatic treachery raised anti-German sentiment in the US to a crescendo. Finally, on April 6, 1917, President Wilson asked Congress for a declaration of war, and the United States formally entered World War I.

In Mexico and on the battlefields of Europe, some young officers of the class of 1915 experienced the sting of combat. Others, including its two most illustrious graduates, remained in the United States performing, to their chagrin, garrison and training duties.

In one of the closest competitions in Academy history, Covell edged Kimble to graduate first in the class of 1915 by a mere three one-thousandths of a point. Covell was commissioned in the Corps of Engineers, served in Hawaii and California, and arrived in France in October 1917, where he was an instructor and held various posts until returning to the United States in 1919. He later became assistant engineer of maintenance in the Panama Canal Zone and retired in May 1940 as a lieutenant colonel. With the outbreak of World War II, he returned to active duty and served as commanding general in the Services of Supply, China-Burma-India Theater. He also served as chief of the Fuels and Lubricants Division, Office of the Quartermaster General, retiring in 1948 with the rank of major general. He died in 1975.

After graduating second, Kimble entered the Corps of Engineers and performed mapping work on the US West Coast. He was deployed to France in the summer of 1917 with the temporary rank of major. By October, he was commanding a battalion of engineers on the Western Front. Although letters to his mother indicate that Kimble's sector was relatively quiet, some of the first German prisoners taken by the US Army during World War I were captured near his position.

In the spring of 1918, Kimble was attached to the staff of the British Fifth Corps. He was present with British forces during the first ten days of the Battle of Picardy from March 21 to 30. There is no direct evidence of Kimble being wounded in action; however, he contracted septicemia following a surgical procedure and died on April 9 at the age of twenty-five. Kimble was the first member of the class of 1915 to die in France.

Anastacio Ver was the second Filipino graduate of the Academy. Vicente Lim, a 1914 graduate, was commissioned in the Philippine Scouts, a unit of the US Army that existed from 1901 until the end of World War II and included Filipino personnel usually under the command of American officers. Lim reached the rank of brigadier general and commanded a guerrilla operation against the Japanese during World War II. He was captured and executed in late 1944. Ver graduated 119th in the class of 1915. He served in his native Philippines during World War I, retired in 1934 with the rank of major due to physical disability, and served with guerrilla units during World War II. He died in 1960.

Luis Esteves, who reportedly tutored Dwight Eisenhower in Spanish at the Academy, graduated ninety-seventh. He encountered a unique obstacle in obtaining his commission. Although Puerto Rico was a US possession, Puerto Ricans were not US citizens in 1915, and a legal question arose as to whether he could be commissioned in the army. Research at the War Department uncovered a precedent. During the Revolutionary War, foreign military men, such as the Marquis de Lafayette and Baron von Steuben, had received commissions in the Continental Army. In 1917, Congress passed the Jones Act, granting US citizenship to Puerto Ricans.

Esteves was initially assigned to the 23rd Infantry. Family members recount that on the evening he joined his unit in El Paso, Texas, Mexican and US troops were firing at one another across the border as Villa was on the loose and tensions were high. The following morning, Esteves crossed the border into Mexico and demanded to see the commander of the Mexican troops.

When Esteves was informed that the Mexican commander was having breakfast and was not dressed, the young lieutenant responded, "This is no time for a military officer to be undressed and having breakfast. Tell him to get dressed immediately and present himself to his office. An officer of the US Army is here demanding to speak with him!"

The Mexican officer dressed quickly and rushed to meet Esteves. The two discussed the situation in Spanish and resolved the issue.[58]

Esteves was a superb organizer and trained Puerto Rican soldiers for service during World War I. On June 3, 1919, due to the continuing illness of his wife, he resigned his commission in the Regular Army. He petitioned for the formation of the Puerto Rican National Guard and was persuaded the following February to take command of its first unit, which later became the 65th Infantry Regiment. Eventually, Estevez rose to adjutant general of the Puerto Rican National Guard and was promoted to major general. During World War II, he commanded the 92nd Infantry Brigade in the Caribbean. He died in 1958.

Admitted to the infirmary with acute influenza on June 6, 1915, Dwight Eisenhower almost missed his graduation but recovered sufficiently to attend. Eisenhower and roommate P. A. Hodgson had both worked on the staff of the *Howitzer*, the West Point yearbook, and the latter wrote of his roommate and close friend, "This is Señor Dwight David Eisenhower, gentleman, the terrible Swedish-Jew, as big as life and twice as natural. . . . At one time he threatened to get interested in life and won his 'A' by being the most promising back in Eastern football—but the Tufts game broke his knee and the promise. Now Ike must content himself with tea, tiddledywinks, and talk, at all of which he excels. . . ."

Hodgson's reference to Eisenhower being a Swedish-Jew is perplexing. Historians tend to agree that it was because of Ike's blond hair and blue eyes at a time when Scandinavians were often the topic of folk humor. The Jewish reference is characteristic of the times as well, as Jews were stereotyped as cunning, crafty, and shrewd bargainers. Hodgson believed Eisenhower possessed each of these traits and, in a day when social anti-Semitism was common, referred to him as a Jew.[59]

Meanwhile, the knee injury that ended Eisenhower's football career nearly terminated his association with the US Army altogether. As graduation approached, he was called to the office of Lt. Col. Henry Shaw, the head of the Academy medical department. Shaw told Eisenhower that he would receive a diploma but that a commission would probably be withheld due to the fact that anyone with a potentially debilitating physical issue could not serve.

"When Colonel Shaw had finished, I said that this was all right with me," Eisenhower wrote years later. "I remarked that I had always had a curious ambition to go to the Argentine (Argentina sounded to me a little like the Old West), and I might go there and see the place, maybe even live there for two or three years. I may have been the first in his experience who was not seriously upset by the possible termination of all military ambitions. He said he would think the matter over."[60]

A few days later, Eisenhower was back in Shaw's office, and the surgeon offered to recommend a commission if he would choose the Coast Artillery as his preference. Eisenhower demurred, explaining that he did not want a commission in the Coast Artillery, which had gained a reputation for long, uneventful postings. Shaw was somewhat taken aback by the abrupt refusal, possibly because he had served in the Coast Artillery himself. At that point, Eisenhower believed his future in the military was virtually nonexistent. However, during a third meeting, Shaw told Eisenhower that a thorough review of his record as a cadet indicated that a riding mishap had contributed to his most serious knee injury. Shaw offered to recommend a commission to the academic board if Eisenhower agreed not to seek service in the Cavalry.

"So I told Colonel Shaw that my ambition was to go to the infantry," Eisenhower remembered. "To which he said, 'All right, I'll recommend you for a commission, but with the stipulation that you will ask for no other service in the Army.' When the time came for me to submit my preference card I put down *Infantry*, first, *Infantry*, second, and *Infantry* third."[61]

In 1946, when Eisenhower was army chief of staff, Col. Herman Beukema, an Academy classmate who became the head of the Department of Economics, Government, and History at West Point in 1930, wrote to him that it had been Colonel Shaw alone who saved Eisenhower's commission. "A medical board in 1915 had you slated for the axe until the chairman [Colonel Shaw] reversed a unanimous vote and carried the case to Washington. . . . I'll tell you the story some time if you are interested."

When Eisenhower responded with great interest, Beukema continued:

[M]embers of the board voted against commissioning you. He [Colonel Shaw] then called in the key people in the Tac [Tactical] Department, the Academic Board, etc., to comment on your cadet record. As a result he reversed the board and carried the split situation to Washington where it was agreed that you "would be a good gamble."[62]

Beukema, incidentally, was married to Lieutenant Colonel Shaw's daughter, Peggy, for nearly forty-five years. Some of the information passed from Beukema to Eisenhower may well have been learned in conversation with his father-in-law. Beukema graduated twenty-sixth in the class of 1915, served along the Mexican border, and was seriously wounded while commanding the 308th Field Artillery Battalion at Pont-à-Mousson, France, on September 9, 1918. He joined the West Point faculty in 1928, founded the Army Specialized Training Program during World War II to provide college education to promising enlisted personnel, became a foremost authority on the philosophy of *Geopolitik*, and retired from the army in 1954 with the rank of brigadier general. He died in 1960.

Eisenhower received his second lieutenant's commission in August 1915, and despite his request for duty in the Philippines, he was assigned to the 19th Infantry Regiment at Fort Sam Houston in San Antonio, Texas. There he met Mamie Geneva Doud, pursued her relentlessly, and finally married her at her family home in Denver, Colorado, on July 1, 1916. Dwight was promoted to first lieutenant on the same day. On September 24, 1917, Mamie gave birth to their first child, Doud Dwight Eisenhower, nicknamed "Icky," shortly after Dwight was transferred to Fort Oglethorpe, Georgia, as an officers' training camp instructor. The child died of scarlet fever in January 1921, and the young parents never fully recovered from their grief.

Eisenhower worked as a regimental supply officer and was promoted to captain in May 1917, a month after the United States entered World War I. On more than one occasion, he had requested transfers to join Pershing's expedition in Mexico but to no avail, and numerous requests for transfer to a command in France were also denied. At one time, he aspired to join the Aviation Section of the Signal Corps. Although the duty was indeed hazardous, a much needed 50 percent pay increase would come along with it.

Mamie's father, wealthy Denver businessman John Doud, realized the hazardous nature of pilot training and frowned on the idea. Icky's pending birth ended the notion completely.

As the war in Europe dragged on, frustration mounted. Eisenhower received a reprimand from one of his commanding officers for the repeated transfer requests, but he stood his ground and eventually earned the respect of his superior. Nevertheless, the young officer's organizational, command, and training skills began to shine. He was transferred to Fort Leavenworth, Kansas, for duty as an instructor. He was miserable the entire time.

Subsequently, Eisenhower was transferred to Camp Meade, Maryland, where the fledgling Tank Corps was being formed. Convinced that with this new weapon his 301st Tank Battalion would soon be fighting in France, breaking the stalemate of trench warfare, his hopes for overseas duty soared. They were quickly dashed again when he was ordered to assume his first independent command at Camp Colt, in Gettysburg, Pennsylvania. Camp Colt was the largest Tank Corps training center in the country, located on the grounds of Gettysburg National Military Park, where the most famous battle of the Civil War had been fought in 1863.

Disappointed that overseas duty continued to elude him, Eisenhower nevertheless dedicated himself to the task at hand. His abilities were recognized, and promotions to major and then lieutenant colonel followed in quick succession in June and October 1918. He wrote:

> The Tank Corps was new. There were no precedents except in basic training and I was the only regular officer in command. Now I really began to learn about responsibility. Although we were part of the Tank Corps, we knew about tanks only from hearsay and newspapers. . . . However, someone in the war zone apparently thought that there might be virtue in letting the Tank Corps recruits and trainees get a preliminary look at the machine that one day we were to operate. Three small tanks were sent to us.

Still, Eisenhower could not shake the thought of overseas duty in wartime. His superior officer in the Tank Corps, Col. Ira C. Welborn, had experienced combat during the Spanish-American War and been awarded the Medal of Honor. Welborn offered to recommend a promotion for Eisenhower to full colonel in exchange for dropping his continuing efforts to go to Europe. As Eisenhower later wrote:

> I declined. I'm ready to take a reduction in rank to the average of my class—to major that is—if the lieutenant colonelcy which I have now stands in the way of my going overseas,' I said. Fate, with its usual bad manners, intervened; I had made no provision for imminent German defeat. I had missed the boat in the war we had been told would end all wars. A soldier's place was where the fighting went on. I hadn't yet fully learned the basic lesson of the military—that the proper place for a soldier is where he is ordered by his superiors.
>
> As for my professional career, the prospects were none too bright. I was older than my classmates, was still bothered on occasion by a bad knee, and saw myself in the years ahead putting on weight in a meaningless chair-bound assignment, shuffling papers and filling out forms, hoping to make colonel before I was retired. If not depressed, I was mad, disappointed, and resented the fact that life had passed me by.[63]

In his frustration, Eisenhower might have taken his own advice, written in his assessment of Omar Bradley that appeared in the 1915 *Howitzer*. "True merit is like a river, the deeper it is, the less noise it makes," Eisenhower quoted an anonymous author. He then said of Bradley, "His most prominent characteristic is 'getting there,' and if he keeps up the clip he's started, some of us will someday be bragging to our grandchildren that 'sure, General Bradley was a classmate of mine.'"

Bradley chose the Infantry upon graduation and was assigned to the 3rd Battalion, 14th Regiment at Fort George Wright in Spokane, Washington. Living with two other lieutenants in a three-bedroom brick duplex, he was soon drawn to the personable officer living in the building's other side. Forrest Harding was a 1909 graduate of West Point and still languishing with the grade of second lieutenant in an Army that was typically slow to promote. Lieutenant Harding initiated gatherings of other young officers in his quarters to discuss infantry tactics and such influences as terrain and logistics. Bradley remembered these discussions as helping him to learn and develop the military craft, and he considered the time spent with Harding to be of great value.

As the cold winter of 1915 set in, soldiers who had gone AWOL (absent without leave) returned to the warmth of the jail at Fort Wright. Since he had taken some basic legal instruction at West Point, Bradley was designated as defense counsel for one of these soldiers, who was also accused of stealing a suitcase. During the trial, Bradley successfully created some doubt about the actual identity of the luggage thief and won an acquittal. When word got back to the stockade, the other thirty-three jailed soldiers clamored for Bradley to represent them as well. For weeks he was overwhelmed with cases, but the load was lifted when he was moved to a seat on the officers' tribunal for court-martial.[64]

In the spring of 1916, the threat of war with Mexico and deployment to the desert Southwest near the town of Douglas, Arizona, postponed Bradley's marriage to Mary Quayle of Moberly. Mary survived a near-fatal bout of typhoid fever, and the two were married in Columbia, Missouri, on December 28, 1916. The 14th Regiment was subsequently withdrawn to Yuma, Arizona, and duty there proved an exercise in misery.

Bradley applied for a transfer to the 14th Regiment's 1st Battalion, then on detached duty in Alaska; however, orders approving the transfer were abruptly cancelled when the United States entered World War I. Instead, the regiment was relocated to Vancouver Barracks, Washington, where it became apparent that he was not going to war.

"The next 16 months were, professionally, the most frustrating of my early Army career," Bradley wrote. "I tried every possible scheme I could dream up to get out of the 14th Infantry and into an outfit bound for France. I sincerely believed that if I did not get to France I would be professionally ruined. Nothing worked. By the luck of the draw, it appeared that I was doomed to sit out the war in the Pacific Northwest."[65]

Early in 1918, the 14th Infantry was again moved. This time the destination was Butte, Montana, where the soldiers were to safeguard the Anaconda copper mines. The mines were vital to the war effort, and labor strife threatened to shut them down. The International Workers of the World had fomented unrest, which culminated in a showdown on the streets of Butte on St. Patrick's Day, 1918. The sight of Regular Army troops with fixed bayonets quelled the disturbance.

Meanwhile, a pregnant Mary gave birth to a stillborn son. Her mother took the infant's body back to Moberly and buried it in the family plot. The young couple was grief stricken.

Promotion to major came in August along with welcome news that the 14th Infantry, at full strength, was to report to Camp Dodge, near Des Moines, Iowa, for training and further assignment to the 19th Infantry Division, followed by deployment to France. Bradley still hoped that he might yet get into the fight. However, the worldwide influenza pandemic of 1918 firmly gripped Camp Dodge. Scores of men became seriously ill, and some died, seriously disrupting the camp's training regimen. Rumors were flying that Germany might well sue for peace.

When word of the armistice came on November 11, 1918, Omar Bradley genuinely felt mixed emotions:

> Mary and I were in downtown Des Moines. There had been several premature "armistices," but now came the real thing. We heard whistles blowing all over town; people surged into the streets wildly celebrating. The war to end all wars was over. I was glad the carnage had stopped, but I was now absolutely convinced that, having missed the war, I was professionally ruined. I could only look forward to a career lifetime of dull routine assignments and would be lucky to retire after 30 years as a lieutenant colonel.[66]

On the first leg of their extended honeymoon trip in late 1916, Omar and Mary Bradley had taken a train from Kansas City to El Paso, Texas, eventually reaching Los Angeles, where they visited members of Mary's family. While in El Paso, they welcomed the New Year with Jo Hunt "Spec" Reaney, a West Point classmate who was serving with the 20th Infantry Regiment. He was a genial host and presented them with a Navajo rug as a wedding gift.

"We returned to Yuma on January 11, 1917," Bradley wrote, "and rented a small furnished house on a hill—two rooms and a screened porch. (The kitchen and bedroom were on the porch.) Mary perked the place up with some curtains and the Navaho [sic] rug Spec Reaney had given us. And so we began forty-nine years of married Army life."[67]

In May 1917, Reaney transferred to a machine gun company of the 42nd Infantry, and in January 1918 he was ordered to the 7th Infantry Regiment, 3rd Division at Camp Greene, North Carolina. The regiment arrived in France on April 15, and by mid-June Reaney had been promoted to the temporary rank of major.

Commanding an infantry company near Château-Thierry, Reaney held positions along the Marne River during two weeks of relative inactivity. At midnight on the morning of July 15, the Germans broke the uneasy calm with a heavy artillery barrage. Another officer met Reaney in his command post sometime later. In a letter to Reaney's mother, the officer wrote:

> He came through the barrage after making arrangements for spare guns and ammunition to go forward. In addition to the high explosive and shrapnel, he had encountered some gas on his way down. The night was hot and blacker than indigo. He stayed with me fifteen or twenty minutes to rest and cool off a bit. He then started out with his orderly, saying that he was going to go over to the other platoon . . . to see that everything was all right. I know that his main idea was to encourage the men by his presence to let them know that they had a company commander who would not ask them to stay at a gun while he remained in a dugout. That was the last any of us ever saw him alive.
>
> Before dawn I had had occasion to return to my P.C. [post of command] and was some thirty meters away from it on my return trip forward, when the concussion of a shell landed me in a ravine. I was overheated and took off a large sheepskin coat I had been wearing. I threw it to one side and it landed on top of a body. It was still too dark to recognize anyone and as it was an urgent necessity for me to get back to my gun position, I didn't investigate.
>
> The next morning the Captain was reported missing. We sent out searching parties. As this little ravine where I had discarded my coat was under direct observation and constant machine gun fire in the daytime, it was not examined until dusk. Then the detail, seeing and recognizing my coat, knowing that I was all right, thought the Captain had been wearing it. They carried him back under cover and it was the Captain. He never suffered; he was killed instantly with his orderly. We buried them side by side.[68]

An at-large appointee to the Academy, Reaney was from Eugene, Oregon. He graduated seventy-ninth in the class of 1915 and was remembered in the *Howitzer* as "a genius for nosing out a rough-house and if there's none to nose out he starts one. . . . His idea of a good time is to have his hat in the gutter, his blouse torn open, his shirt in shreds. . . ." Jo Hunt Reaney was twenty-six years old.

Among those officers of the class of 1915 who experienced extensive combat during World War I, Charles W. Ryder of Topeka, Kansas, compiled an exceptional service record. Ryder graduated thirty-ninth in the class. While his entry in the *Howitzer* alludes to a desire to join the field artillery, he was actually assigned to the infantry. If there was any disappointment associated with the assignment, it is likely that Lieutenant Ryder took it in stride.

Promoted to the rank of captain, Ryder took command of the 1st American Trench Sector near Toul, France, in January 1918, with the 16th Regiment of the 1st Infantry Division. Then from April to July, his command occupied trenches on the Montdidier Front. He was wounded in action on July 21 during the Allied Soissons Offensive and participated in the Argonne Offensive in September and the fighting around the city of Sedan in October.

For gallantry on the day he was wounded, Ryder received the Distinguished Service Cross and the French Croix de Guerre with Palm. His Distinguished Service Cross citation reads in part, "Major Ryder took command of the front-line units and reorganized them under heavy artillery and machine-gun fire. Although wounded in the early operations, he remained in command and directed the attack until all objectives had been taken."

Near the town of Fléville, France, on October 9, 1918, Ryder again distinguished himself under fire. He later received an oak leaf cluster as a second award of the Distinguished Service Cross. The citation reads, "In the attack on Hill 272, after all his runners had been killed or wounded while trying to establish liaison with the front-line companies, Major Ryder advanced alone and personally directed the action of his command although under direct fire from two enemy machine guns. He later personally led the final assault on Hill 272, thereby making possible the success of the entire attack."

After the war, Ryder served with the Provost Marshal General's Department in Paris and in occupied areas of Germany. He was promoted to lieutenant colonel in May 1919.

While commanding a battalion of the 6th Infantry Regiment that was heavily engaged during the Meuse-Argonne Offensive in the autumn of 1918, Maj. John W. Leonard moved forward against German positions. His citation for the Distinguished Service Cross reads: "In action near

Romagne, France, October 14, 1918, Col. [then Maj.] Leonard personally led the assaulting wave in an attack under severe shell and machine-gun fire from the front and flanks. Upon reaching the objective, he directed the organization of the position and by his example of fearlessness rallied his men and kept his line intact." Promotion to lieutenant colonel followed on October 31.

Leonard was wounded in action during the same period and was also awarded the French Croix de Guerre with Palm. Raised in the Old South End of Toledo, Ohio, he graduated eighty-fourth in the class of 1915 and served for the duration with General Pershing's Punitive Expedition in Mexico. With the 6th Infantry throughout World War I, he was also on the frontlines during the action at Saint-Mihiel. After the war, he served with the occupation forces in Germany until 1921.

Following his deployment to Mexico with Pershing, Sidney C. Graves, who graduated seventy-sixth in the class, received a promotion to first lieutenant in the summer of 1916. Within the year, he was in France with the 16th Infantry Regiment. In action in the Bois de Fontaine region on April 29, 1918, he located a German machine gun position that had taken his men under fire.

According to his Distinguished Service Cross citation, "Graves, with three men, voluntarily crawled out to the position of the machine gun in full view and within 100 yards of the enemy lines, shot the gunner, killed the rest of the crew with grenades, and returned with his party without casualty." By July, he had transferred to the 17th Infantry and returned to Camp Meade, Maryland. In mid-August, he was assigned as aide-de-camp to his father, Maj. Gen. William S. Graves, commander of the American Expeditionary Force deployed to Siberia.

On November 18, 1919, while serving as an assistant to the chief of staff of the American Expeditionary Force at Vladivostok, Major Graves earned a second Distinguished Service Cross. "In answer to a call to save noncombatants entrapped in the railroad station at Vladivostok, Siberia," reads the citation, "Major Graves fearlessly entered a zone swept by intense machine-gun and artillery fire of Russian Government and insurgent forces, entered the station, and assisted in locating six noncombatants. He escorted them through the attacking troops to a place of safety."

In the spring of 1920, Graves returned to the United States and took a leave of absence from the army. On July 12, 1920, having also received the French Croix de Guerre and the British Distinguished Service Order, he resigned his commission. In 1921, he married Olga Roosevelt, a distant relative of President Theodore Roosevelt, who had divorced from her first husband a year earlier. In the West Point Association of Graduates annual report issued in 1925, he is listed as "Address not known." Graves worked as an insurance broker and died in Washington, D.C., on September 6, 1974.

William S. T. Halcomb of New York reached the rank of major with the field artillery, serving in the Vosges sector and at Saint-Mihiel. Twice cited for bravery, he received the French Croix de Guerre with Palm. Halcomb resigned his commission in December 1919 and became the factory superintendent for C.D. Durkee & Co., on Staten Island.

James Van Fleet planned to marry soon after graduation. He had met his fiancée, Helen Moore, at West Point in the spring of 1915. His roommate, Benjamin Yancey, was confined to quarters for an infraction of the rules and asked Van Fleet to escort his girlfriend to a social function hosted by Mrs. Logan, who was operating the West Point Hotel at the time. Yancey's girlfriend brought along Helen, a student at Columbia University from Long Beach, California. James and Helen married in Carnegie, Pennsylvania, on Christmas Day, 1915.

Soon after graduation, Van Fleet was ordered to Plattsburg, New York, to join the 3rd Infantry Regiment, the storied "Old Guard," which was the longest-serving active-duty unit in the US Army. He arrived in September 1915 and engaged in training civilian volunteers. By the spring of 1916, the troubles with Pancho Villa brought the 3rd Infantry to Camp Eagle Pass, Texas.

Early in his military career, Van Fleet became familiar with the machine gun, a weapon that was reaping a deadly harvest in Europe at the time. He was promoted to first lieutenant in July 1916, took command of a machine gun company the following spring, and was elevated to captain in May 1917.

In the autumn of that year, Van Fleet was transferred to Fort Leavenworth, Kansas, where he taught machine gun tactics. Hungry for an assignment that would take him to France, his break came when he joined the 6th Infantry Division in April 1918. The division was hurriedly preparing to cross the Atlantic, and he received command of a company in the 16th Machine Gun Battalion, embarking for France on July 5. Two weeks later, he was promoted to major, and in September he took charge of the 17th Machine Gun Battalion.

"We were most anxious to get into battle and have some kind of a record before this armistice was signed," he remembered.[69] By that time, the Van Fleets were the parents of two daughters.

After initial deployment in the Gérardmer sector near the town of Colmar in the Vosges Mountains, the 6th Division was redeployed to the Meuse-Argonne sector. The march was long and muddy as the men of the 17th Machine Gun Battalion dragged their heavy weapons and equipment through steady rain. On November 4, 1918, a week before the armistice that ended the shooting war, the 6th Division was near the frontline in the vicinity of Grandpré as American forces exploited advances during the Meuse-Argonne Offensive. The soldiers were tired and soaking wet, and soon fires were burning despite the fact that the camp was in a combat zone.

German aircraft were overhead, and the enemy pilots noticed the smoke and flames. Within a few minutes, the entire division, strung out along a six-mile front, was being strafed and bombed by German planes. An explosion killed an officer nearby, and bomb fragments ripped into Van Fleet's back and both legs. He was evacuated to an aid station, but his wounds were not serious enough to receive much more than cursory attention. After a few days of shuffling between various facilities, he walked out of a hospital and returned to the 17th Machine Gun Battalion.[70]

Van Fleet was awarded two Silver Stars for heroism in combat along with the Purple Heart for his wounds. There was talk of a promotion to lieutenant colonel and a return to the United States; however, his commanding officer refused to part with a proven leader. The 6th Division remained in France and then moved to occupation duty in Germany before finally coming home in June 1919. By August, Van Fleet, still with the 6th Division, had reunited with his family at Camp Grant, Illinois.

Van Fleet's All-American football teammate, Louis Merillat, who graduated ninety-third in the class, reached the rank of temporary major in the summer of 1918 with the 38th Infantry Regiment, 3rd Division. From the end of May to mid-September, he saw steady combat at Château-Thierry and during the Second Battle of the Marne, the reduction of the Saint-Mihiel salient, and the Meuse-Argonne Offensive. On October 5, Merillat was seriously wounded by bomb fragments and machine gun fire from German aircraft. He spent days in the hospital and eventually recovered.

In November 1915, Merillat had made scandalous headlines. Just days after his graduation from the Academy, he married Ethel Wynn, a beautiful

Chicago socialite. Helen Van Ness, a stenographer from Wooster, Ohio, filed suit against the football hero for breach of contract. Van Ness claimed that Merillat had promised to marry her during their courtship in the autumn of 1913. Van Ness sought $20,000 as a "heart balm" for the emotional distress and embarrassment she had suffered. Merillat and his father hired a formidable lawyer with a growing reputation, Clarence Darrow, as defense counsel.

Van Ness told a Wooster newspaper, "And here I have a ring. . . . Here it is. His West Point ring. It's just about the same as a college fraternity pin. It has the same significance as an engagement ring. It has my birthstone for a setting."

Merillat told an Illinois newspaper, the *Oswego Daily Palladium*, that he had visited Van Ness only a few times and that he informed her their relationship would likely end after Christmas 1914. As for the ring, he retorted that it was worth about $15 and never intended to signify much of anything.

"On one of his trips to the girl's home he wore a ring which he purchased as a present for his aunt," reported the Oswego newspaper. "He spoke of it to Miss Van Ness, and, according to the statement of the lieutenant today, she 'abducted' it, having wished to see it and then kept it. He says he endeavored to get it back, but it was of no use. . . ."

Merillat refused to negotiate a settlement, and after several weeks of excitement, the lawsuit was dismissed.[71]

After leaving the US Army, Merillat played professional football during the 1925 season with the Canton Bulldogs of the fledgling National Football League. He later became a soldier of fortune, and according to a 1948 newspaper article by famed sportswriter Grantland Rice, he was said to have trained soldiers in Iran and China before joining the French Foreign Legion and serving in the fortifications of the Maginot Line during the early days of World War II.

When the US entered World War II, Merillat returned to active duty with the army and served with the rank of colonel as commander of forces in the Miami Beach, Florida, area. During the war, the military occupied ninety hotels in the vicinity, and Merillat returned the last of these to civilian control in the summer of 1946. In April 1948, he died in Chicago at age fifty-five after a yearlong illness.

For most of his life, Joseph McNarney seems to have shunned the spotlight. Little has been recorded of his personal life—no books or lengthy critical essays. The 1915 *Howitzer* alludes to his frequenting of social gatherings but adds that he was rarely accompanied by a young lady.

There is a hint of a significant romance but little more than the tantalizing comment regarding "several 'sight unseen' spooning formations. . . . He goes to most of the hops but is wise enough to let others do the dragging. It is whispered that within the last year, though, he cherished secret thoughts of the Coast. This was at the time when, not satisfied with one picture of a certain person, he begged for another and was rewarded with an exact duplicate of the first."

The *Howitzer* goes on to provide a glimpse of a personality that has been described as dour and colorless: "The Irish in him does not advertise itself in boisterous hilarity, but rather in a quiet sense of humor and the happy faculty of letting the other tell his grind in his own way."

McNarney reported to Vancouver Barracks, Washington, in September 1915 as a second lieutenant of the 21st Infantry Regiment. He was transferred with the regiment to Yuma, Arizona, a few months later. In July 1916, he entered flight training at San Diego, California. Within the year, First Lieutenant McNarney was rated a junior military aviator and promoted to captain in the Aviation Section of the Signal Corps.

McNarney married the former Helen Wahrenberger in San Diego on June 30, 1917, and joined the 1st Aero Squadron at Columbus, New Mexico. He sailed to France in September 1917 and became a student officer of the French Flying School at Avord. He served as an instructor in meteorology and radio telegraphy and rejoined the 1st Aero Squadron in October.

In January 1918, McNarney was assigned to the headquarters of the US Air Service at Chaumont. He directed the 2nd Corps Aeronautical School and moved to Colombey-les-Belles with the assistant chief of air service, zone of advance. Later based at Ourches, he became a flight commander with the 1st Aero Squadron and led operations in the Toul sector. Promoted to major in June 1918, he commanded several Corps air groups during the Château-Thierry, Saint-Mihiel, and Meuse-Argonne Offensives. In a 1966 interview with Forrest C. Pogue, best known for his in-depth biography of George C. Marshall, army chief of staff and later secretary of state, McNarney commented:

> I had observation groups during World War I, in six corps. I would take one man and go to a new corps. Then we would set up an office

and brief the squadron commanders. We would take them through their first battle and then go to another corps. An air officer was not very useful at that time, and no one sent you any information. In the later stages of the war, we got some bomb racks and put them on the planes and would go over the [German] soup lines and drop bombs to scatter the men. There was no great effect, but it was fun to watch them scatter. We lacked the necessary power to break up concentrations of troops, and the fighters stayed busy chasing off other planes.[72]

McNarney returned to the United States in October 1919 to take command of the flying school at Gerstner Field, Louisiana. Helen gave birth to the couple's only child, a daughter named Betty Jo, in 1920.

Harry A. Harvey was a native of McComb, Mississippi, and lived in Memphis, Tennessee. A clean sleeve at the Academy, he graduated 111th and was assigned to the 1st Cavalry Regiment along the Mexican border. On November 5, 1916, he married Ethel Canavan in San Antonio, Texas. In the spring of 1917, he was transferred to the 18th Field Artillery at Fort Bliss, Texas. A son, Harry Canavan Harvey, was born in October of that year.

In the summer of 1918, Harvey was on the frontlines in France, participating in defensive action in the Champagne-Marne area. Commanding Battery A, 8th Field Artillery, on July 14 and 15, Harvey maintained his positions under tremendous German bombardment. During four hours of heavy enemy artillery fire, a nearby ammunition dump was blown up and all communications were knocked out. Throughout the severe pounding, Harvey was conspicuous in directing his men. He was later awarded the Distinguished Service Cross, and the citation reads in part, "Captain Harvey kept his battery in action, exposing himself to concentrated enemy artillery fire in order to replenish his ammunition supply and delivered an effective fire on the enemy."

When the offensive was wrested from the Germans, the 18th Field Artillery moved forward in support of Allied operations near Mont-Saint-Père, Jaulgonne, and Charmel. Two weeks later, the twenty-eight-year-old officer was assigned to command the 2nd Battery, 103rd Field Artillery, with the rank of major. On September 12, 1918, the battery was in action at Saint-Mihiel. American infantry drove German troops from territory in his immediate front, and Harvey set out to reconnoiter the terrain in preparation to relocate his guns to more favorable firing positions. German artillery had previously zeroed in on the ground, and he was killed instantly by an exploding shell.

At the time of Harvey's death, his wife was living in Brooklyn with her parents. In the October 10, 1918, edition of the *New York Times*, his was one of twenty-two brief notices in the newspaper's regular publication of the casualty lists. The young officer was buried in the West Point cemetery.

The tragedy of the Great War took its toll by other means as well. The confines and often unsanitary conditions of military camps exacerbated the spread of the deadly influenza that gripped the globe. Wrote one US Army physician:

> These men start with what appears to be an ordinary attack of *La Grippe* or influenza, and when brought to the Hosp. they very rapidly develop the most vicious type of Pneumonia that has ever been seen, and a few hours later you can begin to see the Cyanosis extending from their ears and spreading all over the face, until it is hard to distinguish the colored men from the white. It is only a matter of a few hours then until death comes. . . . It is horrible. One can stand it to see two or twenty men die, but to see these poor devils dropping like flies. . . . We have been averaging about 100 deaths per day. . . . For several days there were no coffins and the bodies piled up something fierce. . . . An extra long barracks has been vacated for the use of a Morgue, and it would make any man sit up and take notice to walk down the long lines of dead soldiers all dressed and laid out in double rows. . . .[73]

William Berkeley Peebles of Petersburg, Virginia, was a clean sleeve who graduated 149th in the class of 1915 and served with Troop M of the 10th Cavalry during the Punitive Expedition in Mexico. "His experiences were many and varied," read a remembrance written after his death. "At one time he was placed in charge of a party sent out to rescue the men of the Tenth Cavalry who had been cut off from their regiment by the Mexicans; at another time he and his party were cut off from supplies for some weeks, during which time they subsisted on hard corn and such food as could be obtained from the Mexicans."

Peebles transferred to the Aviation Section of the Signal Corps and was designated a junior military aviator. He assisted in the formation of air squadrons and served as an instructor in aerial gunnery, mapping, and topography. In early September 1918, he sailed from New York for France aboard the transport *St. Louis*. The close quarters aboard the ship were a breeding ground for the killer influenza, and he was one of many who contracted the disease. On September 30, five days after his arrival in the port of Brest, he died in Camp Hospital No. 33 of "broncho pneumonia."

Herbert Corbin, nicknamed "Squab" at the Academy, graduated 101st, entered the Coast Artillery, and then transferred to the Field Artillery prior to assignment as aide-de-camp to Maj. Gen. Clarence P. Townsley in the Philippines. Commanding a battery of the 12th Field Artillery, he spent six months at the front in France, near the bloody battlefields and fortifications of Verdun. In the spring of 1918, he was ordered to Fort Sill, Oklahoma, as an instructor. Within a week of contracting influenza in mid-October, he was dead.

On May 15, 1917, Melchior McEwen Eberts, who shared the nickname "Ike" with his classmate Eisenhower, was killed when the plane he was piloting crashed minutes after takeoff from Columbus, New Mexico, en route to Fifth Brigade headquarters in El Paso, Texas. According to an official release, "the aeroplane apparently ran into an 'air pocket' and Lieutenant Eberts was unable to right it. The machine turned over and dived to the ground. Lieutenant Eberts died a few minutes after he was taken from the wreckage." Twenty-seven years old, Eberts, from Little Rock, Arkansas, had graduated 155th in the class.

Graduating 127th, Stanley McNabb of New York City, reported to the 18th Infantry Regiment at Douglas, Arizona, and temporarily served as a company commander. He was killed on December 6, 1915, near his post along the Mexican border, when the car he was riding in plunged down an embankment and crashed. His brother Thomas, a 1909 West Point graduate, had died the previous year.

"To have been in action against Mexican bandits on the border, to have flown over the British, French and Italian fronts as a pilot during the Great War and then to have come home and be killed in an automobile accident was the cruel fate meted out to Major Whitten Jasper East," reads the lament of a classmate written after the twenty-five-year-old died in an automobile accident in Mineola, Long Island, while he was serving at nearby Hazelhurst Field.

From Senatobia, Mississippi, East was nicknamed "Tubby" and graduated seventieth in the class of 1915. His brief but colorful career in the

Aviation Section included responsibility for the Balloon Service of the American Expeditionary Force in France and command of Group A, First Provisional Wing.

Following a West Point career that a fellow cadet described as "Uneventful beyond the making of innumerable friends," John B. Duckstad married Ida Dorothy Zane while on duty in Gettysburg, Pennsylvania. The couple spent two months together as the newly formed 4th Infantry Division was organizing at Camp Greene, North Carolina.

Commanding a machine gun company of the 58th Infantry Regiment, Duckstad reached France in the summer of 1918 and participated in the Second Battle of the Marne near Château-Thierry. In a letter to the young officer's wife, Maj. Gen. George H. Cameron, commander of the 4th Division, wrote, "Here Captain Duckstad not only handled his Company with skill and judgment but executed several hazardous reconnaissances in one of which he alone, of four officers, escaped injury. He scouted personal danger in his aggressive, loyal sense of duty."

After surviving the hazards of combat, Duckstad was killed in a strange accident. General Cameron continued:

> It appears that Major Duckstad, while riding in the side-car of a motorcycle at night, was so badly injured by collision with a truck that he died shortly afterwards. In the highest sense, his death was in the performance of duty and in action before the enemy. To insure the execution of orders, he gave immediate supervision. Near the front, no lights on machines can be permitted for fear of shelling or bombing. The necessity for high speed was urgent and your husband's driver failed to see in time the stationary truck on the road. The poor fellow himself was killed instantly.

According to the author of Duckstad's memorial entry in the Academy's annual report of June 10, 1919, "Along the road were piles of stone and in order to avoid a truck train, the driver swerved the cycle and it ran into one of these piles. The driver was killed instantly and Major Duckstad was thrown into another pile of stone, sustaining a fractured skull. He was rushed to Evacuation Hospital No. 6, but never regained consciousness. He . . . was buried in the Cemetiere des Mont Osches at Souilly. . . . He is survived by his wife [and] a little son Eric Edward Duckstad, whom he never saw. . . ."

In the summer of 1916, George Pulsifer, who had competed so closely with Eisenhower for a coveted appointment to the Academy, arrived at the Signal Corps Aviation School in San Diego, California, for pilot training. He had graduated 116th in the class of 1915, and by the spring of 1917 he was rapidly promoted to junior military aviator, captain, and major. By September, he was in France for duty in the office of the assistant chief of air service. He was soon assigned to the office of the chief of air service, 1st Army Corps.

When George passed away in 1970, his brother Arthur, West Point Class of 1918, recounted:

> Overseas he flew many missions over Germany. He was successful in these flights only to be felled upon his return from one flight by an American soldier sentry posted at a crossroad from the air field to the chateau that housed the flyers. When George flew out on his last mission, such a sentry post was not there. In the dark, George, along with other pilots who rode in the car, passed up the sentry without stopping, as he was not seen. The sentry fired and hit George as he slept in the car.
>
> The bullet lodged in his liver after hitting his spine, paralyzing him below the waist. In his long struggle for survival and mobility, he went through many operations. . . . After some time, George could drive a car and walk short distances with the aid of two canes. . . . This obituary will let his classmates know of his passing and will let those who tried to see him know that it was not because he did not care, or harbored any bitterness, but because of his highly nervous condition and sensitivity to his disability.
>
> His love of West Point stayed with him all his life and was one period of his life that he referred to with great affection.

George Pulsifer spent months in and out of hospitals, particularly at Fox Hills, Staten Island, New York. On September 22, 1920, he was retired from the army with the permanent rank of captain due to "disability contracted in the line of duty."

A severe bout of influenza and pneumonia kept Hubert "Doodle" Harmon out of action during World War I. After graduating 103rd in the class of 1915, he entered the Coast Artillery and transferred to the Aviation

Section of the Signal Corps in the autumn of 1916. He earned his wings the following summer, and he spent three weeks in the hospital in Saint-Maixent, France.

Harmon remained in Germany with the occupation forces until late 1919. Between the wars, he served as an instructor at West Point and held various posts, including command of the 19th Bomb Group. On February 19, 1927, he married Rosa-Maye Kendrick, the daughter of US Sen. John B. Kendrick of Wyoming. He graduated from the Army War College in 1938 and worked in the Operations Division of the War Department General Staff prior to assuming command of the Primary Flying School at Kelly Field, Texas, in 1940, with the rank of colonel. In November 1941, a month before Pearl Harbor, he took command of the Gulf Coast Training Center at Randolph Field, Texas, after promotion to brigadier general.

New Yorker John K. "Jake" Meneely graduated fifty-seventh in the class of 1915 and commanded a battery of the 53rd Coast Artillery Regiment during the Great War. He saw action in the Toul Sector and during the Champagne-Marne, Saint-Mihiel, and Meuse Argonne Offensives. In 1920, Major Meneely resigned his commission to join his wife's family business, the Sutton and Suderly Brick Company of Coeymans, New York.

After the Great War, some officers of the class of 1915 returned to the United States as bona fide war heroes. Others, like Eisenhower and Bradley, contemplated their careers and assessed their prospects as dismal. Some had seen the face of war and left the military in the wake of the experience. Several lost their lives, either directly or indirectly, because of the conflict.

All of these young men had lost something—life, innocence, idealism, or optimism. For the career soldiers, the further tests of the peacetime Army and the wilderness of the interwar years lay ahead.

CHAPTER SIX

The Interwar Years

In the wake of World War I, the strength of the United States Army dwindled. More than four million men had been mobilized for service during the Great War; however, by 1922 Congress had established a maximum strength of only 12,000 commissioned officers and 125,000 other ranks. At its nadir, the manpower of the US Army was approximately nineteenth in the world, slightly smaller than that of Portugal. Many of the junior officers who had received rapid temporary promotions during wartime were reduced in rank to lower grades in the peacetime army as well.

Though at the time the disappointment of missing overseas duty seemed like the death knell for his career, Dwight Eisenhower likely did not fully appreciate the developing command and administrative skills that he had honed during the war years. The Distinguished Service Medal that he was awarded in 1922 in recognition of "unusual zeal, foresight, and marked administrative ability in the organization, training, and preparation for overseas service of technical troops of the Tank Corps" meant that others were beginning to appreciate the promise he had shown during his service at Camp Colt.

Meanwhile, rather than allowing his ambitions of a military career to ebb, Eisenhower redoubled his efforts for advancement. In the summer of

1919, he received approval as one of fifteen War Department observers to take part in a transcontinental motor convoy, the first expedition of its kind. Its purpose was to assess the capability of a mechanized military column to move across the country.

With twenty-four officers and 258 enlisted men participating, the convoy departed from the ellipse south of the White House on July 7, 1919, and covered 3,251 miles in sixty-two days along the so-called Lincoln Highway (later designated US 30), terminating at the Presidio in San Francisco on September 6. Numerous specialized vehicles such as heavy and light trucks, a caterpillar tractor, and five sidecar motorcycles were among the eighty-one assembled vehicles.

The trip was arduous and often frustrating, averaging 58.1 miles per day and 6.07 miles per hour. Nine vehicles were destroyed or damaged to the extent that they could not continue, and twenty-one men had to be left at stops along the way due to illness or injury.

Reported Capt. William C. Greany of the Army Motor Transport Corps: "It frequently was necessary to pull and push the vehicles by man-power over wide areas of gumbo mud in the central states and across the desert lands of the far west, for many hours at a time, and to laboriously construct wheel paths of timber, canvas, sage brush, or grass for long distances. On a number of days the personnel labored from fifteen to twenty-four hours to accomplish the pre-arranged forced-march itinerary."[74]

The experience impressed upon Eisenhower the potential difficulties of logistical movement of a military force. It was a lesson that would serve him well in the years to come. Eisenhower also concluded that the nation's road network should be improved, not only out of military necessity but to provide a means for travelers to move freely around the country.

Following the transcontinental adventure, Eisenhower returned to Camp Meade, Maryland, and the Tank Corps with which he had become so familiar. Soon he struck up a friendship with an impetuous lieutenant colonel, George S. Patton Jr., a combat veteran of World War I who had established the Army Tank School at Langres, France, where some of Eisenhower's former charges had reported for duty overseas, and who then commanded the 304th Tank Brigade in action at Saint-Mihiel in the autumn of 1918.

The two officers were zealous in their advocacy of the tank as an offensive weapon. They familiarized themselves with the mechanics of the tanks that had been used during World War I, took long rides across fields and hills discussing armored tactics, and generally stirred up controversy over the future role of the tank in the US Army. Their assertiveness nearly got both of them court-martialed.

During an inspection visit, Brig. Gen. Fox Conner, a well-known and influential officer who had served as General Pershing's chief of operations during the war, was invited to the Patton quarters for Sunday dinner, along with the Eisenhowers. Conner peppered both officers with questions about the Infantry Tank School and their opinions on the role of armor in future wars. He was impressed with their responses.

Soon enough, Eisenhower heard from Conner again—this time to offer him a post as executive officer in Conner's infantry command at Camp Gaillard, Panama. Eisenhower was thrilled, but his request for transfer was denied by the War Department. Finally, in the summer of 1921, with Conner's friend General Pershing serving as army chief of staff, the transfer was approved.[75]

Conner rekindled an interest in military history that had gone dormant in Eisenhower, encouraging the young officer to read and then asking questions about command situations. Eisenhower remembered that Conner might pose:

> "What do you think would have been the outcome if this decision had been just the opposite? What were the alternatives?" The best chance for such conversations was when we were out on reconnaissance. . . . We would make camp before dark. Close to the equator, the sun sets early and during the long hours before bedtime, between 6:30 and 10:00, we sat around a small campfire and talked about the Civil War or Napoleon's operations.
>
> Our conversations continued throughout the three years I served with him in the isolated post of Camp Gaillard. It is clear now that life with General Conner was a sort of graduate school in military affairs and the humanities, leavened by the comments and discourses of a man who was experienced in his knowledge of men and their conduct. I can never adequately express my gratitude to this one gentleman, for it took years before I fully realized the value of what he had led me through. And then General Conner was gone. But in a lifetime of association with great and good men, he is the one more or less invisible figure to whom I owe an incalculable debt.[76]

While in Panama, the Eisenhowers were thrilled to learn that they were expecting a baby. Mamie traveled to her family home in Denver, Colorado, and Dwight followed as the time of the birth neared. On August 3, 1922, the couple welcomed John Sheldon Doud Eisenhower, and his parents could scarcely tell the difference between photos of John and their beloved and lost Icky.

Before they parted company, General Conner offered another piece of advice. He encouraged Eisenhower to seek a post serving under Col. George C. Marshall, who had served under Conner in France. Conner considered Marshall, an 1899 graduate of the Virginia Military Institute, a genius and recognized the leading role he was destined to play in the army during the next twenty-five years. Such an opportunity did not come until the eve of World War II when then-General Marshall was serving as army chief of staff. Eisenhower later observed, "One of the first things I noticed was that he was a man who had many of the characteristics of Fox Conner."

Promotions were slow in the peacetime army, but by the autumn of 1924 Eisenhower had achieved the permanent rank of major and was ordered, of all places, back to Camp Meade. He had coached football teams off and on since his Academy days, and such was his duty there. Then came orders to transfer to Fort Benning, Georgia, to once again command a tank battalion. Benning was the home of the Infantry School, and Eisenhower petitioned the chief of infantry for admission to the school rather than taking on another dead-end armored command. The request was flatly refused.

Then Fox Conner interceded on behalf of his protégé. A cryptic telegram from Conner read, "No matter what orders you receive from the War Department, make no protest accept them without question." Eisenhower trusted Conner and did just that when orders for recruiting duty at Fort Logan, Colorado, eight miles south of Denver, came through. The Douds were pleased to have their grandson nearby.

Conner's purpose soon became evident. He had bigger plans for Eisenhower. No appointment could be made to the Infantry School without the approval of the chief of infantry; therefore, Conner had arranged for Eisenhower to be transferred to the office of the adjutant general and the Fort Logan assignment temporarily. Subsequent orders directed Eisenhower to the Command and General Staff School at Fort Leavenworth. Prior to reporting in August 1925, Eisenhower wrote to Conner about preparations, and his benefactor responded, "You may not know it, but because of your three years' work in Panama, you are far better trained and ready for Leavenworth than anybody I know."[77]

Completing the Command and General Staff School was no easy task. Those who finished the yearlong course were said to be earmarked for better assignments and potentially higher levels of command in the future. Eisenhower was pleased to see his old friend Maj. Leonard Gerow, and the two studied together. Eisenhower graduated first in a class of 275 officers, many of them senior to him, and Gerow was close behind.

Even before he had completed the course at Leavenworth, Eisenhower was returned to the Infantry and received orders to report to Fort Benning as executive officer of the 24th Regiment. The assignment was short-lived, and in December 1926 he was ordered to report to General Pershing in Washington, D.C., for duty with the Battle Monuments Commission, which had been formed to coordinate the establishment, in France, of American cemeteries and memorials to the fallen of the Great War. Eisenhower was tasked with writing a short guidebook for the commission, and he completed the assignment in a few weeks.

General Pershing praised Eisenhower's work and encouraged him to remain with the commission. However, an opportunity to attend the Army War College at nearby Washington Barracks (now Fort McNair) arose, which Eisenhower preferred. After graduation from the War College in June 1928, a second assignment to the Battle Monuments Commission finally afforded Eisenhower the opportunity to travel to Europe.

The family took an apartment in Paris, and while Dwight revised his guidebook, six-year-old John was enrolled in an elementary school in the French capital. The idyllic experience enabled the family to travel extensively. They visited Belgium, Germany, and Switzerland, and they vacationed for a month in Italy. Major Eisenhower familiarized himself with the land and peoples of Western Europe, and the experience would prove invaluable later in his career.

In November 1929, Eisenhower reported to the War Department for duty as assistant executive to Brig. Gen. George Moseley, whose role as military advisor to the assistant secretary of war included the development of a protocol for mobilization and the conversion of American industry to a wartime footing in the event of another major conflict. Although he no longer reported to Pershing, the famed general, who was heavily engaged in writing his wartime memoirs, asked Eisenhower to review the chapters on Saint-Mihiel and the Argonne.

Eisenhower responded that the diary format was confusing and recommended a narrative style. At Pershing's request, Dwight rewrote the two chapters per his recommendations. Pershing liked Ike's work and told Eisenhower that since he placed a high value on the opinion of Col. George C. Marshall, he would forward the revisions to him for review.

A few days later, Marshall went to Pershing's office, and the two men met for several hours. As Marshall was leaving, he exited through Eisenhower's office.

"For the first time in my life, I met George Marshall," Eisenhower remembered. "He did not sit down but remarked that he read over my chapters. 'I think they're interesting. Nevertheless, I've advised General Pershing to stick with his original idea. I think to break up the format right at the end of the war would be a mistake.' He remarked, rather kindly, that my idea was a good one. Nevertheless, he thought that General Pershing would be happier if he stayed with the original scheme."[78]

Although the short discussion seemed rather innocuous at the time, Marshall must surely have made a mental note that Eisenhower was a junior officer worth watching. Eisenhower, on the other hand, glimpsed something of the man who would exert great influence on his career in the years to come. The two would not meet again for more than a decade, early in 1940. Marshall is remembered for having a keen eye for talent and for recording in a little black book the names of junior officers he believed had promise. Eisenhower joined a growing list that eventually included several of the major commanders in World War II, such as Joseph Stilwell, Omar Bradley, George S. Patton, Jr., Walter Bedell Smith, and J. Lawton Collins.

In his War Department post, Eisenhower traveled around the United States and discussed with corporate leaders the issues surrounding the conversion of industry to a war footing. One of these, financier and presidential advisor Bernard Baruch, would become a lifelong friend. Eisenhower toured manufacturing facilities and, along with Maj. Gilbert Wilkes, a 1909 West Point graduate, served as principal author of a report delivered to the War Department and subsequently to the administration of President Herbert Hoover on June 16, 1930.

Eisenhower wrote, "Our purpose is simple—to see to it that every individual and every material thing shall contribute, in the manner demanded by inherent characteristics, their full share to the winning of any war in which we may become involved."[79]

Clear and concise, the report drew praise, although President Hoover asserted that the United States had no intention of becoming involved in another major war. Later, Eisenhower drafted a congressional resolution, supported by the War Department report, that led to federal legislation prohibiting profiteering during wartime.

Eisenhower, who had languished in the peacetime army with the rank of major for years, still believed that his prospects of promotion and advancement were remote. However, about the time he completed the congressional resolution, he declined an offer from newspaper magnate William Randolph Hearst to take a position as a correspondent on military affairs. The pay of an army major was less than $5,000 per year, and Hearst had intimated that the newspaper job would pay between $15,000 and $20,000. Pay cuts had rippled through the army already. Still, Eisenhower remembered Fox Conner's prediction that another global war would come. He remained in the military.

A changing of the guard in the War Department brought new opportunity. In November 1930, Gen. Charles Summerall stepped down as army chief of staff. He was replaced by Douglas MacArthur, a soldier of great intellect with an ego to match. MacArthur knew Eisenhower was a capable officer, and the workload he handed the major was tremendous at times.

In the summer of 1932, with the nation in the throes of the Great Depression, thousands of World War I veterans, who had been promised a monetary bonus to be paid in 1945, set up a ramshackle camp near the US Capitol. The veterans, dubbed the "Bonus Marchers," were seeking early payment to alleviate the want they suffered as a result of the Depression. When President Hoover ordered the army to disperse the veterans, the active-duty soldiers—some of them mounted and with sabers drawn—did just that. Against Eisenhower's advice, MacArthur was present during the incident and told reporters that the action had quelled a potential "revolution."

The press had a field day. The reputation of the army suffered, and Eisenhower did his best to defend the conduct of the military personnel involved when he penned the official report on the action. Eisenhower deplored the fact that the army had been required to remove its own veterans from the nation's capital by force, and he remained critical of MacArthur's conduct during that affair for the rest of his life.

Nevertheless, MacArthur appreciated Eisenhower's organizational and administrative skills. While he might never admit it, he probably valued Eisenhower's willingness to speak frankly and to express his own opinions. Further, there was a benefit to the fact that the affable Eisenhower was already developing a reputation as a consensus builder, a quality that might prove valuable in a close subordinate, providing some balance to the persona of the headstrong, mercurial MacArthur.

In January 1933, Eisenhower accepted MacArthur's offer of the post of special assistant to the chief of staff. The two men's sometimes turbulent association would last until December 1939, further shaping Eisenhower's career. As the economy continued to suffer, MacArthur defended the limited funding that the army received from Congress. Eisenhower drafted reports and speeches for MacArthur, and his superior commended his work on more than one occasion.

Eisenhower admired MacArthur but also recognized flaws in his personality, particularly in his patrician, pedigreed military presence and his legendary pompousness. During their time in Washington, D.C., MacArthur traveled around the city in a chauffeured limousine. Eisenhower frequently needed to make trips to Capitol Hill and was required to fill out expense-reimbursement forms or return even the pocket change left over from paying cab fare. MacArthur never offered him a ride. Eisenhower never forgot the glaring disparity of treatment between those who had means and those who had struggled financially, like he and Mamie. He also saw MacArthur's towering ego firsthand.

"In several respects, he was a rewarding man to work for," Eisenhower remembered. "When he gave an assignment, he never asked any questions; he never cared what kind of hours were kept; his only requirement was that the work be done. On any subject he chose to discuss, his knowledge, always amazingly comprehensive, and largely accurate, poured out in a torrent of words. 'Discuss' is hardly the correct word; discussion suggests dialogue and the General's conversations were usually monologues."[80]

In 1935, MacArthur accepted an opportunity to return to the Philippines, where he had previously served, to assist in the formation of a Filipino army as the islands achieved commonwealth status en route to independence from the United States. MacArthur considered the islands his home. He persuaded Eisenhower to accompany him, and somewhat ironically, twenty years after his graduation from West Point, Eisenhower was finally going to the locale he had expected as his first military assignment.

Mamie was shocked at the news of the transfer. She remembered her distaste for the tropical climate of Panama and feared that John might be susceptible to potentially fatal diseases, such as the malaria that was common among Americans serving in the Philippines. She declined to accompany her husband initially. It would be a year before the family was reunited, and the strain on the marriage was apparent. In time, however, Mamie began to enjoy the exotic flavor of Manila.

In 1936, after sixteen years as a major, Eisenhower was finally promoted to the rank of lieutenant colonel. MacArthur wrote a glowing assessment of his aide's work, stating, "A brilliant officer . . . in time of war [he] should be promoted to general officer rank immediately."[81]

Yet the relationship between Eisenhower and MacArthur could be explosive at times, and Eisenhower lost trust in his superior when MacArthur asked his aide to prepare an elaborate parade through the streets of Manila to showcase the progress of the Filipino army. Philippine president Manuel Quezon was incensed by the use of scarce finances to stage a parade. When he confronted Eisenhower, the latter suggested he talk to MacArthur, who promptly said that he had no knowledge of the planned event and that Eisenhower had come up with a poor idea on his own. The relationship between the two was never the same.

Eisenhower made repeated requests for transfers, but MacArthur refused. As the end of his tour of duty approached, MacArthur urged him to remain in the Philippines despite their differences. Eisenhower declined, and at long last, on December 31, 1939, the Eisenhower family went home. Before leaving, Dwight turned down a job offer from the Jewish community in Manila for the princely sum of $60,000 per year. He had also politely refused a lucrative offer from Quezon to remain with the Filipino army.

Remembering his long sojourn in the shadow of MacArthur, Eisenhower once remarked, "I studied dramatics under him for five years in Washington and four years in the Philippines."[82]

In January 1940, Lieutenant Colonel Eisenhower took command of the 1st Battalion, 15th Infantry at Fort Lewis, Washington. It was the field post he had so desired, and he took the opportunity to stretch his command legs. In June 1941, he protested a transfer to Fort Sam Houston, Texas, as chief of staff of the Third Army. He was incensed at the prospect of another desk job, but Gen. Walter Krueger, commander of the Third Army, insisted that Eisenhower take it, so much so that he made the specific request directly to General Marshall, who had become army chief of staff on September 1, 1939, the day war erupted in Europe.

Although the coming of war had been foreseen and the ranks of the peacetime US Army had expanded considerably, there had been no real opportunity to determine the extent of the army's field capabilities. In the autumn of 1941, large-scale maneuvers were planned in Louisiana. Eisenhower, in his role as Third Army chief of staff, was responsible for planning its participation in the exercise. When the time came to put Eisenhower's plan in motion, the Third Army decisively routed the opposing Second Army. In October, Eisenhower was promoted to the temporary rank of brigadier general. At long last, his star was on the rise.

When Eisenhower agreed to accompany MacArthur to the Philippines in 1935, he had been allowed to choose another officer to share some of the significant responsibilities of working for the general. He chose West Point classmate James Basevi Ord, who had served in the islands in the late 1920s. The two had been friends for more than twenty years, and when time permitted they reminisced about their days at the Academy, particularly the pranks they had played and the time they had spent walking off their punishments.

Ord was outgoing and full of life. He graduated sixty-sixth in the class of 1915 and was wounded in action at Parral during the Punitive Expedition in Mexico. A recommendation for the Medal of Honor followed, and two years later he received the Distinguished Service Medal. His citation reads, "For exceptionally meritorious service to the Government in a duty of great responsibility, as follows: While serving as second lieutenant, 6th Infantry, attached to the 13th Cavalry, in action at Parral, Mexico, April 12, 1916, after being himself wounded, he dismounted from his horse under heavy fire, placed a wounded man on a horse, and assisted him from the field."

On the morning of January 30, 1938, Ord took off on a flight to the town of Baguio, north of Manila on the Philippine island of Luzon. Rather than requesting a more seasoned pilot, as Eisenhower suggested, Ord allowed a Filipino student flier to take the controls. As the plane approached Baguio, Ord asked the pilot to fly low over the house of a friend so that he could drop a note tied to a rock on the lawn to announce his arrival. The inexperienced pilot lost speed, and the engine stalled. As Ord leaned out of the aircraft, it crashed into a nearby hillside, crushing him.

Eisenhower was grief-stricken. He soon lamented, "Even yet, three months after his death, I cannot fully realize that he is never again to come walking into the office with his cheery 'Top of the morning, Comra-a-ade!'"[83]

The rapid demobilization of the US Army after World War I left Camp Dodge, Iowa, nearly deserted. Omar Bradley's 14th Regiment was the only unit of any consequence remaining there within a month of the armistice, and soon he was gone as well. A posting to Camp Grant, Illinois, included a disturbing term as a member of the court during the trial of sixteen black soldiers indicted for raping a white woman. During the course of the trial, Bradley was ordered to Columbus Barracks, Ohio, in preparation for deployment to Siberia. However, a previously issued War Department directive that no member of the tribunal was to be transferred until the trial was concluded saved Bradley from an assignment he dreaded.

The Bradleys were fond of the Pacific Northwest, and in the spring of 1919 an opportunity to work as an instructor with an ROTC (Reserve Officers' Training Corps) program at a university in that region seemed ideal. When Bradley filled out his request for such duty, a slight mistake derailed the plan:

> In a box on the application designating location preferred, I typed in "Northwest," assuming that to mean the states of Washington and Oregon. My request for ROTC duty was granted, but unknown to me, in those days the states of Washington and Oregon were designated "Pacific Northwest." My choice, "Northwest," denoted the area of North and South Dakota. As a result of the misunderstanding, on August 25, I was assigned to be an assistant professor of military science and tactics at South Dakota State College (of Agriculture and Mechanic Arts) in Brookings, a small city in the eastern part of the state.[84]

A frigid year in Brookings was followed by an unexpected assignment to West Point as an instructor of mathematics. Before leaving South Dakota, Bradley was asked to suggest a replacement at the college. He recommended Academy classmate James Van Fleet.

While at West Point, the Bradleys led a quiet life, refraining from the Prohibition-era parties that included bathtub gin and bootleg whiskey since neither Omar nor Mary smoked or drank alcohol. Omar played poker to augment their meager $300 or so monthly salary, and Mary played bridge. Following a second miscarriage, Mary gave birth to a healthy daughter, Elizabeth, in late 1923. The following spring, Bradley was promoted to major. He would remain in that grade for the next twelve years.

During his four years as a faculty member at West Point, Bradley began to read military history and familiarize himself with the Civil War. The campaigns of Union general William T. Sherman impressed him. Sherman had conducted a campaign of movement, rather than the stalemate of trench warfare that had recently been experienced on the Western Front during World War I. Appointed to the Infantry School at Fort Benning in 1925, he discovered renewed optimism. Bradley reflected:

> It slowly dawned on me that my failure to get to France had not ruined me professionally after all. The emphasis at Benning was on open warfare or "war of maneuver," General Sherman's specialty. The trench warfare of France was not only not relevant. It was disdained. My classmates who had served in France had great difficulty adjusting to these concepts. They had fixed, inflexible ideas, whereas I, who had been denied the experience, still had an open mind and I grasped the theories under discussion more easily.[85]

Bradley finished the Infantry School second in his class. He spent the next three years in Hawaii, where, among other duties, he commanded the 1st Battalion, 27th Infantry Regiment, and worked with the National Guard and army reserve organizations in the islands. Bradley perceived the National Guard duty as something of a dead end and, rather than apply for an extension of the three-year Hawaiian tour, asked for an assignment in the States. Meanwhile, the family did enjoy the leisurely pace of life in Hawaii, and Bradley dabbled in the stock market.

The yearlong Command and General Staff School followed in 1928, and Bradley, like most every other junior officer in the army, believed that completion virtually assured promotion to colonel before retirement. In fact, so much emphasis had been placed on final class standing that some officers had actually resigned their commissions or even committed suicide when they failed to finish strongly. Just as Bradley entered the course, the army abolished the publication of class standing, hoping to curb the fierce competition.

The following year, Bradley fortuitously turned down an opportunity to return to West Point as treasurer of the Academy. Instead, he chose to accept a post at Fort Benning as an instructor of tactics and weapons at the Infantry School. It was there that he met George C. Marshall for the first time. Bradley recalled upon his return:

Not only had the Fort Benning Infantry School changed for the better physically, it had changed spiritually and intellectually. The architect of the latter changes was the most impressive man I ever knew, one of the greatest military minds the world has ever produced: George Catlett Marshall, then a lieutenant colonel and assistant commandant in charge of the academic department at the school. My association with Marshall began during this tour at Fort Benning and, with brief gaps, continued for more than two decades. No man had a greater influence on me personally or professionally. No man served his country more nobly or perfectly, or sought so little public credit.[86]

At the end of his first year at Fort Benning, Bradley was named head of the weapons section by Marshall and became one of his primary assistants. In the spring of 1930, Omar and Mary traveled to West Point and "had a grand time" visiting with old friends during the fifteenth reunion of the class of 1915.

While at Fort Benning, Bradley singled out two episodes that he considered significant in elevating his standing with Marshall. The first was the flawless conduct of a weapons demonstration that was completed in about half the allotted time. The second was his "discovery" of a young captain, Walter Bedell Smith, who presented all the characteristics of a fine instructor and future staff officer. Shortly after Marshall noted that Smith would make a fine instructor but that he believed the young man's talent was yet unrecognized, he found on his desk a request from Bradley for Smith's assignment to the weapons section. Bradley had submitted the request several days before Marshall's observation, recognizing Smith's potential before Marshall did.

When Bradley's four years at Fort Benning came to an end, he made a difficult decision, opting to attend the Army War College at the risk of being pigeonholed as a staff officer for the rest of his career. He wanted to be a field commander, but the War College was the highest level of the army's peacetime educational experience, and Major Bradley deemed the investment worth the risk. Meanwhile, his foray into the stock market had come to grief with the Great Depression, and he was forced to take out a loan to cover his losses.

In early 1934, an old friend, Simon Bolivar Buckner, who was serving as commandant of cadets at West Point, asked Bradley to return to the Academy as an instructor of tactics and planning. Mary was thrilled, and the assignment lasted four years. In the summer of 1936, Bradley was finally promoted to lieutenant colonel. By 1938, he appeared in line for the post of commandant of cadets. Instead, the new superintendent, Brig. Gen. Jay Benedict, chose Bradley's West Point classmate, Lt. Col. Charles "Doc" Ryder.

Bradley refused to be bitter, later saying that he was content to complete his term at West Point as an instructor. Since the tour at the Academy was considered a troop assignment and he had completed the army's available educational options, his next post was likely to be administrative. He reported to the General Staff in Washington, where Marshall was already in line to ascend to the chief of staff post, and was assigned to G-1, the personnel section.

When Marshall was appointed chief of staff in 1939, he reorganized the General Staff and assigned a close group of officers to triage the mountain of reports and statistics that were regularly funneled upward. The pace of reorganization and preparedness quickened as war erupted in Europe, and Bradley became one of the assistant secretaries who distilled lengthy assessments to single pages for Marshall's review.

"I had worked closely with Marshall at Fort Benning for three years," Bradley later wrote. "I knew his wife, Katherine, and his stepchildren. I knew he valued my judgment and professionalism. And yet I was still in awe and some fear of the man. I was never at ease when I made a presentation."[87]

For the next two and a half years, Bradley worked for Marshall, a hard taskmaster who often acknowledged good performance with a simple grunt or nod. Nevertheless, Marshall was fair and demonstrated an uncanny ability to judge the potential of the officers with whom he came in contact.

By the spring of 1941, Bradley considered it imperative that he secure a troop command as war loomed. He tentatively accepted an offer to return to West Point as commandant of cadets.

Marshall approved the transfer, then several days later engaged Bradley in conversation.

"Bradley, are you sure you want to go to West Point?" I gave him my reasons for accepting the job. He glanced idly out the window and then said, "How'd you like to have Hodges' job." My heart went to my throat. Courtney H. Hodges was now a brigadier general and

commandant of the Infantry School at Fort Benning. I did not hesi-
tate a second. I said, "Sir, that's a new situation. I would much prefer
Hodges' job." Marshall said, "All right. Bring in Bryden [Deputy Chief
of Staff Maj. Gen. William Bryden] and we'll fix it up."[88]

When Bradley arrived at Fort Benning in late February 1941, his wife pinned
the star of a brigadier general to his collar. After five years as a lieutenant
colonel, Bradley skipped the grade of colonel and became the first member
of the class of 1915 to achieve general officer rank. He reminded himself
that the promotion was officially temporary. Nevertheless, it was significant
and, as it turned out, enduring.

Major James Van Fleet returned to the United States in the spring of
1919, following duty with the occupation forces in Germany. For the next
thirteen years, he held various teaching positions with ROTC programs and,
as both Eisenhower and Bradley had done, coached football. His first postwar assignment was at Kansas State University in Manhattan. Then, over
the howling objections of administrators, he transferred to South Dakota
State in January 1921 to replace Bradley.

The accommodations were meager, and Van Fleet was actually separated
from his family for a time because their apartment was simply too tiny. A
smallpox outbreak came with the spring and kept the children confined to
the limited space. Within the year, a request for transfer to the University of
Florida in Gainesville was approved, and for the next seven years Van Fleet
served as commandant of cadets at the campus while coaching the Gators
football team, first as an assistant and then as head coach.

In 1924, the Florida football team traveled to West Point to play the
Black Knights. After the officials waved off a Florida touchdown in the third
quarter, Army scored in the game's waning moments to seal the 14–7 victory. Helen was said to have observed that the Corps of Cadets cheered for
Florida as much as they did Army and was told by a friend, "This game
was Van Fleet against [Army football coach John] McEwen, and everybody
likes Van the best." Florida finished the season with eight wins, two ties,
and the single loss to Army. It was by far the program's best performance
to date.[89]

In January 1925, the satisfying tenure at the University of Florida came
to an end. Van Fleet was detailed to Panama to command the 1st Battalion,
42nd Infantry Regiment. He guided the battalion through training, and

its performance during jungle maneuvers was outstanding. In December, Helen gave birth to the couple's third child, a son named Jimmy, at her parents' home in California.

In 1928, Van Fleet was ordered to attend the advanced course of the Infantry School at Fort Benning. He renewed his several friendships with West Point classmates, including Bradley, and completed the course. However, he was still dogged by difficulties in the classroom that seemed to evaporate when he was in actual command of troops in the field. Based on his academic performance, the army recommended no further schooling.

The Infantry School experience was followed by a request to return to the University of Florida, where Van Fleet's former ROTC position was vacant. He served there until 1933, when he was assigned to command the 2nd Battalion, 5th Infantry Regiment, at Fort Williams, Maine. He was also involved with the formation and administration of the local Civilian Conservation Corps, a public works organization developed as part of Pres. Franklin D. Roosevelt's massive New Deal, which was intended to revive the US economy during the Great Depression. In October 1936, he was promoted to lieutenant colonel.

In the autumn of 1939, Van Fleet was back at Fort Benning, commanding the 1st Battalion, 29th Infantry Regiment. After two decades in the army, his grasp of infantry tactics was solid, and his battalion performed well in exercises, live fire demonstrations, and maneuvers. By the summer of 1941, he was promoted to colonel and given command of the 8th Regiment, 4th Infantry Division. The 8th Regiment was already the guardian of a proud tradition that dated back to the late eighteenth century.

When Joseph McNarney came home from Europe in October 1919, he reported to Gerstner Field, Louisiana, as a flight instructor. A month later, he was transferred to Langley Field, Virginia, first as a student and then as an instructor at the Air Corps Tactical School. After completing the Command and General Staff School at Fort Leavenworth, he served with the Air Section of the War Department General Staff until 1930, when he was admitted to the Army War College.

After finishing the War College in August, McNarney was assigned to March Field, California, as commander of both the Primary Flying School and the 7th Bomb Group and executive officer of the 1st Bomb Wing. He coordinated the relocation of the Primary Flying School to Randolph Field, Texas. In August 1933, he became an instructor at the Army War College.

Eighteen months later, McNarney was assigned to the General Head-quarters Air Force, at Langley Field. The concept of a General Headquarters considered the requirements of an organizational command structure in the field, and a GHQ Air Force had been organized for the first time in 1924. On March 1, 1935, a peacetime GHQ Air Force became operational under veteran airman Frank Andrews, who had been elevated in rank from lieutenant colonel to temporary brigadier general with the assignment.

After World War I, the air service had been recognized as a combatant branch of the US Army; however, it suffered tremendous postwar cuts, as 163 of its 185 squadrons were disbanded. Nevertheless, the movement for an independent air force stirred persistent controversy at the highest levels of the military, and several petitions to establish a separate air force had failed.

Andrews was allowed to choose his own staff, and he selected Maj. Joseph McNarney as his G-4 in charge of planning and logistics. At the time, McNarney was a combat veteran "who commanded observation squadrons in France during the war, had written a book on air tactics and was well regarded in the War Department. Noted for the caliber of his intellect and the dourness of his manner, McNarney kept his own counsel on the issue of independence."[90]

Andrews was also an associate of George C. Marshall, and it is likely that McNarney came to the attention of the future army chief of staff prior to his appointment to GHQ Air Force. McNarney's work at Langley Field was impressive, and it was followed by an appointment to Hamilton Field, California, that lasted less than a year.

By 1939, McNarney had hit the fast track. He was again in Washington, D.C., working in the War Plans Division of the War Department General Staff and then with the Joint Army-Navy Planning Committee. In the spring of 1940, he was promoted to colonel and appointed to the American-Canadian Permanent Joint Board on Defense.

Of course, McNarney soon learned that Marshall was a dominating force. In his 1966 interview with Marshall biographer Forrest C. Pogue, he recalled:

When I was in War Plans, I had to go to see General Marshall several times. The first time I went to see General Marshall, I laid out some plans we were working on. He made some remark about what he wanted. I said, "Jesus, man, you can't do that." He looked startled. I thought he would put me out. However, I talked to the SGS, Colonel Ward [Marshall's secretary, Colonel Orlando Ward]. He said, "It's OK. He likes for people to speak out."

I was head of the War Plans branch, and most of my dealings were with the Navy. I worked with Kelly Turner [Adm. Richmond Kelly Turner, then director of Navy War Plans], who was a bastard. I would cuss him out. He was an S.O.B. and didn't want anyone's ideas but his own.[91]

The industrious Edmund DeTreville "Det" Ellis, who delivered laundry and sold coal to pay for his education at the University of South Carolina, reached the rank of first sergeant, played polo, and graduated seventy-second in the class of 1915 prior to serving with the Cavalry and Quartermaster Corps between the world wars. In the mid-1920s, he attended the Army Industrial College and the Quartermaster School. From 1924 to 1926, he was detailed to Harvard University, where he received a master's of business administration degree to go along with his two bachelor of science degrees. During the 1930s, he held various posts with the Quartermaster General's office.

The class of 1915 was not immune from scandal during the interwar years, and one of its finest graduates was the victim in a tragic death that remains shrouded in mystery. The son of Maj. Gen. Adelbert Cronkhite, Alexander Pennington Cronkhite graduated seventh in the class and served as an instructor and surveyor with the Corps of Engineers at various locations around the United States. In early 1918, he was promoted to the temporary rank of major, and in October he moved to Camp Lewis, Washington, with the 213th Engineers.

During a training exercise on October 25, 1918, Cronkhite separated from the other soldiers in his formation. A few moments later, gunshots reverberated. Another officer, Capt. Robert Rosenbluth, moved toward the area when he heard the shots and shouted in a jovial manner at Cronkhite, who was shooting cans with a .45-caliber revolver. Rosenbluth turned away just as another shot rang out. He ran to the scene and discovered Cronkhite mortally wounded by a single round. An enlisted man, Sgt. Bugler Roland Pothier, was also nearby, although his exact location was unknown at the time. Within minutes, Cronkhite was dead.

An autopsy determined that the fatal wound had entered Cronkhite's chest three inches from his right nipple and exited at the waist on his left side. A formal inquiry followed and ruled the death accidental. Cronkhite was known for his outstanding marksmanship and for his ability to draw, cock, and shoot a handgun in one motion. The board of inquiry theorized that Cronkhite was demonstrating his quick-draw prowess. It reasoned that he had been weakened by a severe bout of influenza a few days earlier, and as he fired and the recoil loosened his grip, the gun turned in his hand and then accidentally discharged.

The possibility of suicide was raised but quickly discounted, and following an elaborate funeral in the Camp Lewis Chapel, Cronkhite's body was sent to West Point for interment.[92]

Major John Easter Harris, a West Point classmate, eulogized Cronkhite in the 1920 Annual Report of the Association of Graduates. "'Buddy,' as he was known to everyone, early attracted the attention of his classmates. . . . A smile, a flash of wit, a rollicking laugh, and an infectious, bubbling boyishness—these were 'Buddy'; a serious student, a care-free play-fellow, a keen soldier, and a leader beloved of his men."[93]

The twenty-five-year-old major's distraught parents questioned the findings of the inquiry, and when Maj. Gen. Cronkhite returned home from France, where he had commanded the 80th Infantry Division during World War I, he asserted strongly that his son could never have shot himself. The body was exhumed, and a medical examiner found that Major Cronkhite, who was right-handed, could not have shot himself in the right chest. After a round of appeals from the general that went all the way to the White House and President Warren G. Harding, the US Justice Department opened an investigation.

On March 17, 1921, Sgt. Bugler Pothier confessed to FBI agents that he had shot Major Cronkhite by accident. Five days later, he changed his story and said that he had shot Cronkhite intentionally at the direction of Captain Rosenbluth, who was arrested on March 23. The supposed motive for Rosenbluth's order was concern that Major Cronkhite was preparing a case for his demotion for poor performance.

By the summer of 1921, Major Cronkhite, a distant cousin of famed television news anchor Walter Cronkite, had been dead nearly three years, and his father was agitating for the case to be brought to trial. Meanwhile, federal charges against Rosenbluth and Pothier were dropped after it was determined that the incident had not occurred on government property since the deed conveying the tract from Pierce County, Washington, to the federal government had not been recorded at the time.

Pierce County Prosecutor J. W. Selden reviewed the evidence, and at the end of the year decided that the case had no basis for trial. Still, the affair was not over. In the autumn of 1922, a grand jury convened in Tacoma. Based on testimony from numerous witnesses, an actual visit to the area where the incident occurred, and the available evidence, both Rosenbluth and Pothier were indicted for murder and rearrested.

As delays mounted, General Cronkhite's public criticism of the army's handling of the investigation reached fever pitch in the spring of 1923, resulting in a reprimand from the secretary of war. In late 1922, the *Dearborn Independent* newspaper, owned by the wealthy and virulently anti-Semitic Henry Ford, published a series of articles implying that Rosenbluth was merely a part of a much larger Jewish conspiracy and a Communist sympathizer. On the other hand, future president Herbert Hoover, who headed the American Relief Administration, showed support for Rosenbluth, who had worked for the agency in Russia after leaving the army in 1919.

Finally, it was determined that the defendants would be tried separately, and Pothier's trial began on September 30, 1924.

The pivotal testimony during the proceedings was that of Capt. Eugene Caffey, who physically demonstrated that, contrary to prior determinations, Major Cronkhite might well have accidentally shot himself. Pothier was quickly acquitted, and the charges against Rosenbluth were soon dismissed.

Through the years, interest in the mystery of Major Cronkhite's death has ebbed and flowed; however, the tragedy of the event itself has lingered. In 1922, the 213th Engineers erected a small obelisk near the site where the fatal shooting occurred. General Adelbert Cronkhite was forced into retirement in 1923 after his criticism of the army had become too much of a public embarrassment. In 1937, he died a shattered man.[94]

In the spring of 1931, the fifteen-year military career of Maj. Metcalfe Reed came to an abrupt end. Born in Colorado, Reed spent his childhood in the Philadelphia area and was appointed to the Academy by Senator Hamilton Fish Kean of New Jersey. Reed graduated 102nd in the class of 1915, played football and basketball, and attained the rank of sergeant. Following graduation, he commanded a motorcycle detachment at Douglas, Arizona, and served as battalion quartermaster of the 11th Infantry. During World War I, he saw action at Château-Thierry, Saint-Mihiel, and in the Argonne. He returned to the United States in 1919 as an inspector and instructor assigned to the New York National Guard. Reed married Zella Wiedeman in

St. Louis on June 30, 1921, and by the end of the decade, he had been posted to Fort Thomas, Kentucky, near Cincinnati, Ohio, and then commanded the 2nd Battalion, 21st Infantry Regiment at Schofield Barracks, Hawaii.

While stationed in Hawaii, Reed was court-martialed and called back to Fort Thomas for arraignment and trial. The charges and specifications included forgery, fraud, and falsifying statements to his commanding officer. In the winter of 1928, while posted to Fort Thomas, Reed borrowed $300 from the Fidelity Loan and Investment Company of Columbus, Georgia, signing the note and representing that Chaplain Ralph W. Rogers had also "indorsed" or guaranteed the loan. Reed was further accused of failure to pay debts owed to individuals, the Cincinnati Club, a Newport, Kentucky, bank, and the French Bros. Bauer Co., a local provider of dairy products.

The amount of money totaled $464.07, approximately $7,100 today with adjustments for inflation. Reed was found guilty of all three charges and five of the eight accompanying specifications. These included the signature forgery and intent to defraud the Fidelity Loan and Investment Company, owing money to four of the individuals or businesses specified in the complaint, and falsifying a statement to his commanding officer that all personal debts had been paid or satisfactory arrangements had been made to pay them prior to his departure from Fort Thomas.

Reed was sentenced to be dismissed from the army, and following review by the appropriate authorities, including President Herbert Hoover, Secretary of War Patrick J. Hurley, and Army Chief of Staff General Douglas MacArthur, the sentence was imposed. "Major Metcalfe Reed (O-3855)," the order read, "ceases to be an officer of the Army at 12 o'clock midnight, April 6, 1931."[95]

Three weeks after his dismissal, Reed traveled to San Francisco, where he boarded the steamer *Maui* for the weeklong voyage to the Honolulu area. He and Zella remained in the islands, and Reed took a job as a salesman with the Graystone Corporation. The couple had two sons, David and Thomas, born in 1935 and 1937, respectively. Metcalfe Reed died on June 29, 1959. David Reed passed away in 2007.

Contacted by telephone, seventy-seven-year-old Thomas Reed, who resides in Pearl City, Hawaii, said he knew virtually nothing of his father's service record. "All that happened before I was born, and my mother and older brother were very secretive about it. I was just a little boy during World War II, but I remember that my father was a big man. He drove a 1937 Buick, and the lights were painted out except for little slits. I remember going on family outings when he would drive that car and that he may have worked for Kemper Insurance."

A twenty-year veteran of the US Coast Guard, Thomas Reed retired with the rank of chief petty officer. From the time he joined the Coast Guard in 1955 until his father's death, he was not close with the family. "I was in the service, and after they told me he was going to die, they sent me home to see him."

At the time of his dismissal, Metcalfe Reed was thirty-nine years old. Whether any extenuating circumstances, such as financial hardship, existed in his sad case is unknown.

In June 1940, when the members of the West Point class of 1915 gathered for their twenty-fifth reunion, fifty-eight of them were present and seventeen brought their wives. Bradley and Van Fleet attended. Eisenhower and McNarney did not. During the past quarter century, more than fifty of their number had died or left the service due to physical disability or resigning their commissions. The class presented a stained glass window, titled "Hosea," to the Academy chaplain as a memorial to the Class of 1915, and it was installed on the east side of the chapel.

On the evening of Sunday, June 9, the wives of Charles Ryder and Herman Beukema, both of whom were serving at West Point at the time, hosted a dinner for the ladies, while the classmates, six full colonels among them, assembled for their banquet. There was talk of war. Japan had been conducting a military adventure on the Asian continent since 1931, and war had broken out with China in 1937. Hitler's legions had overrun Poland, and now the Nazi juggernaut was battering British and French forces into submission. Within two weeks of the festive gathering, German soldiers would be goosestepping along the Champs-Élysées in Paris.

For now, there was precious time for laughter and remembering. Classmate Clesson H. Tenney wrote:

> After much persuasion Doc Ryder was finally forced to his feet in order to tell the clamoring group whether or not the Corps had gone to hell. Doc's story was that while the close personal touch with which we were familiar in our own time, no longer existed, nevertheless, the other things which make the Corps what it is have not

suffered by reason of this change. . . . After all the food and liquor in sight had been consumed the party broke up into small groups devoted to reminiscing and settling the affairs of the nation.[96]

Among those who had been lost during the intervening years was Maj. Harry Benson Anderson, who had graduated 114th in the class and was killed in a plane crash on February 20, 1919, in Cochem, Germany, when the captured German Fokker fighter he was flying "became unmanageable while several thousand feet in the air . . . Expert aviators [later] reported to the commanding officers that some part of the German made machine probably broke in the air causing the machine to fall."[97]

Charles Calvert Benedict of Nebraska had executed the memorable high-low hit with Eisenhower against Jim Thorpe during the football game against Carlisle Institute and graduated fifty-fourth in the class of 1915. He died in a plane crash at Langley Field on May 7, 1925. According to one eulogist, ". . . he met his death while participating in an aerial attack on a captive balloon, falling on the airdrome in sight of his comrades."[98]

Joseph Francis Dunigan was remembered for his heroics in the 1913 Army-Navy baseball game, during which he broke his nose while playing for the injured captain of the Army team, and scored the winning run. Dunigan died in a hunting accident at Camp Lewis, Washington, on October 19, 1921, a week before the mysterious death of Cronkhite there. He had graduated twenty-eighth in the class, served with the Punitive Expedition, and commanded the 313th Artillery Regiment in the Meuse-Argonne during World War I.

Major Henry Harold Dabney of Montana graduated 153rd and was posted to Tientsin, China, with the 15th Infantry Regiment during civil strife in the mid-1920s. He died of pneumonia brought on by influenza on January 4, 1926, after refusing treatment as he commanded troops charged with protecting American citizens caught in the fighting. His commanding officer, Lt. Col. George C. Marshall, wrote that he had died in the "midst of a career of great promise."

Little is known of the deaths of Charles Hosmer Chapin (September 1929) and Edwin Alexander Bethel (September 1934). Major Chapin, who graduated 130th, served in the Coast Artillery at Fort Kamehameha, Hawaii, and was retired for disability in the line of duty in 1925. Bethel, who graduated twelfth and attended the French equivalent of West Point, the

École Supérieure de Guerre in Paris, from 1928 to 1930, died while a student at the Army War College in 1934. He was forty-one years old.

While serving as a battalion commander with the 319th Field Artillery in the Meuse-Argonne during World War I, Maj. John Wallace went aloft in an observation balloon to direct the fire of his guns. A German fighter plane blazed away and set the balloon on fire, forcing Wallace and the balloon pilot to jump. Wallace survived that brush with death in wartime, and while on leave after graduating from the War College he died in a tragic accident in San Antonio, Texas, on July 2, 1938. Wallace, who had graduated thirty-fourth in the class of 1915, was slated for duty in the Philippines.

One of the few qualified aviators in the army on the eve of World War I, John Ellis Rossell had graduated sixty-seventh in the class and remained in the United States during the war, training others to fly. Major Rossell was the commanding officer at Mitchel Field on Long Island in 1918. The following year, he resigned his commission and accepted a position as secretary and service manager for Penny and Long Inc., Southern Factory Branch of the American Motors Corporation in Greensboro, North Carolina. Rossell died on November 8, 1939, at the age of forty-six, and his biographer wrote:

> Not being sent to France was one of the greatest disappointments of his life. . . . After the War and until his resignation in 1919 he pioneered in radio telephones for use in aeroplanes. He always contended that leaving the Service was the greatest mistake of his life, and he always longed to return to the Army in which he had been brought up. Among the happiest moments of his life were those when he rejoined his classmates at reunions.[99]

Lieutenant Colonel Edward C. McGuire, who graduated eighty-eighth in the class, died suddenly on June 24, 1940, while on duty at the Presidio in San Francisco, California. A veteran of the Somme, Saint-Mihiel, and Meuse-Argonne campaigns during World War I, he received the British Distinguished Service Order. On September 17, Lt. Col. Layson Enslow Atkins, the plebe who had joined Eisenhower in the irate corporal's quarters wearing "full dress coats" and not another stitch of clothing, died at the age of forty-eight following an unspecified illness of at least four months' duration. Tommy Atkins graduated twenty-fifth in the class of 1915 and served with the Punitive Expedition and overseas during World War I.

As the momentum of global war increased and it appeared that the United States was being inevitably drawn into the conflict, the officers of the West Point class of 1915 were deep into middle age. The memories of their days at the Academy remained vivid, but the army had changed. They had changed. There was more change to come, and while these men anticipated that they were on the threshold of momentous events, none of them reckoned just how significant their roles in those events would be.

PART IV

True Mettle

CHAPTER SEVEN

The Coming of War

O n the afternoon of Sunday, December 7, 1941, Dwight Eisenhower was exhausted. The Louisiana Maneuvers had just been completed, and after returning to Fort Sam Houston, he settled down for a long nap, leaving orders that he was not to be disturbed.

Within a few minutes, those orders were disobeyed with the alarming news that the Japanese had attacked Pearl Harbor and other American military installations in Hawaii. The United States was at war. As the army leadership swung into responsive action, Eisenhower's plans for Christmas leave at West Point to visit with son John, who was then a plebe, were dismissed.

Five days after the Japanese attack, the telephone in Eisenhower's office clanged. "'Is that you, Ike?'" he remembered the caller asking. "'The Chief says for you to hop a plane and get up here right away. Tell your boss that formal orders will come through later.' The 'Chief' was General George Marshall, and the man at the other end of the line was Colonel Walter Bedell Smith, who was later to become my close friend and Chief of Staff throughout the European operations."[100]

During the flight from Texas to Washington, D.C., Eisenhower considered the implications of a staff assignment during wartime. Throughout his career, he had endeavored to command troops in the field. Now, just as the

United States had entered World War II, he had been ordered away from a troop assignment to the War Department. Years later, he called the message a "hard blow."

There was little time to contemplate personal preference, though. When Eisenhower arrived at Marshall's office on the morning of Sunday, December 14, he was ushered in, "and for the first time in my life talked to him for more than two minutes."

Marshall presented an overview of the bleak strategic situation in the Pacific and the obvious peril in the Philippines. The Japanese were certainly planning to take the islands, and without substantial resupply and reinforcement, the American and Filipino forces there could be expected to put up a spirited resistance that was destined to fail. Marshall inquired matter-of-factly, "What should be our general line of action?"

Drawing on his card-playing experience, Eisenhower was poker faced. He asked for a desk and a few hours to contemplate the question, utilizing his unique understanding of the situation in the Philippines gleaned from his years of service there. He concluded that the islands could not be reinforced sufficiently to hold the Japanese at bay but that everything that could be done to support the troops there should be done.

Eisenhower told Marshall, "It will be a long time before major reinforcements can go to the Philippines, longer than the garrison can hold out with any driblet assistance, if the enemy commits major forces to their reduction. But we must do everything for them that is humanly possible. The people of China, of the Philippines, of the Dutch East Indies, will be watching us. They may excuse failure, but they will not excuse abandonment."

Eisenhower further asserted that the base of Allied operations in the Pacific should be established in Australia and that the aerial supply routes from there to Hawaii should be preserved at all costs.

Marshall listened to the short, succinct report and snapped, "I agree with you. Do your best to save them."[101] In all likelihood, the chief of staff had already come to the same conclusions. Eisenhower had passed his test with flying colors and contributed heavily to his rapid rise in rank and responsibility.

Before the two parted company, Marshall offered a glimpse of his perspective on command. "Eisenhower," he stated, "the [War] Department is filled with able men who analyze their problems well but feel compelled always to bring them to me for final solution. I must have assistants who will solve their own problems and tell me later what they have done."[102]

Two other factors contributed significantly to Eisenhower's ascent in late 1941 and early 1942. Marshall had initiated a massive overhaul and reorganization of the army's command structure, and Eisenhower's West Point classmate Maj. Gen. Joseph McNarney was placed in charge of the undertaking. The chief of staff had also asked an old friend of Eisenhower's from West Point for a list of ten officers he thought best qualified to lead the new Operations Division of the War Department General Staff.

Brigadier General Mark Clark was an ambitious staff officer destined to command the Allied Fifth Army during the Italian Campaign in World War II. He was a graduate of the Class of 1917 who had been assigned to Eisenhower's barracks at the Academy, and he emphatically responded to Marshall's request with only one name. "Ike Eisenhower. If you have to have 10 names, I'll just put nine ditto marks below."[103]

In December 1941, Eisenhower attended the first meeting of the newly formed Anglo-American Combined Chiefs of Staff. During three weeks of talks in Washington, D.C., the Arcadia Conference reinforced a consensus that Nazi Germany, which had declared war on the United States on December 11, would be the priority while Japan would be contained and dealt with as resources permitted. Recognizing Eisenhower's promise, Marshall made it possible during the conference for his protégé to gain exposure to both the British and American senior military and political leaders.

In February 1942, Eisenhower succeeded his longtime friend Leonard Gerow as assistant chief of staff in charge of war plans. Although his new role was one of great responsibility, Eisenhower envied Gerow, who received promotion to major general and command of the 29th Infantry Division. In March, Eisenhower was named chief of the newly created Operations Division. He was promoted to the temporary rank of major general, reflecting briefly that he had achieved the grade that most army officers of the day considered the pinnacle of an exceptional military career.

The spring of 1942 was a time of incredible challenge, and serving as the chief war planner for the US Army required Eisenhower to work long hours. Tempers, including Eisenhower's, were often short. While his staff formulated plans for both the European and Pacific Theaters, he did all he could do to allocate scarce resources to the embattled Philippines, where his old boss MacArthur howled that his command had been abandoned. The horrible truth was that the Philippines would be lost. It was only a matter of time.

Meanwhile, Eisenhower's staff worked feverishly on operations that might relieve the pressure on the embattled Soviet Red Army, which had been fighting the Nazis on the Eastern Front for a year. Operation Sledgehammer constituted an emergency landing in Western Europe in the event of an imminent Soviet collapse. Operation Bolero outlined the massive troop and supply buildup in Great Britain that would be necessary in support of any major offensive in Western Europe. Operation Roundup was the precursor of the Allied invasion of Northern France that later became known as Operation Overlord.

Growing in urgency were the plans for the Allied invasion of North Africa, known as Operation Torch. The impetus for Torch had grown out of pressure to assist the Soviets in their fight to the death with the Nazis in the East by establishing a second front. Although Soviet Premier Josef Stalin had demanded action, the British had insisted that an attack against Nazi-occupied France involving an amphibious operation across the English Channel could not be mounted with any expectation of success prior to 1944. Marshall and most American senior officers were frustrated by the circumstances but acquiesced. Operation Torch was scheduled for the autumn of 1942.

On March 10, Eisenhower's father, David, died in Abilene. Although he had never been exceptionally close to his father, Dwight felt the loss deeply. However, the exigencies of war prevented his attending the funeral. He sent a telegram to his mother and locked himself away for several hours on the day of his father's funeral to meditate and pray.

Within weeks, word reached the War Department that the heroic defenders of Bataan and Corregidor had surrendered. The Philippines had fallen. On orders from President Franklin D. Roosevelt, MacArthur and his wife and young son had been spirited out of immediate danger aboard a Navy PT boat. Left to the bitter end, Gen. Jonathan Wainwright had surrendered more than eighty thousand troops to the Japanese. It remains the largest capitulation in American military history.

In late May, Marshall's growing concern about the implementation of Operation Bolero prompted him to send Eisenhower on a fact-finding mission to England. Eisenhower and Mark Clark determined that the performance of the American command then in place was inadequate.

Their chauffeur was a young woman named Kay Summersby, with whom Eisenhower was later and most likely incorrectly linked.

The American officers met with the British chiefs of staff and described ongoing preparations for Operation Roundup, which, at the time, they were still projecting for early 1943. Eisenhower asserted that the most pressing item of business was the naming of a commander for the invasion.

When one of the British officers posed the question to Eisenhower as to who he thought would be best to lead Roundup, he considered the fact that in 1943 the British would initially supply the preponderance of the troops committed to the invasion. He remembered Marshall's high opinion of Adm. Lord Louis Mountbatten and mentioned his name as an individual who had been studying amphibious operations for some time and was also thought of as vigorous, intelligent, and courageous. Eisenhower made the statement without realizing that Mountbatten was seated across the table from him. A moment of embarrassment was followed by an introduction, and the two officers became great friends.

Eisenhower and Clark also made their first acquaintance with feisty British Lt. Gen. Bernard Law Montgomery while observing an exercise in Kent, southeast of London. It was the beginning of a contentious relationship for Eisenhower, one that would require all the tact, diplomacy, and charm the man from Kansas could muster. Clark remembered that Montgomery arrived extremely late for a briefing:

> He shook hands stiffly, making it very clear that we were mere major generals while he was a lieutenant general. He told us, "I'm sorry I'm late, but I really shouldn't have come at all. I'll make it brief." He turned to a big map on the wall and, with a pointer, started showing us where the troops were, the German troops and his. Ike took out a pack of cigarettes, lit one and in a minute or so, Montgomery, not turning around, said, "Who's smoking?" "I am, sir," said Eisenhower, and Montgomery said, "Stop it. I don't permit it here." Ike dropped the cigarette on the floor, stepped on it, and looked at me, very red faced. Monty took a few minutes more, then said, "That concludes my presentation. Sorry to be so abrupt." He shook hands, and out we went.[104]

When he returned to Washington on June 3, Eisenhower stopped short of recommending the removal of the entire American command structure in

England and starting from scratch. Nevertheless, he recommended that a headquarters be established to spearhead the coordination of the buildup. Marshall set Eisenhower at once to producing a job description for the officer who would command the growing US military presence in Europe. As Marshall read through the description a few days later, he asked Eisenhower for a recommendation to fill the post.

Eisenhower had already considered the available choices and responded that his friend and classmate McNarney was the man for the job. He wrote, "I believe that General McNarney has the strength of character, the independence of thought, and the ability to fulfill satisfactorily the requirements of this difficult task."[105]

McNarney was indeed a brilliant organizer, and the choice was solid. At the time, however, he had just completed the reorganization of the War Department that Marshall had mandated and been elevated to deputy chief of staff in the previous ninety days. Marshall would not release him for duty in the European Theater.

When Marshall sought the opinions of other officers concerning a European Theater commander, Eisenhower's name came up more than once. Marshall had also been in close contact with Eisenhower for several months. The chief of staff appreciated the fact that his protégé, unlike so many other officers of excellent talent who seemed to lose their composure during direct communication with him, was never tongue-tied or awestruck in his presence. Although he possessed a fiery temper, Eisenhower had learned to keep it under control. His wide grin and affable manner made him instantly likable. Already Marshall knew that the successful prosecution of coalition warfare required a leader with a rare set of skills—soldier, diplomat, and consensus builder.

Eisenhower later recalled that when he presented his overview of the European Theater commander's responsibilities to Marshall, "I remarked to General Marshall that this was one paper he should read in detail before it went out because it was likely to be an important document in the further waging of the war. His reply still lives in my memory: 'I certainly do want to read it. You may be the man who executes it. If that's the case, when can you leave?' Three days later General Marshall told me definitely that I would command the European Theater."[106]

At this juncture, Eisenhower's primary mission was two-fold: energize Operation Bolero and prepare for Operation Torch, seeing to it that the buildup for the cross-Channel attack that was surely to come proceeded apace and ensuring the success of the landings in North Africa. Command of the Normandy invasion itself was not part of the package. In fact, that important role, as far as Eisenhower knew, might well be reserved for Marshall himself. Nevertheless, Eisenhower's success in his new post was critical to winning the war. It carried with it the double-edged sword of prestige and responsibility second only to that of the chief of staff.

Eisenhower's effective date as commander of US Forces, European Theater of Operations was June 25, 1942. Less than a year earlier, he had been an obscure lieutenant colonel. At dinner on the evening of his appointment, Eisenhower told Mamie that he would be returning to London and that this time it would probably be for the duration of the war. She asked, "What post are you going to have?" He grinned and responded, "I'm going to command the whole shebang."[107]

Contrary to the closely held beliefs of many contemporary observers, the initial second front against the Nazis was not to come in Western Europe. Plans for Operation Torch were well underway in the summer of 1942. The amphibious operation was scheduled for November 8. Eisenhower's first test as a coalition commander loomed ahead.

When Omar Bradley took command of the Infantry School at Fort Benning in February 1941, a crisis for the foot soldier existed—not in manpower but in leadership. While the draft swelled the ranks of the active-duty army, reserves, and National Guard, a shortage of junior officers and instructors was bound to become worse. To address the problem, Marshall had proposed the establishment of Officers Candidate Schools (OCS) to train selected personnel for command responsibilities.

General Hodges had established an OCS at Fort Benning, but it was not up to the standards that were obviously necessary to serve the intended purpose. Now, at Marshall's behest, Bradley set about overhauling the existing school and expanding the concept across the country against a headwind of both vocal and passive opposition within the army command structure. Bradley remembered:

> . . . I drew up a sort of assembly-line plan that would enable us to expand the Benning OCS program twenty-fourfold . . . I took my plan to Washington and presented it to Hodges—now chief of infantry—and to G-1 [personnel]. Because of the widespread underlying prejudice against OCS in general (the graduates had already

been derisively tagged "ninety-day wonders"), I got nowhere until I decided to go over everybody's head and take the plan directly to Marshall. He was impressed—and pleased—and promptly gave the plan a green light.[108]

Bradley's overhaul of the OCS program was tremendously successful and supplied large numbers of qualified junior officers for service around the globe in the coming war. The program remains a component of the army's development of young officers, and the term OCS is familiar lexicon for both soldiers and civilians.

"The Fort Benning OCS became the model, or prototype, for all future OCS's, carefully studied and copied by representatives from the other branches. The school turned out countless thousands of junior officers who went on to fill the infantry ranks in Europe and the Pacific. I consider the founding of the Fort Benning OCS my greatest contribution to the mobilization effort," Bradley concluded.[109]

During his tenure as commandant of the Infantry School, Bradley witnessed the growth of the armored and airborne branches of the army. One officer who stepped forward among the tankers was Col. George Patton, the longtime friend of Eisenhower who had tried unsuccessfully to lure Ike back into the Armored Corps in 1940. The early airborne effort was led by Maj. William "Bud" Miley, whom Bradley had previously assisted with the procurement of equipment for his parachute soldiers. In 1941, Lt. Col. Willis C. Lee, acknowledged as the father of the army's Airborne Corps, came to command the Provisional Parachute Group at Fort Benning.

On the afternoon of December 7, 1941, Omar and Mary Bradley were out on their lawn doing some gardening. A friend stopped by and broke the startling news of the attack on Pearl Harbor. Bradley remembered one of Marshall's visits to Fort Benning sometime earlier. He had asked Bradley's thoughts on a replacement as Infantry School commandant when he was handed command of a division. Bradley had been a brigadier general for only a few months. Command of a division would mean a promotion to major general and recognition of a job well done, as most divisions were going to officers who were senior to Bradley.

In late December, orders were cut to activate three infantry divisions. Bradley was given command of the 82nd. Among the staff members he chose was Joseph M. Swing, a classmate at West Point and a "crusty disciplinarian," who assumed the duties of artillery commander. When he arrived at Camp Claiborne, Louisiana, Bradley was dismayed by the lack of physical training in the 82nd Division. He instituted an immediate regimen and required his staff—and even himself—to take part. During one exercise, the forty-nine-year-old major general lost his grip on a rope swing and fell unceremoniously into an open sewage ditch. The incident became legendary among the men of the 82nd. Bradley also brought Sgt. Alvin York, the well-known hero who had served with the 82nd Division and received the Medal of Honor during World War I, to deliver an inspirational address to the men.

Bradley was proud of the progress the 82nd had made and referred to the division as his "pride and joy." Summarily, though, it was taken away. In the spring of 1942, Marshall recognized the lack of progress that many of the National Guard infantry divisions were making after their call-up. Among these was the 28th, a Pennsylvania unit that had been activated in January 1941. More than a year later, in June 1942, Bradley became the third commanding general of the 28th Division in a six-month period. The following month, his beloved 82nd was designated the army's first airborne division and relocated to Fort Bragg, North Carolina.

Bradley quickly assessed the issues confronting the 28th Division—chiefly, a manpower drain as young noncommissioned officers were detailed for OCS and then sent to other units upon graduation, or groups of officers were taken to form the command cadres of other units. He ended the manpower drain and requested experienced commanders who were capable of leading the 28th Division's transformation.

Physical fitness again was a top priority, and Bradley instituted a series of lengthy hikes, working the troops up to a grueling twenty-five-mile nocturnal march. The commanding general took part in the march and completed it while, often, men half his age could not. He laughed, "One soldier said to me, 'Who the hell ordered this march?' I replied, 'I don't know, but they ought to hang the S.O.B.'"[110]

By August, the 28th Division had made great strides. Relocating to Camp Gordon Johnson in Carrabelle, Florida, the unit engaged in amphibious training, and Bradley believed that Marshall would make good on an earlier promise that his faithful service in training divisions for combat duty would be rewarded. On his fiftieth birthday, February 12, 1943, he received word from Marshall that at long last he would command a corps. Within days, Bradley received orders to take over X Corps based at Temple, Texas. Then, once again, the unexpected happened.

Bradley's telephone rang, and Gen. Alexander Bolling, G-1 (personnel officer) for Gen. Lesley McNair, commanding general Army Ground Forces, was on the other end of the line. Bradley remembered, "He said cryptically, 'We're cutting orders for you today, Brad. You're going overseas on extended active duty. Not the division—just you.' I was understandably flabbergasted. I said, 'I've just received orders to Temple, Texas, to—' Bolling broke in, 'Oh, that was yesterday.' I composed my voice and said, 'Well, what kind of clothes? Which way do I go?' I meant Africa or the Pacific, holding my breath, devoutly hoping it would be Africa. It was against regulations to discuss troop movements (in this case, me) on an open telephone. Cagily, Bolling said, 'Remember your classmate? You're going to join him.' Eisenhower! Africa.'"[111]

Bradley's 82nd and 28th Divisions went on to render distinguished service during World War II. The 82nd Airborne jumped into Sicily, Normandy, and the Netherlands, while the 28th Infantry, its distinctive red keystone unit patch nicknamed the "Bloody Bucket," fought in the Hürtgen Forest, the Battle of the Bulge, and Alsace.

On the eve of US involvement in World War II, Joseph McNarney was already a staff officer of proven capability. He was promoted to the rank of colonel in March 1940 and to brigadier general in April 1941. Within a month, he was assigned to a group of Army observers detailed to London under the command of Maj. Gen. James E. Chaney, who had previously served as an observer in the city during the Battle of Britain in 1940.

Chaney selected McNarney as his chief of staff. While continuing a dialogue that would facilitate the introduction of American air assets to the European Theater when the United States entered the war against the Nazis, the group scouted suitable locations for major air bases that soon enough would be home to a host of US heavy bombers and fighters participating in the air assault on Fortress Europe.

During his 1966 interview with Forrest C. Pogue, McNarney remembered that he was summoned to Washington, D.C., by Marshall and left London on December 7, 1941, expecting six weeks of temporary duty. As he sat aboard a train from London, someone mentioned that Pearl Harbor had been attacked. His reaction was nonbelief. Pogue wrote, "He said they were crazy to tell such a story."[112]

A youthful Dwight Eisenhower poses in West Point cadet uniform for his graduation portrait. Popular among his fellow cadets, Eisenhower delighted in mischief and received a large number of demerits during his four years at the Academy. He ranked ninety-fifth in conduct and graduated sixty-first in the Class of 1915. *US Army, Dwight D. Eisenhower Presidential Library and Museum*

Returning from mess, cadets march past the Academic Building on the campus of the United States Military Academy. Designed by Richard Morris Hunt, the foremost American architect of the nineteenth century, the structure is also referred to as the West Academic Building. Occupied in 1895, the Academic Building combines elements of the old library and barracks. *Library of Congress*

Japanese Adm. Heihachirō Tōgō (left) stands with Maj. Gen. Thomas Henry Barry, superintendent of the United States Military Academy, during Tōgō's visit to West Point in August 1911. The hero of the Japanese naval victory at the Battle of Tsushima during the Russo-Japanese War, Tōgō reviewed the Corps of Cadets, which included members of the Class of 1915. *Library of Congress*

The army offense runs a sweep around the right end during a 6–0 football loss to powerful Yale on October 19, 1912. Three weeks later, Dwight Eisenhower's promising football career was cut short by a devastating knee injury in a game against Carlisle Institute, which featured the great athlete Jim Thorpe. For the rest of their lives, Eisenhower, Omar Bradley, and other members of the Class of 1915 considered their athletic experiences essential in building character and teamwork. *US Army, Dwight D. Eisenhower Presidential Library and Museum*

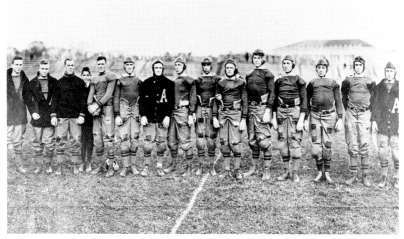

Members of the 1912 West Point football team gather on the field with Cullum Hall looming in the background. Members of the class of 1915 include Dwight Eisenhower, second from left; Louis Merillat, seventh from left, wearing an A sweater; Omar Bradley, second from right; and Leland Hobbs at far right, wearing an A sweater. The 1912 football team finished the season with a 5–3 record, losing to Yale, Carlisle Institute, and Navy. *Library of Congress*

First Lieutenant Dwight D. Eisenhower and his new wife pose for their wedding portrait shortly after the ceremony, which took place on July 1, 1916. Mamie Geneva Eisenhower, née Doud, was the daughter of wealthy Denver businessman John Doud, and the wedding took place at the Doud family home. Dwight was promoted to the rank of first lieutenant on the same day. *US Army, Dwight D. Eisenhower Presidential Library and Museum*

Major Leland Hobbs was serving as a personnel officer in Washington, D.C., when he posed for this photograph in 1929. The 1915 *Howitzer* yearbook noted that Hobbs "gave no display of athletic ability" during his high school days. At West Point, however, Hobbs lettered in football, basketball, and baseball during each of his four years. He graduated forty-sixth in the class of 1915, rose to the rank of major general, and commanded the 30th Infantry Division during heavy fighting in Normandy in World War II. *National Archives and Records Administration*

Major Jo Hunt Reaney was killed in action in France on July 15, 1918, while commanding an infantry company near Château Thierry during World War I. Reaney graduated seventy-ninth in the class of 1915 and presented a Navajo rug to newlyweds Omar and Mary Bradley as they traveled to California following their marriage in December 1916. *United States Military Academy Library, West Point*

Major General Henry J. F. Miller served as commander of the US Air Service Command in Europe until he was sent home for a breach of security prior to the D-Day landings of June 6, 1944. Miller was relieved of duty and reverted to his permanent rank of colonel by 1915 West Point classmate Gen. Dwight Eisenhower. *Library of Congress*

General Dwight Eisenhower, supreme commander of Allied forces in Europe, chats with troopers of the 502nd Parachute Infantry Regiment, 101st Airborne Division, prior to their departure for Normandy. Eisenhower visited the troops on the evening of June 5, 1944, offering encouragement as senior Allied commanders expected heavy casualties among the three airborne divisions that took part in the D-Day operations. *National Archives and Records Administration*

On April 12, 1945, Generals Bradley (left) and Eisenhower (right) inspect paintings stolen by the Nazis and hidden in a salt mine in Merkers, Germany. Peering over Eisenhower's shoulder is Lt. Gen. George S. Patton, commander of the US Third Army. *National Archives and Records Administration*

In October 1944, US Army Chief of Staff Gen. George C. Marshall (left) congratulates Gen. Joseph McNarney after presenting him with the Distinguished Service Medal and the Legion of Merit for his service in numerous significant roles, including the reorganization of the War Department command structure and serving as deputy supreme commander and commanding general of US forces in the Mediterranean Theater of Operations. *George C. Marshall Foundation*

Commander of the US Eighth Army in Korea Gen. James Van Fleet is shown with his four-star rank and the Eighth Army patch emblazoned on his helmet. Among the general's prominent decorations are the Combat Infantryman's Badge and the ribbons to the Distinguished Service Cross, the Silver Star, the Bronze Star, and the Purple Heart. *George C. Marshall Foundation*

General Eisenhower (left) and US ground forces commander Lt. Gen. Omar Bradley (center) confer with Maj. Gen. J. Lawton Collins (right), commander of the US VII Corps, in France on July 4, 1944. At the time of the meeting, Allied troops were engaged in fierce fighting against determined German resistance in Normandy. At the end of July, the Allies launched Operation Cobra, resulting in a breakout from the Norman hedgerow country. *US Army, Dwight D. Eisenhower Presidential Library and Museum*

On December 14, 1961, Gen. James Van Fleet (second from left) met with President John F. Kennedy (third from left), Secretary of the Army Elvis J. Stahr Jr. (far right), and Army Chief of Staff Gen. George H. Decker (far left) in the Oval Office. Van Fleet served as a special consultant to Stahr and assessed the capabilities of American special forces. *Abbie Rowe, White House Photographs, John F. Kennedy Presidential Library and Museum*

In 1950, Dwight and Mamie Eisenhower purchased this farmhouse and surrounding acreage in Gettysburg, Pennsylvania. During the presidential years, it served as a retreat from the rigors of Washington, D.C., and a location to welcome world leaders. The two-hundred-year-old house underwent extensive renovations that were completed in 1955, and the Eisenhowers retired to the property in 1961. Today, it is preserved by the National Park Service as the Eisenhower National Historic Site. *Gettysburg Foundation*

McNarney flew from Britain to the Portuguese capital of Lisbon, a hotbed of intrigue and espionage, and waited four days for the Thursday arrival of the Pan Am Clipper flying boat that would carry him across the Atlantic to Washington. Marshall was moving quickly to assemble his talented lieutenants. McNarney departed Lisbon on the same day that Eisenhower received his defining telephone call from Bedell Smith.

In the early days after the US entered World War II, nerves were raw. As McNarney came down the elevator to board the flying boat that Thursday morning, one of the crewmen remarked that his was the last such flight out of Lisbon because the Portuguese government intended to intern Americans for the duration of the war. "I became disturbed," McNarney admitted. The flight was delayed for hours. A telephone call from Pan Am headquarters cleared the departure at 9:00 p.m.; however, local authorities did not permit takeoff until 2:00 a.m. local time.

The flying boat lumbered across the harbor and lifted into the darkness. Hugging the coast of Africa briefly, it then turned southwest to Brazil and on to Jamaica, Bermuda, and New York. Bone tired, McNarney at last reached Washington and arrived at Marshall's office breathless.

At the time, Marshall was evaluating the need to restructure the War Department, streamlining reporting and decision making. McNarney was already tapped to play a key role in the process, but the attack on Pearl Harbor had gotten in the way. McNarney recalled that when he reported to the chief of staff, Marshall said, "'McNarney, you are going to Hawaii on the Roberts Board.' I had no baggage; just the clothes I was in. He said I was to leave the next day."[113]

The Roberts Commission made the first official inquiry into the circumstances surrounding the Japanese attack on Pearl Harbor. Authorized by executive order on December 18, 1941, the five-man board of inquiry was headed by US Supreme Court justice Owen J. Roberts. The commission held meetings in both Washington and Honolulu and interviewed 127 witnesses, including Marshall himself.

On January 23, 1942, the Roberts Commission delivered its report to President Roosevelt. Its conclusions are still controversial today. Foremost was the culpability of the senior army and navy commanders in Hawaii, Maj. Gen. Walter Short and Adm. Husband Kimmel. The report stated:

In the light of the warnings and directions to take appropriate action, transmitted to both commanders between November 27 and December 7, and the obligation under the system of coordination then in effect for joint cooperative action on their part, it was a dereliction of duty on the part of each of them not to consult and confer with the other respecting the meaning and intent of the warnings, and the appropriate measures of defense required by the imminence of hostilities. The attitude of each, that he was not required to inform himself of, and his lack of interest in, the measures undertaken by the other to carry out the responsibility assigned to such other under the provisions of the plans then in effect, demonstrated on the part of each a lack of appreciation of the responsibilities vested in them and inherent in their positions as commander in chief, Pacific Fleet, and commanding general, Hawaiian Department.[114]

Historians have reached differing conclusions as to the real responsibility that Short and Kimmel shouldered for the Pearl Harbor disaster, and congressional hearings and resolutions have sought to exonerate them. However, McNarney asserted to Pogue that he was recommended for the position on the Roberts Commission by Gen. Henry "Hap" Arnold, chief of the Army Air Forces, and it is doubtful that the appointment took place without Marshall's blessing. The nation was at war. The reputations of Marshall and the War Department were at stake, and McNarney was Marshall's man on the Roberts Commission, guarding both.

Before Marshall ascended to the post of chief of staff in 1939, he realized that the bureaucracy of the Army General Staff would be paralyzing in time of war. He commented, "It had become a huge, bureaucratic, red-tape-ridden operating agency. It slowed everything down [and had] lost track of its purpose for existence."[115]

However, when Marshall sent McNarney to Hawaii, he had said nothing of the pending reorganization. "I spent two weeks in Hawaii," McNarney remembered. "At the conclusion of the Roberts Board report, he told me that he wanted me to head the committee to reorganize the War Department. Too many people were reporting to him, and it took too long to get any paper through the War Department. Everybody had to concur. About 28 people had to pass on matters. He said, 'I can't stand it.'"[116]

Two officers, Lt. Col. William K. Harrison and Maj. Laurence S. Kuter, had already begun hammering out a new framework that Marshall wanted to resemble the structure of some of the largest and most successful corporations in the United States. More than sixty officers were reporting directly to Marshall, while at least thirty major and 350 minor army commands were beneath him in the existing cumbersome hierarchy.

Marshall knew that a long, procedurally driven overhaul would sink under its own weight—particularly if those who were to be negatively impacted were given time to formulate a response. To avoid the morass of turf defending and interference from military and civilian quarters, he needed swift action. For Marshall's reorganization to be successful, it had to be done quickly, efficiently, and in cold blood. He turned to McNarney.

"General Marshall . . . was grim at times," McNarney said of his boss. "He put the fear of God into people just by looking at them. He was a fine operator. If he wanted something done, he would tell you what it was, and you went and did it. He didn't tell you how. He gave authority and responsibility. He didn't have time to do more. It was not intended that he should solve all problems. That was what the staff was for. He knew how a staff should operate. He seldom relaxed. I recall only once, at a party together, that he ever relaxed with me. He was usually strictly business."

A month after Pearl Harbor, Marshall appointed McNarney to lead the way with the reorganization because, Pogue wrote, he needed an experienced officer who was a "tough hatchet man with a rhinoceros hide [and] the nerve to push through the reorganization in the face of the rugged infighting that was almost certain to follow."[117]

McNarney began his task on January 25, 1942, and in about a week the basic plan was presented to Marshall. The changes were sweeping and hit the War Department like a tidal wave. Recalled McNarney:

Nothing was done to ease the change. The General Staff had started to expand, with G-1 having over 100 people; G-2 not so bad; Operations [G-3] 100; G-4 large. They were not policy people but were trying to make policy. By fiat, I said G-1, G-2, G-3, and G-4 can have 10 General Staff people and 20 helpers and no more. I went along with commanding generals of the three forces [Army Ground Forces under Lt. Gen. Lesley McNair; Army Air Forces under Lt. Gen. Henry "Hap" Arnold; Army Services Forces under Lt. Gen. Brehon Somervell] and wiped out the chiefs of arms in the Coast Artillery, Field Artillery, Infantry, and Cavalry and cut off the heads of the chiefs of Ordnance, Engineers, and Chemical Warfare. The exception was JAG [Judge Advocate General].[118]

McNarney was not finished yet. "With the aid of the assistant JAG, I wrote the executive order putting all this into effect and cut down the number reporting to him [Marshall] to about six," he recalled. He discussed the changes with Marshall for about a half hour and gained approval. When McNarney told the chief of staff that it cut the jobs of two of his deputies, Marshall retorted, "Is that enough?" When the reply was affirmative, Marshall told McNarney, "You do it."

After Marshall's approval, McNarney went to Secretary of War Henry L. Stimson, and then to President Roosevelt. The meeting with Roosevelt was anything but routine.

"He was in the dentist chair," McNarney commented. "The girl receptionist took it to him and said, 'They want approval right away.' He was mad. I got bawled out over the telephone. I had merely told her it had top priority. The President asked Marshall the next day, 'Who is McNarney; you had better fire him.' General Marshall said, 'When I find people who get things done, I won't fire them.'"[119]

McNarney convened a committee that did not vote or debate. Its purpose, he told them, was to put into effect the executive order that authorized the reorganization. He remembered that Somervell had the most challenging job during the implementation. "We had our disagreements," McNarney remarked. "He would get red and then white. Sometimes he would say, 'I won't do it.' I would say, 'The hell you're not!'"[120]

The only combat arms chief to put his objection to the change in writing was Maj. Gen. Robert M. Danford, head of the Field Artillery. He cried on Marshall's shoulder and wrote that the Field Artillery should remain horse-drawn because horses could feed off the land, while "motor trucks" could not.

With the reorganization, careers ended. Many old soldiers went, with a bang or a whimper, into retirement. It was a peacetime purge that prepared the War Department to successfully prosecute World War II. Although McNarney certainly incurred the wrath and enmity of many as he ruthlessly executed the plan, there was no doubt that Marshall, who once told Pogue that his lieutenant was a "merciless man," respected his willingness to carry out orders like a good soldier without regard for personal gain.

In doing so, McNarney did achieve recognition. In January 1942, he was promoted to major general. In March, he was named deputy chief of staff. In June, he was promoted to lieutenant general. When the construction of the Pentagon was completed in January 1943, he was the first member of the staff to move into a new office—next door to Marshall.

In response to the German U-boat threat off the coast of the United States, McNarney directed Gen. Henry "Hap" Arnold of the Army Air Forces to organize the First Antisubmarine Army Air Command in September 1942. Its mission of "the location and destruction of hostile submarines" was later expanded to attacking enemy submarines "wherever they may be operating." The initiative was effective.

In June 1943, McNarney overcame inter-service rivalry and hammered out the Arnold-McNarney-McCain Agreement, which vested full responsibility for antisubmarine warfare with the US Navy while the Army Air Forces would retain control of all long-range bombing forces defending the Western Hemisphere. The agreement was held up for a month by Chief of Naval Operations Adm. Ernest J. King, but Marshall interceded, threatening to go directly to President Franklin D. Roosevelt. King agreed to the proposal.

In October 1944, McNarney transferred to the Mediterranean Theater as deputy supreme Allied commander and commander of all US forces in the region. In March 1945, he was promoted to full general.

In a radio broadcast to the American people on the evening of December 29, 1940, President Roosevelt proclaimed that the nation, in defense of its own shores, would become the great "arsenal of democracy." In so doing, the industrial might of the United States would support the British war effort through expansive programs that eventually evolved into Lend-Lease, the lifeline of war materiel that sustained Great Britain and other Allied nations through the war years.

Although the United States did not formally enter World War II for another year, the logistics of reequipping its own armed forces had to be balanced with the needs of its allies. This monumental task required reinvention of the army's logistical systems, and at the forefront was Henry Spiese Aurand. A Pennsylvanian, Aurand graduated twentieth in the class of 1915. Initially with the Coast Artillery, he spent World War I as a student of the Army Ordnance School and in various assignments, including the Sandy Hook Proving Grounds in New Jersey. In the mid-1920s, Aurand wrote the distribution protocol for the army mobilization plan. In 1932, he wrote the Ordnance Field Manual that was later revised and in use by the army throughout World War II.

Aurand was a brilliant thinker who distilled complex problems to their components with dexterity. In the spring of 1940, he was named chief, Plans and Requirements, Army G-4, War Department General Staff. He held numerous other titles during the reorganization of the army logistics programs. He worked closely with the British to quantify and deliver war materiel to the embattled nation prior to and during Lend-Lease while calculating with great accuracy the US industrial and production requirements that were collectively referred to as the Victory Plan for World War II.

Maintaining the flow of materiel to Lend-Lease recipients without compromising the needs of the US Army and refusing to retool US production to foreign military specifications were near miraculous accomplishments, and Aurand's contribution to victory, although somewhat obscure, can scarcely be measured. During his tenure with the War Department General Staff, he worked with three classmates, Brig. Gen. Clesen Tenney (who had graduated seventy-seventh), Brig. Gen. Victor Vaughn Taylor (122nd), and former West Point roommate Albert W. "Doc" Waldron (thirty-second).

In an April 21, 1974, interview with Maj. William O. Morrison, Aurand stated:

> The Supply section was headed by an old friend of mine named Jeff Keyes [West Point Class of 1913 and later Lt. Gen. Geoffrey Keyes], who somehow or other slid out of the General Staff and back to the troops. And who should come in to replace him—my West Point roommate Doc Waldron, and this made working together very easy. But when the requests for foreign assistance began coming in a year and a half before Lend-Lease, we had to work so very closely together and . . . decided that we'd make it one section. And I think I ranked Doc Waldron five files and said I was the section chief and he was the exec. And for a while he was a little mad about it but we had known each other too long and too well to make any difference. . . .[121]

When the Allied push against stubborn Japanese resistance in New Guinea stalled during fighting at Buna and Gona in the autumn of 1942, Gen. Douglas MacArthur, supreme commander of Allied forces in the Southwest

Pacific Area, ordered a change in command, sacking Maj. Gen. Edwin F. Harding, commander of the 32nd Infantry Division. Harding's replacement was the division artillery officer and Aurand's old roommate, Brig. Gen. Doc Waldron, who had garnered a coveted combat assignment.

On December 5, 1942, Waldron was with his frontline units during heavy fighting near Buna and was seriously wounded by a bullet in the shoulder. For the action, he received the Distinguished Service Cross, the citation reading in part that "many leaders of small infantry units became casualties and the units became disorganized. Brigadier General Waldron, with complete disregard for his own safety, moved along the line of the assault platoons under heavy fire from enemy snipers, machine guns, grenades and mortars. By his personal example, calm bearing and utter fearlessness, he inspired the men to great effort."

Waldron's leadership was recognized with promotion in the field to major general, but the wound left him permanently disabled, precipitating his retirement from the army in 1946 after duty with the headquarters of the Army Ground Forces. He later led the Veterans Administration Hospital in Palo Alto, California, and was an active leader in the local Republican Party.

Waldron died in 1961, and Aurand's *Assembly* tribute was glowing: "He loved the great outdoors, and fished and hunted with the most skilled even after his wound had left him without a joint in his right shoulder. After his second retirement, he spent many hours in his wood-working shop carving and painting beautiful, life-like, wooden ducks for use as decoys, which he gave unstintingly to any friend who visited him. Also, he was a bird-watcher who kept a feeding box outside the window by his favorite chair and he could identify all the birds which accepted his hospitality."[122]

Prior to US entry into the war, the appearance of neutrality had to be maintained during clandestine discussions with representatives of the British military in Washington, D.C. "The fact that the British were in touch with the War Department, and military British at that, had to be kept completely secret," Aurand remembered. "The British rented some apartments on K Street not far from the Army-Navy Club as individuals. They were not permitted at the start to come to the munitions building at all. When I went to see them I walked down the alley between K and I streets and went up a fire escape, which fortunately had been anchored to the ground so we didn't have to raise and lower the last flight down. The principle [*sic*] task at that time was to match the US surpluses with the British needs."[123]

Perhaps Aurand's greatest contribution to the war effort was his role in the procurement of the "quarter-ton truck 4X4," better known as the ubiquitous jeep. The original design from the Bantam Company was rejected by an infantry board as unsuitable for a mobile gun mount. When a friend asked Aurand to take a look at the vehicle, he made some suggestions for improvement.

"In my mind, it was absolutely unsuitable for a machine gun mount," Aurand said. "But what a pretty little truck. . . . Well, I knew nothing about automotive design, but I began asking a few dumb questions and they are always harder to answer than smart ones—and by the time this was over, much to the red faces of the salesmen, I had sold the Quartermaster General's office on buying some."[124]

During a demonstration of the jeep a few days later, General Marshall rode up on his horse and asked about the little truck. Aurand recalled that he asked an officer, "'Well, what you got there?'" When the officer responded, "'Oh, I don't know. This is called a quarter-ton truck 4X4,'" Marshall shot back, "'Well, buy one for each regiment.'"[125]

An estimated 650,000 jeeps were produced between 1941 and 1945.

In January 1941, Aurand was promoted to brigadier general, and this was followed in September with a second star. During World War II, he served as commanding general of Sixth Service Command in Chicago from 1942 to 1944. In late 1944, he was transferred to France as commander of the Normandy Base Section. During the Battle of the Bulge, his command delivered outstanding service, allowing significant numbers of troops to enter combat to eliminate the German breakthrough. He was also a pioneer in the deployment of black troops, giving them greater autonomy and responsibility than ever before.

At the end of World War II, Aurand was commanding general, Services of Supply, China Theater. While visiting rear-echelon headquarters at Lashio, Burma, in June 1945, he pinned the second star of major general rank on the collar of West Point classmate Douglas Lafayette Weart. At the time, Weart was serving as commander of rear-echelon troops in the theater. He had previously been posted to the Panama Canal Zone and as chief of staff of the Caribbean Defense Command. Weart, who had graduated tenth in the class, was a veteran of the Punitive Expedition and served four campaigns during World War I. He retired due to disability in 1951 and died in Washington, D.C., in 1975.

In 1946, Aurand became the last commander of the US Africa–Middle East Theater responsible for concluding postwar operations. He went on to head Army Research and Development and then served as director of logistics following the creation of the Department of Defense. He was promoted to lieutenant general in January 1948 and assumed the post of commanding general, US Army Pacific the following year, then continued in that role through much of the Korean War. Aurand retired in 1952 and died in 1980. He was survived by two sons, Maj. Gen. Henry S. Aurand Jr. (West Point Class of 1944), and Vice Adm. Evan Peter Aurand (US Naval Academy Class of 1938).

Major General Henry B. Sayler, Eisenhower's chief ordnance officer in the European Theater, reported for duty in England on June 25, 1942. Directly responsible for the buildup of bombs, bullets, weapons, explosives, and other materiel for the D-Day invasion, Sayler commanded more than 150,000 soldiers engaged in the effort. At its peak, ordnance poured into England at a rate of fourteen tons per minute and was temporarily warehoused in twenty-one storage depots, nineteen vehicle parks, twenty-two maintenance depots, and eight ammunition depots. Ordnance soldiers assembled up to one thousand vehicles per day, and following the Normandy landings they delivered ammunition within one thousand yards of the frontlines as 212,000 tons came ashore during the first six weeks of the campaign.

Sayler graduated thirty-seventh in the class of 1915, entered the Coast Artillery, and served in France during World War I. He transferred to the Ordnance Department in 1921 and spent the rest of his career there. From 1945 to his retirement in 1949, he served as director of research and development. His two sons, Henry Jr. and John, graduated from West Point in 1943 and 1949, respectively. He died in 1970.

While several of his West Point classmates were earning stars, James Van Fleet was an infantry officer commanding the 8th Regiment, 4th Infantry Division. An experiment in assigning halftracks, light tanks, and other vehicles to its regiments led to the division being designated a provisional motorized division for participation in maneuvers in Louisiana and the Carolinas. When the reports on its performance during the exercises were less than compelling, the 4th was returned to traditional infantry division status.

At the age of fifty, Van Fleet was considerably older than most of his officers and men. Nevertheless, he took pride in staying physically fit and participated in rigorous training. Some friends and even family members openly wondered why he had not been promoted to brigadier general, and while Van Fleet sought to maintain the morale of his regiment, his own began to sag at times. The 4th Division was routinely being raided for trained officers and replacement troops who were then assigned to other outfits. Unit cohesion suffered, and elements of the division were often required to start training all over again from scratch.

Rumors of combat deployment circulated routinely as the 4th Division relocated from Fort Benning to Fort Gordon, Georgia, and then to Fort Dix, New Jersey, Camp Gordon Johnson on the Florida coast for amphibious training with the US Marines, and Fort Jackson, South Carolina. Along the way, Van Fleet speculated that the division had become so adept at training soldiers that its destiny was to remain stateside for the duration of the war doing just that. Rumors of deployment during the North African campaign came to nothing. Mark Clark stopped by to reassure Van Fleet that his name was on the list for promotion to brigadier general, but all remained inexplicably silent on that front as well.

Amid his own frustration, Van Fleet did his best to maintain morale and hold the 8th Regiment together. Fed up with the training and itching to get into the war, one of the regiment's best young officers, Lt. George Mabry, asked for a transfer to the Army Air Forces. Van Fleet asked the lieutenant if he had ever flown in an airplane. When the young officer replied that he had not, the colonel said, "Well, you better get over and withdraw that application. You might get sick in an airplane."

Mabry did. He remained with the 8th Regiment and later became one of the most distinguished officers of the 4th Infantry Division.[126]

On December 1, 1943, the orders came for the 4th Division to embark for Europe. Soon enough, all the amphibious training in Florida made sense. When the troops reached England in January 1944, everyone down to the lowest private knew that the unit was to participate in the coming liberation of Europe.[127]

Before the Japanese attack on Pearl Harbor, its architect, Adm. Isoroku Yamamoto, warned that he would run wild in the Pacific for six months. After that, he would make no guarantees. His words were prophetic, and during the first half of 1942, the Japanese juggernaut marched from victory to victory. On the Asian continent, the great cities of Hong Kong and Singapore fell. The Japanese became masters of the Dutch East Indies. Their territorial gains stretched to the Solomon Islands in the south, and until the great US naval victory in the Battle of Midway in June, their navy was supreme in the Central Pacific.

When the Philippines fell, three members of the class of 1915 were among those taken prisoner and subjected to the harrowing ordeal of the Bataan Death March. The Japanese were unprepared for the thousands of American and Filipino prisoners they had captured, and summary executions and torture became commonplace. Along the fifty-five-mile route from Mariveles at the southern end of the Bataan Peninsula to San Fernando, those who could not continue were shot or bayoneted where they fell. Heat, thirst, starvation, exhaustion, and Japanese cruelty claimed thousands. Packed onto railroad cars, the prisoners were transported to Capas and then forced to march the final eight miles to a makeshift prison at Camp O'Donnell, where conditions were deplorable.

Approximately ninety thousand American and Filipino prisoners began the Death March on April 9, 1942, and they died at a rate of up to fifty per day. When the march was over, fifty-four thousand had survived only to be subjected to wretched captivity at the hands of the Japanese.

Colonel Alfred S. Balsam graduated 112th in the class of 1915. Born in Birmingham, Alabama, he attended Birmingham College for two years prior to entering West Point with the Class of 1914. He had performed well in mathematics previously, but his grades in the subject slipped at the Academy, and he was turned back for deficiency, becoming a member of the following class. During World War I, he remained in training posts in the United States. In 1939, he was named Philippine Division Quartermaster and commanding officer of the 12th Quartermaster Regiment. He arrived in Manila with his wife, Emily, and enjoyed the duty for a time, playing tennis in the tropical heat.

By the time his tour was completed in July 1941, the situation in the Far East had become unstable. All officers were ordered to remain at their current posts due to the threat of war with Japan. Emily returned to the United States, and Alfred was appointed quartermaster of the I Philippine Corps. The following spring, an arduous odyssey began for the fifty-three-year-old officer.

"In the prisoner-of-war ordeal which followed for some three and a half years, commencing with the Bataan Death March, Alfred's tennis toughened health undoubtedly enabled his survival while many younger men died," read commentary written by a friend after Balsam's death in 1974 at age eighty-six. "However, his digestion was ruined. He kept a diary on paper scraps in his own code. Some years after release, he discovered that he had forgotten the code!

"The senior officer group in which he was held was first shipped to Taiwan, then moved to Beppu, Kyushu, then to Northern Manchuria. At the end of the war they were at Mukden, where the Russians freed them in August 1945. Returned to the United States, Alfred was hospitalized and was retired on 30 November 1946 for physical disability."[128]

Colonel Stuart C. MacDonald arrived in the Philippines in November 1941, aboard the army transport *Coolidge*, and within weeks of his arrival war erupted. Standing five feet five inches tall and known as "Shorty," he served as the chief of staff of the Southern Luzon Force and later with I Corps, surrendering in April with the bulk of the American and Filipino troops on Bataan. After surviving the Death March, MacDonald was transferred to various prisoner-of-war camps in Taiwan, Japan, Korea, and Manchuria.

In October 1944, MacDonald was among a group of American officers crowded into the hold of the *Oryoku Maru*, a Japanese troopship that had been converted to a prisoner transport. Conditions aboard such vessels were notoriously awful, and they earned the collective nickname "Hell Ships." The *Ōryoku Maru* was anchored in Keelung Harbor, Taiwan, and the Americans were shoved into the dark, dank hold of the ship on October 9. Beginning on the 12th, American bombers hit the harbor for three consecutive days, and the prison ship was rocked by near misses. MacDonald was remembered for his coolness during the harrowing raids and for his comment that such was a "hell of a way" to spend his fifty-third birthday.

McDonald graduated one hundredth in the class of 1915 and died in 1970 in Pompano Beach, Florida, at the age of seventy-eight. Two months after his narrow escape aboard the *Ōryoku Maru*, the unmarked Hell Ship was sunk off the Philippine coast by planes from the aircraft carrier USS *Hornet*. Two hundred prisoners were killed.

Following his ordeal during the Death March and captivity, Col. Marshall Henry Quesenberry, who graduated 162nd in the class of 1915, wrote to his classmates via the Association of Graduates' *Assembly* newsletter. "No longer useful, I was turned out to pasture, and I like it," he stated in 1949. "My son was killed in action in Germany. Having a wife, step-son, and a couple of fine grandchildren, I have no complaint."[129]

Quesenberry retired to San Jose, California, attended reunions of his West Point class, and died in 1960.

Lieutenant Colonel Carl E. Hocker, the commander of the 61st Coast Artillery Regiment, an antiaircraft unit, was in bed with influenza at Fort Sheridan, Illinois, when he heard the news of the Pearl Harbor attack. At once, he put on his uniform and headed for his office. When word came to mobilize, physicals were required. Years earlier, Hocker's hearing had been impaired during the firing of heavy guns, and the condition worsened as he supervised the target practice of three-inch antiaircraft weapons.

Hocker's daughter, Peggy Hocker Small, wrote that the doctor who pronounced her father unfit for service and recommended his retirement had only recently been drafted into the army. She reasoned that a more seasoned physician might have found it within him to spare the career officer such a painful verdict.

Hocker, who graduated eighty-third in the class of 1915, held the rank of cadet captain and broke Academy records in the shot put and discus as a member of the track and field team. Prior to receiving the bad news, he seemed destined for significant command responsibility. He attended the Command and General Staff School and commanded the 59th Coast Artillery Regiment on Corregidor in Manila Bay during the 1920s. He graduated from the Army War College and worked on the staff of Gen. Hugh Drum, commander of the US Army, Pacific, at Fort Shafter in Hawaii.

Although retirement had been recommended, Colonel Hocker had friends in high places and remained active as the artillery officer of the X Corps in Texas. When the Corps deployed overseas, however, he was retired for physical disability. Hocker's daughter wrote:

> He watched the action of World War II from his home in little Sherman, Texas. He never got over the disappointment and the hurt of not being on active duty during the war. He was proud of the glory that came to his classmates. . . . Had it not been for his trouble with his hearing, or had some regular army doctor examined him that bleak day in 1942, without any doubt, Carl Ernest Hocker would have been among the General Officers of the class of 1915. There was never any question in the minds of his contemporaries that he would wear stars.[130]

Carl Hocker died in 1963 at the age of seventy-two.

During the opening months of US involvement in World War II, a number of officers from the class of 1915 were recalled to active duty. The need for experienced officers to train troops and take over command and staff positions in the United States was critical as troops deployed overseas.

One of these officers was Eisenhower's West Point roommate, P. A. Hodgson. Highly intelligent and an outstanding athlete, Hodgson appeared destined for great achievement. He served with the Corps of Engineers in the US but did not deploy to Europe during World War I. Beginning in 1920, he spent two years on duty in the Far East, and during his return to the United States aboard the army transport *Thomas*, he met his future wife, Anne.

After duty on the Pacific coast and in the Desert Southwest, he graduated from the Command and General Staff School in 1930. Engineer postings in Washington, D.C., and Kansas City, Missouri, followed, at which point he returned to the Command and General Staff School at Fort Leavenworth as an instructor. By the summer of 1941, however, Hodgson's old affliction—arthritis—returned to haunt him. He was transferred to Fitzsimons General Hospital in Aurora, Colorado, for treatment, and he remained there for several months. Orders were cut to retire him for physical disability effective February 28, 1942.

While Hodgson was in the gloaming between active duty and retirement, he relocated to San Antonio, Texas. Following the attack on Pearl Harbor, his lifelong friend Dwight Eisenhower stepped in and helped to facilitate a change of his retirement to December 31, 1941, with reactivation on January 1, 1942. Hodgson served as executive officer of Fort Sam Houston, Texas, until August 1945, and he received a promotion to colonel and the Legion of Merit. While he continued to serve, his health further deserted him, and P. A. was visibly in decline.

A second retirement followed, this time to the Bay Area of California. In Hodgson's later years, the arthritis crippled him to such an extent that he was stooped and able to see only a few feet ahead as he tried to walk while in great pain, from which he was never entirely free. When Hodgson succumbed on October 7, 1955, to complications from his lifelong illness, Eisenhower wrote, "In P.A.'s passing I have lost one of my oldest and best friends; one who always had my admiration, respect, and deep affection. I shall miss him more than I can say."

Hodgson's story is a poignant example of unrealized potential among those of the West Point class of 1915. There was life and death, and somewhere in between lay the threshold of momentous human events. To some, fate deals the cruelest of blows.

During the war years and beyond, Hodgson maintained contact with Eisenhower through written correspondence. The two confided in one another.

Just days after the Operation Torch landings, Eisenhower keenly felt the weight of his first major operational command. He wrote to Hodgson:

> I can say . . . that high command, particularly Allied Command, in war carries with it a lot of things that were never included in our text books, in the Leavenworth course, or even in the War College investigations. I think sometimes that I am a cross between a one-time soldier, a pseudo-statesman, a jacklegged politician and a crooked diplomat. I walk a soapy tightrope in a rain storm with a blazing furnace on one side and a pack of ravenous tigers on the other. If I get across, my greatest possible reward would be a quiet little cottage on the side of a slow-moving stream where I can sit and fish for catfish with a bobber. In spite of all this, I must admit that the whole thing is intriguing and interesting and is forever presenting new challenges that still have the power to make me come up charging.[131]

In the depths of uncertainty, Eisenhower was resilient. He had to be. The road ahead appeared interminably long. No doubt, writing to his friend of many years provided emotional relief from time to time. Fifteen years after P. A. Hodgson's death, his brother and sister donated two hundred pages of correspondence between the two men to the Dwight D. Eisenhower Presidential Library in Abilene.

CHAPTER EIGHT

Brave Men and Black Sheep

By the time the landing craft ramps had slammed down on the beaches of North Africa and American troops were engaged with the Axis in the European Theater, their British allies had been fighting the Italians and the Germans on the continent for five years. General Erwin Rommel, the commander of the vaunted *Panzerarmee Afrika*, had already earned the reputation of a military genius and the nickname "Desert Fox."

When Dwight Eisenhower arrived in London and established his headquarters at Grosvenor Square in the summer of 1942, he set about dispelling an air of defeatism that pervaded the Allied command structure in London. The fortress city of Tobruk and its thirty thousand Commonwealth defenders surrendered to Rommel on June 21, but just four days later Eisenhower told his subordinates that pessimism would not be tolerated and those who persisted in their negative point of view would be relieved.

At the same time, the new commander of the European Theater of Operations began to forge cooperation among the American and British officers under his charge. He worked to gain the trust of the British and cultivated a lasting friendship with Prime Minister Winston Churchill. He regularly visited the troops in their camps scattered across southern England to let them know his care and concern firsthand. He worked with the media, assuring reporters early on that he would keep them informed to the best of his ability without compromising the need for secrecy.

"We're here to fight! Not to be wined and dined," Eisenhower, who was promoted to lieutenant general in July, told his staff. He chose Brig. Gen. Walter Bedell Smith as his no-nonsense chief of staff, requested Lt. Cmdr. Harry C. Butcher as his naval aide, and further surrounded himself with officers whom he knew and believed he could count on. Although he was reluctant to abandon the Roundup or Sledgehammer options for an invasion of Western Europe in 1943, Eisenhower committed to Operation Torch.

The North African campaign that followed provided a primer for Eisenhower. He learned quickly. The challenges of logistics and supply were daunting, as nearly 120,000 troops, the bulk of them American, were marshaled for amphibious assaults along more than 1,200 miles of French North African coastline. The three-pronged landing included the Western Task Force under Eisenhower's old friend George Patton at Casablanca, elements of the British 78th and the US 34th Infantry Divisions commanded by his West Point classmate Maj. Gen. Charles "Doc" Ryder at Algiers, and the US 1st Infantry and 1st Armored Divisions and 509th Parachute Infantry Regiment under Maj. Gen. Lloyd Fredendall at Oran. To complicate matters, the armed forces of the Vichy government might surrender quickly and welcome the Allies, or they might stand and fight. No one really knew what to expect.

Within five days of the landings, Eisenhower struck a deal with Adm. Francois Darlan for Vichy forces to lay down their arms. Amid political wrangling among the Free French under Gen. Charles de Gaulle, Gen. Henri Giraud (whom the Roosevelt administration favored), and Darlan's Vichy government, Eisenhower's compromise drew strong criticism, although it was the most pragmatic solution at the time. In far-off Washington, Marshall supported Eisenhower, and his decision was at least somewhat vindicated by the low casualty figures experienced during the landings.

During their January 1943 conference at Casablanca, Roosevelt and Churchill conferred with Eisenhower, who explained his willingness to accept responsibility for the Darlan deal. The commander's stock soared. Within days, it was decided that with the successful conclusion of the North African campaign, the Allies would then invade Sicily, and Eisenhower was named to lead Operation Husky, scheduled for midsummer.

The inexperienced American soldiers in North Africa performed poorly in their early combat encounters with the enemy. In mid-February, the Germans hit American positions hard at Sidi Bouzid in Tunisia. Within a week, Rommel again turned on the Americans, this time at Kasserine Pass. The results were disastrous. Fredendall had failed to order his II Corps command to prepare defensive positions and detached himself from the front, locating his headquarters a hundred miles from the lines.

The defeats at Sidi Bouzid and Kasserine Pass cost the Americans several thousand killed, wounded, and captured and resulted in the loss of nearly two hundred tanks. Despite his previous assertions that ineffective and derelict officers would be ruthlessly removed from command, Eisenhower failed to follow his own instructions. Prior to the defeat at Sidi Bouzid, he had inspected Fredendall's forward positions. When he returned to II Corps headquarters, he was incensed but stopped short of issuing direct orders to Fredendall to shore up his defenses.

"I immediately sent for the corps commander and in plain language told him of my dissatisfaction with his defensive arrangements," Eisenhower wrote. "I was in the midst of an urgent directive about the organization of our position when he told me that the Germans had already attacked through Faid Pass; in fact they had captured the entire garrison only two hours after I left it. The events above initiated a battle that became known later as Kasserine Pass. We suffered a driving penetration into our thin line in the south and it was ten days before we finally regrouped and drove the Nazis back to where they had started. This was a painful lesson for green commanders and green troops."[132]

On the eve of the disasters at Sidi Bouzid and Kasserine, Eisenhower was elevated to the rank of full general; however, as he reflected on events he found little to cheer him. Moved to action, he sacked Fredendall and brought Patton in to command II Corps. It was his old tanker friend who revived discipline and morale among the American troops and brought their first significant victory against the Germans at El Guettar at the end of March.

One bright spot in the midst of the Kasserine catastrophe was the performance of the 9th Infantry Division's artillery, led by Eisenhower's classmate Brig. Gen. Stafford Leroy "Red" Irwin. When called to action on February 17, 1943, Irwin led his command on a 777-mile march toward the oncoming Germans, exploiting their Kasserine breakthrough. Ordered to hold an area called the Thala defile, Irwin made contact on the 21st with a small British force consisting of three platoons of the 26th Rifle Brigade, twenty-four light tanks, and a few artillery pieces.

The following morning, the Germans attacked the Thala defile with tanks and infantry supported by Stuka dive bombers. Red Irwin's guns slugged it out with the enemy, depressing their muzzles low to fire point-blank as the German tanks approached their positions. They repulsed the enemy attack. The 9th Division Artillery was awarded the Distinguished Unit Citation, and Irwin received the Silver Star.

Irwin, who had graduated fortieth in the class of 1915 and became well known as a cartoonist because of the illustrations he published in several issues of the *Howitzer*, was a veteran of the Punitive Expedition and highly experienced as an officer and instructor in Field Artillery prior to World War II. Irwin commanded the 5th Infantry Division when it arrived at Utah Beach on July 9, 1944, and in combat at Metz. During the Battle of the Bulge, the division moved sixty-nine miles to the north and attacked the Germans on the southern shoulder of the penetration. In April 1945, Irwin took command of the XII Corps, and by V-J Day his troops had made contact with the Soviets in Czechoslovakia.

After the war, Irwin served as commander of the V Corps and of Fort Bragg. In 1948, he was appointed director of the Intelligence Division of the General Staff. Two years later, he was promoted to lieutenant general. Following a serious heart attack, he retired in 1952. He died in his sleep three years later; Maj. Gen. John B. Wogan, Irwin's classmate, wrote a moving memorial:

> After his retirement Red, with his wife Clare and their two children, lived quietly in their lovely home on Kimberly Avenue, Asheville, North Carolina, where they were gracious and generous hosts to their many friends. In spite of his high honors and great accomplishments Red remained the same modest gentleman and warm friend I had known throughout our service. Master of his own time now he set up a studio in his home and indulged in his life long ambition—water color.

Wogan also reflected on a day long past on a desert battlefield and noted with a measure of pride, "The German attack was stopped and Rommel's drive through Kasserine was halted. It was halted by Red Irwin's 9th Division Artillery. . . ."[133]

As the fighting in North Africa wore on, the stress of a volatile political situation and inexperience in field command took their toll on Eisenhower. Marshall made a trip to Casablanca and proposed that Eisenhower utilize trusted officers to report on conditions and progress in the theater. At the top of Eisenhower's list of thirteen such officers was Maj. Gen. Omar Bradley.

Patton's elevation had occurred after Clark refused to take command of II Corps, telling Eisenhower that he considered it a demotion from his post as deputy commander in the Mediterranean. Eisenhower never forgot the apparently self-serving decision that Clark made in North Africa. When Patton initially arrived at II Corps headquarters, he found Bradley there and asserted that he refused to have one of Eisenhower's "spies" in his midst. When Patton requested Bradley as deputy commander of II Corps, the change was made.

Allied warships, submarines, and aircraft assailed Rommel's supply lines, and the combat efficiency of German and Italian forces in North Africa steadily eroded. Rommel found himself squeezed in the vise of Anglo-American spearheads advancing from the west and the thrust of Montgomery's British Eighth Army in the east, which had begun with Montgomery's great victory at El Alamein on the Egyptian frontier in October 1942.

By the spring of 1943, the Eighth Army had pursued the retreating enemy across a thousand miles of North African desert into Tunisia, and Rommel had been recalled to Berlin and subsequently appointed to command the German defenses along the coast of Western Europe. In May, the remaining Axis forces in North Africa, under Gen. Jürgen von Arnim, surrendered. The Allies captured 275,000 enemy troops. Eisenhower remembered:

> When Von Arnim was brought through Algiers on his way to captivity, some members of my staff felt that I should observe the custom of bygone days and allow him to call on me. The custom had its origin in the fact that mercenary soldiers of old had no real enmity toward their opponents. . . . A captured commander of the eighteenth century was likely to be, for weeks or months, the honored

guest of his captor. . . . For me World War II was far too personal a thing to entertain such feelings. Daily as it progressed there grew within me the conviction that as never before in a war between many nations the forces that stood for human good and men's rights were this time confronted by a completely evil conspiracy with which no compromise could be tolerated.[134]

Eisenhower's attention was already turned to the coming invasion of Sicily, set for July 9, 1943, less than two months away.

One of the American divisions that had been roughed up during the affair at Kasserine was Ryder's 34th, a National Guard division that had been organized primarily with troops from the Plains states and the northern Midwest. In the early phase of Operation Torch, Ryder had commanded a combined force of British and American troops. In a pre-planned arrangement, the higher position was later turned over to a British officer, and Ryder reverted to full-time command of the 34th.

After Kasserine, a further stain on the unit's reputation occurred in early April while the 34th was temporarily under British command and failed to capture an objective. Neither Patton nor Bradley endorsed the British plan involving the 34th Division, and when it failed they came to Ryder's defense.

Bradley was forthright in his criticism of Ryder but knew his strengths as well. "Ryder, an expert tactician, had his faults. In trying too hard to be a nice guy, he was too easy on his subordinates, some of whom were incompetent. As a result, the division suffered. He blamed the poor showing of the division [at Kasserine] on Fredendall, who, Ryder claimed, had ordered him to take the wrong positions—low ground rather than high. In this case, I had to side with Ryder."[135]

The fiasco while under British command occurred during an ill-conceived strike at the German right flank. The 34th Division was unsupported on its own flanks and raked by German artillery, forcing a retirement. British General John T. Crocker blamed Ryder for the failure and sharply criticized the 34th Division in the press. Patton was furious.

Bradley recalled that Patton wrote in his diary of Ryder's "impossible mission," adding: "Ike is more British than the British and putty in their hands. . . ."

When the British went so far as to assert that the 34th Division should be removed from the field and sent to a rear area for training with British officers in command, Patton and Bradley joined forces. "There was little indication that Ike cared," Bradley wrote later, "so Patton and I undertook to avert what would surely have been the destruction of the division and the professional ruin of Doc Ryder, a valuable tactician."

Patton penned a strong letter in support of Ryder, and Bradley flew to the headquarters of Field Marshal Sir Harold Alexander, Allied commander in the Middle East, to plead their case. "I gave Ryder high marks and faulted Crocker's battle plan," remembered Bradley. "What the 34th needed most, I stressed, was a victory to restore its self-confidence. 'Give me the division,' I pleaded, 'and I promise you they will take and hold their very first objective.'"[136]

As the fighting progressed, Patton was ordered to commit his energy to the preparations for the Sicily invasion, and Bradley was elevated to command of II Corps. The opportunity for the 34th Division to reclaim its honor came on April 26, the third day of a renewed offensive. The Germans were well entrenched atop Hill 609, named as such due to its height in meters, and blocked the advance of the main II Corps thrust.

"Get me that hill," Bradley bluntly told Ryder, whose personal courage he had never doubted. Three times, the American infantry assaulted the high ground, only to be repulsed. Finally, on April 30, Ryder's men, supported by artillery and seventeen tanks, claimed the summit of Hill 609. For more than a day, they held it against German counterattacks.

Bradley beamed. "I was immensely pleased with this victory at Hill 609. I was pleased, too, for Doc Ryder's 34th Division. As I had expected, the victory restored self-confidence to the division, and no one ever again would question its courage. In fact, it went on to become one of the finest infantry outfits of World War II."[137]

Ryder led the 34th Division during Operation Avalanche, the invasion of the Italian mainland at Salerno in September 1943, and through heavy fighting during the arduous campaign that followed. The 34th Division spent more than six hundred days on the frontlines in Italy and participated in the battles around Cassino and Anzio.

In September 1944, Ryder was promoted to command of the IX Corps in preparation for the anticipated invasion of Japan. With the end of the war, the Corps performed occupation duty on the northern island of Hokkaido. Ryder briefly commanded the Eighth Army in Japan and returned to the United States in 1948. Two years later, he retired from the army and settled in Massachusetts. He died of a heart attack on August 17, 1960. His wife, Ida, remained in close contact with the class of 1915 for many years.

Donald Angus Davison was another member of the class of 1915 who provided exceptional service in North Africa. Davison graduated nineteenth and entered the Corps of Engineers. He was appointed chief aviation engineer in the theater and located suitable sites for airfields and other installations. He later was posted as air engineer at Army Air Forces Headquarters, but he died suddenly in Bangalore, India, on May 6, 1944.

With the campaign in North Africa behind him, Eisenhower had survived his sternest command test to date. While some observers, including Marshall, criticized him for displaying caution rather than audacity, he maintained the delicate balance between overcommitting his forces, particularly the inexperienced American troops, and rushing into an impetuous offensive thrust that might prove disastrous. At the same time, he managed to hold a coalition fraught with backbiting, finger pointing, and massive egos together. His effort to avoid showing favoritism to his fellow American commanders has sometimes been judged as working in the converse, favoring the British at the expense of his own countrymen.

Although there was little enthusiasm for Operation Husky among the top American commanders and even less for the subsequent invasion of the Italian mainland that Churchill continually advocated, the campaign in North Africa had demonstrated that the American troops were not yet ready for a cross-Channel invasion in 1943. In addition, there were shortages of landing craft, equipment, and supplies.

The buildup continued in Britain. In March 1943, British Lt. Gen. Frederick Morgan was named chief of staff, supreme Allied commander (COSSAC) and became the principal planner of Operation Overlord, the invasion of Normandy, which did incorporate some elements of its predecessor, Operation Roundup. During the Washington Conference in May, the invasion was tentatively scheduled for the spring of 1944.

Patton and Montgomery submitted rival plans for the invasion of Sicily, and over Patton's pointed objections Eisenhower chose the British plan. Montgomery was to land British troops of the Eighth Army at Syracuse on the southeastern corner of the island, while Patton landed at Gela with

US Seventh Army forces positioned to protect Montgomery's flank in a drive directly to Messina in the northeast. The hope was that the 380,000 Axis troops in Sicily might be cut off and forced to surrender. Already distrustful of the British and determined to gain his share of glory, Patton charged that Eisenhower had ceased being an American and become an "Ally."

Operation Husky began on July 10, 1943, and lasted for five tough weeks. Eisenhower again relied on his subordinate commanders to exercise tactical control of the battle and manage its pace. Montgomery was characteristically slow, while Patton developed his supporting role into an offensive of his own, racing northwest to capture the city of Palermo and then turning east and reaching Messina on August 17. Granted, Montgomery had faced stiff German opposition along the direct coastal route to Messina, but in the interest of preserving the tenuous alliance Eisenhower chose to refrain from demanding quicker action from the Eighth Army commander.

Already sown in North Africa, the seeds of discord between Patton and Montgomery blossomed to full flower in Sicily as each tried to upstage the other. By the time Patton reached Messina, the bulk of the German and Italian forces in Sicily had already evacuated to Italy across the narrow strait that separated the two landmasses.

Meanwhile, Eisenhower's mercurial old friend had placed his career in jeopardy with the now famous incidents in which he slapped soldiers suffering from combat fatigue while visiting field hospitals in Sicily. Eisenhower reprimanded Patton but defended the retention of the old-horse cavalryman in command. He sent Patton a strong letter that read in part, "I clearly understand that firm and drastic measures were at times necessary in order to secure the desired objectives. But this does not excuse brutality, abuse of the sick, nor exhibition of uncontrollable temper in front of subordinates. I must so seriously question your good judgment and your self-discipline as to raise serious doubt in my mind as to your future usefulness."[138]

Eisenhower knew that Patton's command presence was essential to the war effort and had no intention of relieving him. In his effort to retain such a fighting general, he sought and received the tacit support of both Marshall and Secretary of War Stimson. Again, however, Eisenhower had failed to fully exercise command and control. Despite its limited success, the Sicily operation had been poorly planned and poorly executed.

Looking at his own performance in Sicily, Eisenhower recognized that he had overestimated the enemy's strength and therefore proceeded too cautiously. He also noted that landing too far from Messina had given the enemy time to escape. These were hard but useful lessons for the days to come.

While planning for the invasion of Normandy continued, the Allied leaders decided at the Quebec Conference in August 1943 to press forward with landings on the Italian mainland. As Allied troops conquered Sicily, Benito Mussolini, the fascist dictator of Italy, was deposed. He was replaced by Gen. Pietro Badoglio, who proposed that his country would surrender to the Allies in exchange for a guarantee that Allied troops would occupy Rome before German soldiers could take control of the city or destroy it.

Eisenhower favored a deal with the Italians, even as Hitler sent more German troops into the country. Eisenhower knew that he could not guarantee the capture of Rome on Badoglio's timetable. While Allied soldiers were en route to their landing point near Salerno, Badoglio began to waffle on his commitment to surrender. This time, Eisenhower rose to the challenge and acted decisively. Preemptively, he announced that the Italian government had surrendered. Badoglio was left with no choice but to acquiesce.

The invasion of Italy began in early September with Montgomery's Eighth Army landings at Reggio di Calabria and Taranto, followed by Mark Clark's Fifth Army landings at Salerno less than a week later. The Salerno landings faced strong opposition, and German counterattacks came close to driving Clark into the sea. Timely naval gunfire from the supporting fleet helped save the day, while rear-echelon soldiers—clerks, bandsmen, and cooks—had to take up rifles and defend some positions.

The situation at Salerno did stabilize, but the fight was a precursor to the arduous, bloody campaign that ensued. The mountainous terrain and swift rivers of Italy presented natural obstacles, while the weather was often inhospitable. At war's end, some fighting was still going on in the north. Clark remained in the Mediterranean, commanding the Fifth Army and then the 15th Army Group. It was apparent, however, that the Italian campaign would soon become a sideshow. It was a matter of time before the invasion of Western Europe became the focus of the Allied war effort.

In early September, Eisenhower called Bradley to a meeting at Alexander's command post, a group of tents in an olive grove at Cassibile, near Syracuse. Bradley was mystified as to why he had been summoned.

Bradley later wrote:

> Ike emerged from his tent, apologized for keeping me waiting and
> invited me inside for a private conference. I still had not the slightest
> inkling of what he had to tell me, although I was beginning to gain
> the impression that it must be something big and urgent. He came
> right to the point: "I've got good news for you, Brad. You've got a
> fancy new job." As I sat in silence he told me what it was. I could not
> have been more stunned or elated. It was going to grow into the most
> important combat job in the US Army in World War II. No soldier
> could have wished for more. I was to leave as soon as possible, first to
> London, then to the States to recruit a full army staff.[139]

Bradley eventually took command of the First Army and then the 12th
Army Group during operations in France.

At the time, Eisenhower may well have been unsure of his own future.
Virtually everyone expected Marshall to be named commander for the
cross-Channel invasion. With Bradley leading the First Army, Eisenhower
might be sent to Washington as chief of staff of the army, a disappointment in light of the events that were rapidly shaping the course of the war
in Europe.

For Patton, his career still reeling, Bradley's new assignment and the
notification that Seventh Army was to be disbanded [which did not occur]
meant that he had been passed over for higher command and was benched,
at least temporarily. Montgomery was named commander of Allied ground
forces for Operation Overlord and arrived in London in January 1944.

At the end of November, President Roosevelt traveled to Teheran, the
capital city of Iran, for the first conference of the Big Three, which included
the president, Prime Minister Churchill, and Soviet Premier Josef Stalin.
Roosevelt and Churchill confirmed their resolve to open a second front in
Europe. The time had come to name a commander for the largest seaborne
operation of its kind in history. Early discussions had centered on a British
commander since the invasion would be launched from southern England
and the British were more experienced, having been at war since 1939.

Slowly but surely, the perspective changed as Roosevelt raised the point
that American public opinion would demand an American commander,
particularly since the United States would supply the lion's share of the men

and materiel for the invasion. Grudgingly, Churchill accepted the inevitable, and Marshall became the frontrunner. There was no doubt that the chief of staff wanted to lead the invasion, and Roosevelt wanted to reward Marshall for his years of loyal and essential service. As late as November, he had said the same to Eisenhower.

At Teheran, Stalin pressed the British and American leaders for a firm commitment to Operation Overlord, part of which would include the naming of the supreme commander for the invasion. When Stalin asked Roosevelt point-blank, "Who will command Overlord?" Roosevelt responded that a decision had not been made and turned to Adm. William Leahy, his personal chief of staff, whispering, "That old Bolshevik is trying to force me to give him the name of our supreme commander. I just can't tell him because I haven't made up my mind."[140]

True to form, Marshall never actively sought the invasion command, never asked for it, and on more than one occasion assured Roosevelt that he would support the president's decision whatever it was. On Sunday, December 5, Marshall visited Roosevelt in Cairo. He later said that he told Roosevelt that the issue "was too great for any personal feeling to be considered. I did not discuss the pros and cons of the matter. If I recall, the president stated in completing our conversation, 'I feel I could not sleep at night with you out of the country.'"[141]

On the morning of December 7, 1943, two years to the day after the Japanese had plunged the United States into war at Pearl Harbor, Roosevelt had come to his decision. Eisenhower wrote years later, "In early December, I had received word the president would return to the United States through our area. I went to Tunis to meet him. The President arrived at midafternoon and was scarcely seated in the automobile when . . . he said, 'Well, Ike, you are going to command Overlord.'"[142]

Sometime later, it was reported that Roosevelt chose Eisenhower because he was the best "politician" among the leading candidates, and even though there had been moments of discord, inter-service rivalry, and squabbling among British and American commanders, the Allied team was winning with Eisenhower at its head. Since the beginning of the war, Eisenhower had honed his administrative and organizational skills and utilized his charming personality to keep the fragile coalition together. Despite setbacks and shortcomings, his generals had advanced from victory to victory on the battlefield.

One towering strength that Eisenhower possessed was absolute self-lessness, a refusal to advance his own career at the expense of the greater good. He had seen this admirable trait in Marshall and emulated it. For Eisenhower, the mission was always the priority, overriding everything else. Those who sought personal glory or to advance their own careers first harbored a character flaw that was impossible to overlook. He despised it in Patton and Clark but recognized their contributions to the war effort. He abhorred it in MacArthur. An unwavering commitment to the ultimate victory, forsaking personal advancement and accolades, was necessary in a supreme commander. In combination with his likability and organizational acumen, it is reasonable to conclude that Eisenhower had no peer.

After a brief, two-week trip to Washington, a family reunion in Kansas, and a short visit with Mamie to see their son John, now a cadet at West Point, Eisenhower arrived in London in January 1944 to establish Supreme Headquarters Allied Expeditionary Force (SHAEF). With the experience of North Africa, Sicily, and Italy, there was working knowledge of the supply, movement, and deployment of great armies. American and British officers worked together in greater harmony and cooperation than in the past. However, there remained a mountain of planning to complete.

Eisenhower's top land, sea, and air commanders for Overlord were all British—Air Chief Marshal Sir Arthur Tedder was deputy supreme commander, Montgomery would command the ground forces, Adm. Bertram Ramsay commanded the naval forces, and Air Marshal Trafford Leigh-Mallory commanded the air forces. Still, more than 1.5 million Americans had come to Britain since early 1943, and Eisenhower had learned to assert his own command presence.

During a fight over ultimate control of the air forces, Eisenhower stepped into the controversy and declared that he alone would have the final say in how they were used—that neither Leigh-Mallory nor American Gen. Carl Spaatz would be the final authority. He refused to back down and threatened to resign. He had Marshall's support throughout the ordeal and won the day. Concerns over the availability of landing craft needed and discussions as to the size of the invasion front in Normandy resulted in the postponement of D-Day from early May to June 5, 1944.

Operation Overlord was warfare on a massive scale. Nearly 160,000 American, British, and Canadian troops would assault Hitler's Atlantic

Wall defenses, five divisions across five Norman beaches code-named, west to east, Sword, Juno, Gold, Omaha, and Utah. Two American airborne divisions, the 101st and Bradley's old 82nd, along with the British 6th Airborne, would go in first to secure vital exits and neutralize German strongpoints behind the beaches. More than five thousand warships, transports, and supply ships would be involved, while the skies would be filled with Allied bombers and fighters, hitting German fortifications and troop concentrations and providing cover against any German aircraft that might venture aloft.

Secrecy was of the utmost importance. A breach of security might compromise all of Overlord and result in the deaths of thousands of men. A naval officer attending a cocktail party began talking too much. When the indiscretion was discovered, the offender was reduced in rank and sent home. Eisenhower wrote to Marshall, "I could cheerfully shoot the offender myself."[143]

Major General Henry J. F. Miller, the head of the 9th Air Force Service Command, attended a dinner party at London's Claridge Hotel in mid-April. According to an article that appeared in *Time* magazine on June 19, 1944, two weeks after the invasion, "Cocktails were sipped; all those present, including three or four women, were in uniform. . . ." Miller then began "telling someone about the tough time he was having to get certain crucial supplies. The date promised, he said, was too late. Henry Miller was quoted as saying: 'On my honor the invasion will come before June 15.'"[144]

When word of the breach reached Eisenhower, the supreme commander was livid. It did not matter that Miller was a member of the class of 1915 and had been a teammate of Omar Bradley on the West Point baseball team. Miller was demoted to his permanent rank of lieutenant colonel and sent home immediately. As Miller departed, Eisenhower wrote to him, "I know of nothing that causes me more real distress than to be faced with the necessity of sitting as a judge in cases involving military offenses by officers of character and good record, particularly when they are old and warm friends."[145] *Time* concluded:

> White-haired, personable Henry Miller, one of the Air Force's best maintenance experts, has always been a popular and respected officer. He left a host of stunned friends behind him in London. This babbling episode occurred two months ago, but disclosure of the

case was held up until last week. Then Lieut. Colonel Miller was discovered in an army hospital at Coral Gables, Fla., where he was said to be "suffering from serious physical ailments . . . not connected with his overseas service." Two days later Lieut. Colonel Miller left the hospital on 30 days' leave, destination unannounced.[146]

A native of New Jersey, Henry J. F. Miller graduated 110th in the class of 1915. He was well known in the army as an aircraft maintenance engineer. Prior to going overseas, he developed and led the Army Air Forces' procurement program at Wright Field in Dayton, Ohio. A year before the incident in London, his wife of twenty-one years, Helen, had died. On November 30, 1944, he was retired from the army due to physical disability. In December 1948, he was promoted to brigadier general on the retired list, and he died on January 7, 1949, at the age of fifty-eight.

Miller never recovered from his indiscretion on the eve of Operation Overlord. His memorial in *Assembly* reads:

> Henry was a completely honest soul—probably too honest for this troubled world of corruption and double-dealing. This same honesty of purpose and speech which had characterized him all through his service led him into difficulties during the latter part of his Army career—difficulties and heartbreaking disappointments, from which he emerged saddened and disillusioned perhaps but with his high ideals of conduct still intact and courage undaunted.[147]

One of the most difficult command decisions Bradley made prior to D-Day involved classmate Maj. Gen. Roscoe Woodruff, commander of the VII Corps, one of three American Army Corps slated for the Normandy campaign. Woodruff was cadet first captain and graduated fifty-sixth in the class of 1915. Bradley referred to Woodruff as a "fraternity brother," but he worried that he had no experience in amphibious landings or in commanding large formations of troops in combat—an interesting observation since Bradley's own experience was still somewhat limited in 1944.

In consultation with Eisenhower, Bradley gave VII Corps to Maj. Gen. J. Lawton "Lightning Joe" Collins (West Point 1917), who had come to the European Theater after leading the 25th "Tropic Lightning" Division on Guadalcanal. Major General Charles Corlett (West Point 1913) also relocated from the Pacific, where he had led the 7th Infantry Division in the capture of Kwajalein in the Marshall Islands. After Woodruff was given temporary command of the XIX Corps, that post was handed to Corlett.

"We made the decision to give him [Corlett] the XIX Corps and send Woodruff home," recalled Bradley. "Woodruff was naturally bitter, but he went on to achieve a distinguished record as a division commander in the Philippines. . . ."[148]

Woodruff did succeed as a combat commander, leading the 24th Infantry Division with distinction during the fighting on the islands of Leyte, Luzon, and Mindanao in the Philippines. After the war, he commanded I Corps in occupied Japan and XV Corps at Fort Polk, Louisiana. His forty-two-year career ended with retirement in 1953, and he died in 1975 at the age of eighty-four.

With D-Day set for June 5, 1944, the combined British and American senior military commanders had done virtually everything in their power to assure the success of the D-Day invasion. One thing they could not control, though, was the weather. Eisenhower remembered that as D-Day approached, the atmosphere around his headquarters was as gloomy as the forecast. Eisenhower wrote:

> When the commanders assembled on the morning of June 4 the reports we received were discouraging. Low clouds, high winds, and formidable wave action were predicted to make landing a most hazardous affair. The meteorologists said that air support would be impossible, naval gunfire would be inefficient, and even the handling of small boats would be rendered difficult. Admiral Ramsay thought that the mechanics of landing could be handled, but agreed with the estimate of the difficulty in adjusting gunfire. His position was mainly neutral. General Montgomery, properly concerned with the great disadvantages of delay, believed that we should go. Tedder disagreed.[149]

This was no time for a decision by committee. Eisenhower could listen to the opinions of others, but he could not defer to them on this, the greatest of questions. He ordered a twenty-four-hour postponement. Throughout the day and night, high winds and rain buffeted southern England and the waters of the English Channel.

In the early darkness of June 5, the commanders ventured to another conference at Southwick House near Portsmouth. There, Eisenhower remembered an "astonishing" weather report. A brief period of calmer weather presented a window of opportunity to launch Overlord on June 6. The supreme commander shouldered the weight of a decision that was his alone, unleashing Allied military might against the coastline of Normandy.

"No one present disagreed, and there was a definite brightening of faces," Eisenhower recalled, "as without further word, each went off to his respective post of duty to flash out to his command the messages that would set the whole host in motion."[150]

On the evening of June 5, Eisenhower visited troops of the 101st Airborne Division, talking with them and reassuring them with his characteristic grin. He stayed with them until around midnight, when the last of them had boarded their transport planes and lifted into the night sky. The weight of command had left him exhausted on the eve of the great test. He smoked constantly, up to four packs of cigarettes a day, and was plagued by throat infections and recurring digestive trouble. Outwardly, however, he was charismatic and optimistic.

Several weeks earlier, members of the supreme commander's staff had written an order of the day to be printed so that each soldier would have a copy to carry with him. Eisenhower made a number of changes to the original text and condensed it to a brief commentary that resonated in its simplicity. He also recorded the message, one minute and thirty-eight seconds long, for broadcast on the day of the invasion. It read:

Soldiers, Sailors and Airmen of the Allied Expeditionary Forces!

You are about to embark on the great crusade, toward which we have striven these many months. The eyes of the world are upon you. The hopes and prayers of liberty-loving people everywhere march with you. In company with our brave Allies and brothers-in-arms on other Fronts you will bring about the destruction of the German war machine, the elimination of Nazi tyranny over oppressed peoples of Europe, and security for ourselves in a free world.

Your task will not be an easy one. Your enemy is well trained, well equipped and battle-hardened. He will fight savagely. . . . The tide has turned! The free men of the world are marching together to victory!

I have full confidence in your courage, devotion to duty and skill in battle. We will accept nothing less than full victory!

Good luck! And let us all beseech the blessing of Almighty God upon this great and noble undertaking.[151]

Reports slowly trickled into Southwick House. The airborne operations had gone well despite the troops being widely scattered and descending into Normandy far from their drop zones. Generally, good progress was made on the invasion beaches, although Montgomery's major D-Day objective, the city of Caen, would not fall for another month. Of the greatest immediate concern was the hotly contested landing at Omaha Beach, where elements of the US 1st and 29th Infantry Divisions suffered heavy casualties.

Bradley waited anxiously aboard his command ship, USS *Augusta*, as the drama at Omaha unfolded. He was aware that the landings of the 4th Infantry Division at Utah Beach had encountered light opposition, even though the actual landings were in the wrong location. He wrote years later:

Omaha Beach, however, was a nightmare. Even now it brings pain to recall what happened there on June 6, 1944. . . . Omaha Beach remained a bloodbath for too long. Six hours after the landings we held only ten yards of beach.

The whole of D-Day was for me a time of grave personal anxiety and frustration. . . . I gained the impression that our forces had suffered an irreversible catastrophe, that there was little hope we could force the beach. Privately, I considered evacuating the beachhead and directing the follow-up troops to Utah Beach or the British beaches. . . . I agonized over the withdrawal decision, praying that our men could hang on.[152]

As the terrible morning wore on at Omaha, small groups of American soldiers, often commanded by sergeants or corporals since their officers were dead or wounded, began to move forward. As at Salerno, naval gunfire provided critical support. Only at midafternoon was Bradley reasonably assured that some progress was being made at Omaha and finally able to dispense with the thought of evacuation.

On June 8, Bradley waded ashore on Omaha Beach, inspecting the scene of the savage fighting that had occurred there just hours earlier. That day, his daughter Lee married Lt. Hal Beukema, the son of Bradley's Academy classmate Herman Beukema, in the West Point Chapel.

The fortunes of war smiled on the Americans at Utah Beach. Enemy fire was relatively light and inaccurate. The well-trained 8th Regiment was the first to hit the beach at Utah, and its commander, fifty-two-year-old Col. James Van Fleet, was at the head of his troops. Brigadier General Theodore Roosevelt, Jr., the son of the twenty-sixth president of the United States and assistant commander of the 4th Division, was also present. As the two officers met one another on the beach, Roosevelt pointed out that a single building that had been designated as a reference for the left of the landing area was actually on the right. The 8th Regiment was coming ashore south of its intended location.

A quick conference followed to determine the proper course of action, either to continue landing on this relatively calm stretch of beach or divert the following assault waves to the originally designated beach. Ironically, the current location was one that Van Fleet had originally preferred, but he had been overruled by the navy due to the perceived shallowness of the water. Some controversy persists as to who actually made the decision.

Roosevelt has been credited historically as saying, "We'll start the war from right here." Van Fleet's account differs. He wrote in an unpublished memoir, "We faced an immediate and important decision. Should we try to shift our entire landing force more than a mile down the beach, and follow our original plan? Or should we proceed across the causeways immediately opposite where we had landed? I made the decision. 'Go straight inland,' I ordered. 'We've caught the enemy at a weak point, so let's take advantage of it.'"[153]

Just after 9:30 a.m., Van Fleet radioed Maj. Gen. Raymond O. "Tubby" Barton, commander of the 4th Division, that his troops were advancing steadily. By nightfall, the 8th Regiment had pushed approximately six miles inland. Near the end of June, Van Fleet was personally observing the progress of his troops. Venturing too close to the frontline, he was grazed across the stomach by a German bullet and evacuated to a field hospital. He stayed only long enough for the wound to be dressed.

Soon afterward, Bradley and Barton visited the 8th Regiment command post. Bradley grinned, "Van, I came here to decorate you, but I ought to court martial you. You are AWOL; you left that hospital without being discharged."

Bradley then presented Van Fleet with the first of three Distinguished Service Crosses he would earn during the coming months. The citation reads in part, ". . . in action against enemy forces from 6 to 8 June 1944 in France, in the initial landing and assault upon the European continent, Colonel Van Fleet quickly organized his troops and pushed them rapidly across the beach in an orderly and determined manner, brushing aside resistance and thereby greatly expediting the early establishment of the Division beachhead."[154]

In August, Van Fleet was promoted at long last to brigadier general. The circumstances surrounding the promotion are intriguing to say the least. Bradley asserted that he had direct involvement in clearing up a longtime misunderstanding:

> Van Fleet was . . . an absolutely superb soldier and leader. . . . I simply could not understand why Marshall and McNair had not given Van Fleet command of a division; I had to assume that he had some very bad mark in his record or had angered them in some way. In not too long, I found out the answer. Marshall, so forgetful about names, had confused Van Fleet with a man who had a remarkably similar name and a problem with the bottle. Marshall apparently passed the mixup on to McNair. When McNair arrived in France for an inspection, he asked me, "Who's been unusually good?"
>
> "Van Fleet has probably been the most outstanding," I replied. "It's too bad that he has a drinking habit isn't it?" McNair said. I exploded in rare profanity. "Jesus Christ! You got the wrong guy. Van Fleet is a teetotaler." "What?" McNair exclaimed disbelieving. "The man you are talking about is—, not Van Fleet, I know him, too." I was soon able to right this egregious injustice. I got Van Fleet promoted and later gave him a division. That set him on his way, ultimately to four-star rank.[155]

Van Fleet biographer Paul Braim asserted a different perspective on the circumstances surrounding the delay in promotion. He wrote, "Van Fleet, on hearing of this story, strongly doubted its veracity, stating that Marshall and he had been together on many social occasions and that Marshall knew very well that [Van] was a teetotaler."

Further, Braim speculates that Marshall may indeed have developed a negative impression of Van Fleet because the latter had requested to return to ROTC duty at the University of Florida in both 1929 and 1940, twice declining to attend the Command and General Staff School at Fort Leavenworth. The two officers had known one another and been neighbors at Fort Benning in earlier years as well; however, Van Fleet had never served in a staff position or with Marshall in Washington.[156]

Regardless, Van Fleet's ascent to the highest levels of field command was rapid. Shortly after his promotion, he was named assistant commander of the 2nd Infantry Division, serving in that capacity through the breakout at St. Lo and the capture of the French port city of Brest. He took command of the 90th Infantry Division in October 1944, was promoted to major general the following month, and led the unit of Patton's Third Army during the bitter fighting at the fortress city of Metz and the Battle of the Bulge. He briefly commanded XXIII Corps in England and then led III Corps during the drive from Remagen, the encirclement and reduction of the Ruhr Pocket, and the Third Army advance into Bavaria and Austria.

A major contributor to the success of Patton's rapid drive across France and its magnificent performance during the Battle of the Bulge was Brig. Gen. John French Conklin, chief engineer of the Third Army. Conklin had graduated thirteenth in the class of 1915 and had served with Patton as chief engineer of I Armored Corps in North Africa. He was promoted to brigadier general in 1945 and later served in Japan. He retired in 1951 and died in 1973.

From Normandy to V-E Day, British and American forces faced eleven months of arduous combat, closing in on the German frontier and then driving into the heart of the Third Reich from the west as Soviet Red Army spearheads advanced relentlessly toward Berlin from the east. Although Eisenhower's subordinate commanders, particularly Patton and Montgomery, were often at odds with one another and he was continually criticized privately for favoring British rather than American interests, he held the Allied command structure together.

Although the opportunity for a greater victory slipped away, the Normandy campaign concluded with the reduction of the Falaise Pocket in the summer of 1944. Allied forces dashed across France, liberating Paris in August. In September, Eisenhower diverted from his broad-front strategy, approving Montgomery's plan for a bold stroke of combined land and airborne troops through Holland and into the Ruhr, the industrial heart of Germany. Operation Market Garden ultimately failed. There was bitter fighting in the Hürtgen Forest, followed by Hitler's desperate gamble in the Ardennes at the end of the year, resulting in the epic Battle of the Bulge. At the height of the Bulge, Eisenhower's promotion to five-star general of the army rank was confirmed.

In the spring of 1945, the Allies crossed the Rhine, and the final push to Berlin was on. At this juncture, Eisenhower was already contemplating the strategic value of racing the Red Army to the German capital. Politicians were shaping the postwar map of Europe. Early in March, he learned that the Red Army was across the Oder River, and in some locations less than thirty miles from Berlin. On March 19, he invited Bradley to accompany him to Cannes, on the French Riviera, for a few days of rest. While there, Eisenhower sought the counsel of his West Point classmate.

Eisenhower asked Bradley what he thought about an all-out push for Berlin. True to form, Bradley replied frankly that the effort would cost one hundred thousand casualties and added perceptively that it was "a pretty stiff price to pay for a prestige objective, especially when we've got to fall back and let the other fellow take over."[157]

In a slight breach of protocol, Eisenhower cabled Soviet Premier Stalin and informed him that the Western Allied armies intended to annihilate the German forces in the Ruhr. The capture of Berlin would be left to the Red Army. Of course, an outcry followed, particularly from Gen. William Simpson, whose Ninth Army had been primed for the drive to Berlin. The wisdom of Eisenhower's decision, however, has stood the test of time. It saved American lives and hastened the final victory.

American troops were to advance no further than the River Elbe, where they met the Red Army at the town of Torgau in Saxony on April 25, 1945. Twelve days later, on May 7, 1945, the German high command surrendered at a schoolhouse in Reims, France. The Soviets were not satisfied with the proceedings and demanded another surrender ceremony in Berlin the following day.

After the signing at Reims, Col. Gen. Alfred Jodl, chief of the operations staff of the German high command, was brought before Eisenhower, whose disdain for the Nazis was boundless. The Allied supreme commander remembered, "I said, 'You will, officially and personally, be held responsible if the terms of this surrender are violated, including its provisions for the

German commanders to appear in Berlin at the moment set by the Russian high command to accomplish the formal surrender to that government. That is all.' He saluted and left."[158]

Several members of the SHAEF staff tried their hand at composing an appropriate message to be sent to the Joint Chiefs of Staff confirming the German surrender. Eisenhower looked them over, discarded them all, and wrote simply, "The mission of this Allied Force was fulfilled at 0241, local time, May 7th, 1945. //signed// Eisenhower."[159]

At any given time, numerous members of the class of 1915 were active in the European Theater of Operations during World War II. Their contributions in combat command, logistics and supply, and administration were instrumental in achieving the final victory.

Major General Leland Stanford Hobbs took command of the 30th Infantry Division in July 1942 and led the unit throughout the war. He had graduated forty-sixth in the class of 1915 and lettered in baseball, basketball, and football in each of his four years at the Academy. A veteran of the Punitive Expedition against Pancho Villa, he took part in a skirmish against the Mexican bandits at Nogales just five months after graduation.

The 30th Division arrived in France on June 11, 1944, less than a week after D-Day. During Operation Cobra, the breakout from the hedgerow country of Normandy, the division suffered heavy losses due to errant bombing by American planes. The friendly fire also took the life of General McNair, the highest-ranking American officer killed in action during World War II.

During the first week of August 1944, the Germans attempted to stem the tide of American arms that flooded the French countryside following the breakout. A strong counterattack pressed the 30th Division in the vicinity of Mortain, and its 2nd Battalion, 120th Regiment was surrounded by the 2nd SS Panzer Division at Hill 314. The 30th Division line held, and the defenders of Hill 314 sustained casualties in excess of 40 percent.

The 30th Division later participated in the Battle of the Bulge and the capture of Aachen, the ancient seat of government of the Holy Roman Empire of Charlemagne. Hobbs later served as commander of the 2nd Armored Division and deputy commander of the Third Army. He commanded IX Corps on occupation duty in Japan from 1949 to 1950, and he returned to the United States as deputy commander of the First Army. He retired in 1953 and pursued a successful second career with Colonial Trust Bank in New York City. He died in 1966.

In September 1944, Maj. Gen. John W. Leonard landed with the 9th Armored Division in France, where he had received the Distinguished Service Cross twenty-six years earlier. During the Battle of the Bulge, the division fought at St. Vith and opened a vital link to the embattled Belgian crossroads town of Bastogne. On March 7, 1945, Leonard led the division to the west bank of the Rhine at Remagen, where troops of the 27th Armored Infantry Battalion found the Ludendorff railroad bridge intact and established the first Allied crossing of the mighty river.

Promoted to lieutenant general, Leonard commanded the 2nd Armored Division, the Armored Center and Armor School at Fort Knox, Kentucky, V Corps, and the XVIII Airborne Corps at Fort Bragg, North Carolina. He served as senior military attaché in London, and he retired in 1952. He died in 1974.

Teammates for a brief period in the backfield of the Army football team, Vernon Prichard and Dwight Eisenhower remained close throughout their lives. Prichard graduated 134th in the class and rode into Mexico with the Punitive Expedition before seeing combat near Verdun and Saint-Mihiel during World War I. Between the wars, he served as a military science professor at Yale University, where he helped coach the football team. With rapid wartime promotion, he received his first star in February 1942. In early September, he gained his second.

On July 17, 1944, Prichard took command of the 1st Armored Division in Italy, where rugged terrain limited the effectiveness of tanks and most of his first winter was spent directing the operations of the division's three armored infantry regiments. In the spring of 1945, the 1st Armored Division spearheaded the offensive that broke through the German lines and opened the gateway to the Po Valley, ideal country for tanks. In less than two days, the division advanced 150 miles. As he rolled along, Prichard received seven minor wounds and earned the Purple Heart. Bullets twice tore through the knit cap he was wearing, and he was finally persuaded to put on a steel helmet.

After the war, Prichard was returned to his permanent rank of colonel for two years. In the spring of 1948, Omar Bradley, now chief of staff of the army, appointed Prichard chief of the army's Public Information Division in Washington, and he regained his brigadier's star. The following March, he was again a major general.

On July 10, 1949, the fifty-seven-year-old Prichard and his wife, Charlotte, joined their friends Colonel and Mrs. Anthony Drexel Biddle and a few other guests for a cruise aboard a small yacht on the Potomac River. Moments after the yacht pulled away from the dock, it was rocked by an explosion. The *Assembly* newsletter account reads, "Colonel Biddle rescued his wife and Charlotte—and the latter's first thought was of her husband. Looking frantically about among the wreckage, she saw him floating nearby and called to Colonel Biddle. The latter plunged in again and swam to the General. He was dead when Biddle reached him."[160]

Although he had seen plenty of action as a young artillery officer during World War I, John Beugnot Wogan, who had graduated seventy-fifth in the class, did not return to France as a fighting man until January 1945, at the head of the 13th Armored Division, which he had activated and trained since July 1942. A colonel when World War II broke out, he was rapidly promoted to major general during progressive assignments with the 1st, 2nd, and 5th Armored Divisions prior to taking the 13th.

During the last month of the war, Wogan drove 13th Armored in an effort to cut off the retreat of German troops in the Ruhr Pocket. On April 14, Wogan was at the head of the 46th Tank Battalion when his vehicle came under fire from a strong German roadblock defending a bridge across the Dhunn River. Wogan, the battalion commander, and a company commander were seriously wounded. While its commanding general recuperated, the 13th Division charged on, reaching the Austrian town of Braunau am Inn, Hitler's birthplace, on May 2, and setting up a command post in the very house where the recently deceased *Führer* was born.

The severity of his wound forced Wogan to retire in 1946, although he remained active in civic affairs in the Asheville, North Carolina, area. He worked for a time as the manager of a nearby veterans hospital. For many years, he served as secretary of the class of 1915, maintaining contact with classmates and their families, gathering news, and submitting regular updates to *Assembly*. He died in 1968.

In October 1942, Wogan's classmate Vernon Evans joined the 13th Armored Division. For the next year, Evans, who had graduated fifty-fifth in the class of 1915, led the division's Combat Command B. From there, he transferred to the China-Burma-India Theater as deputy chief of staff and later chief of staff. After the war, he rose to theater commander. He later became inspector general of European Command and chief of the US Military Mission to Iran. He retired in 1953 with the rank of major general and died in 1987 at the age of ninety-four.

Another member of the Army football team, Thomas Larkin gained the coveted "A" as a varsity player and achieved the rank of cadet captain at West Point before graduating twenty-first in the class of 1915. Larkin chased Pancho Villa in Mexico and received a Silver Star for the high-risk reconnaissance work he had performed during the Second Battle of the Marne in World War I. Between the wars, he traveled to Japan as an assistant military attaché and completed the Army Industrial College, Command and General Staff College, and War College.

When World War II broke out, Larkin requested a transfer from the Panama Canal Zone, where he was supervising a major engineering program, the Third Locks Project. In the spring of 1942, he went to London as Services of Supply chief of staff. He participated in Operation Torch and was named commanding general, Services of Supply, North African Theater in February 1943. Two months later, he was promoted to major general.

Larkin held significant command responsibilities during operations in Sicily and Italy and provided key planning support for Operation Anvil-Dragoon, the invasion of southern France. In August 1944, he was named commander of Southern Lines of Communication, European Theater, and in April 1945 he was elevated to chief of staff of the Communication Zone and deputy commander. After returning to the United States, he was named the 36th quartermaster general of the army in January 1946. In March 1949, he was promoted to lieutenant general and received his last assignment as director of logistics, US Army.

Larkin retired at the end of 1952 but continued in service, participating in an economic survey of West Berlin and the construction of manufacturing facilities in Western Europe. For his work, he received the Secretary of Defense Meritorious Civilian Award in 1960. He died in 1968. A son, Air Force Lt. Harrison Larkin, was killed when his plane crashed in 1950.

In the Pacific and China-Burma-India Theaters, airmen of the class of 1915 shouldered significant command responsibility, shaping strategic and tactical operations and maintaining the vital supply links to troops in the field over thousands of treacherous miles from India to embattled China.

In mid-1943, Maj. Gen. George E. Stratemeyer began a stint of thirty-three months of overseas duty. Stratemeyer was born in Cincinnati, Ohio, and spent his childhood in Peru, Indiana. He graduated 147th in the class of 1915 and was the champion middleweight boxer of the Cadet Corps. He held numerous training and command posts during World War I and through the interwar years and received his first star with the appointment as executive officer to Air Corps Chief Gen. Henry "Hap" Arnold. He commanded the India-Burma sector and served as air advisor to Gen. Joseph Stilwell, the American theater commander. By the end of the war, he was a lieutenant general commanding the Army Air Forces in the China Theater.

In the spring of 1944, Maj. Gen. Thomas Hanley took charge of China-Burma-India Air Service Command, and in July 1945 he assumed command of Army Air Forces in India and Burma. Hanley had graduated 124th in the class of 1915. Too small for the varsity football team, he was "hammered around on the Scrubs" for three years, according to *Assembly*. After the war, he led the combined Army-Air Force Recruiting Service. Following retirement in 1952, he was one of the organizers of Florida Atlantic University. He died in 1969.

The abrupt redirection of the career of Brig. Gen. Earl Larue Naiden is somewhat controversial. Naiden was a pioneer aviator and attended flight school in early 1917 with no fewer than twenty-five of his West Point classmates. As chief of staff of the Tenth Air Force, Naiden provided crucial leadership in the formation of the air supply route from India to China that came to be famously known as "The Hump." He is also credited with assisting Gen. Claire Chennault in the deployment of the famed American Volunteer Group, nicknamed the "Flying Tigers," fighter pilots who harassed the Japanese in the skies above war-torn China.

In August 1942, General Stilwell relieved Naiden of his command, replacing him with Maj. Gen. Clayton Bissell. Some accounts of the event state that Naiden was relieved for financial impropriety, while others assert that he was suffering from a stomach ailment and required hospitalization. Naiden served briefly in the Solomon Islands as chief of staff to 1915 classmate Maj. Gen. Hubert Harmon. He returned to the United States in early 1943 and later assumed command of the 317th Wing, Fourth Air Force. He was killed in a plane crash in Redmond, Oregon, on September 20, 1944, and buried in Arlington National Cemetery.

Naiden's gravestone reflects the rank of colonel, and his handwritten records with the West Point Association of Graduates, submitted by a relative in 1951, note only that his rank of brigadier general was terminated on November 6, 1942, "by reason of physical disability." In the absence of documentation related to a demotion, it is reasonable to conclude that Naiden simply reverted to his permanent rank of colonel. If in fact the reduction in rank was a demotion, it was related either to the alleged financial impropriety or a serious run-in the supposedly abrasive airman had with a British officer.

Naiden graduated sixty-eighth in the class of 1915 and was noted as an excellent golfer, winning the army championship in 1926.

One of the most stirring episodes of World War II in the Pacific was the liberation of the civilian prisoners held in the Japanese internment camp at Los Baños, southeast of the Philippine capital of Manila on the island of Luzon. The task fell to the 11th Airborne Division, commanded by Maj. Gen. Joseph Swing, who had graduated thirty-eighth in the class of 1915.

Swing was a veteran of World War I, and after returning from France in 1918, he served as aide to Army Chief of Staff Gen. Peyton C. March. He married the general's daughter, Josephine Mary, that summer. While organizing the artillery of the 82nd Infantry Division under Omar Bradley, he was introduced to the concept of airborne operations. In February 1943, he was placed in command of the 11th Airborne Division. During the next five years, Swing led the 11th Airborne through activation, training, combat, and occupation duty in Japan.

On January 31, 1945, Swing and the glider regiments of the 11th Airborne landed on Luzon, and three days later the 511th Parachute Infantry Regiment dropped nearby. The division's mission was twofold: open a second front in the advance to Manila, driving from the south while elements of the Sixth Army pushed from the north, and liberate the 2,147 internees at Los Baños, 1,575 of whom were Americans. While fighting the Japanese south of the Philippine capital, Swing and his staff devised the plan for the liberation of the camp, located forty miles behind enemy lines.

The complex operation included airborne and amphibious assaults by 11th Airborne troops and Filipino guerrillas. A "flying column" of truck-mounted glider troops would race to the gates of the prison while other forces held the Japanese, who were present in significant numbers in the vicinity, at bay. The internees would be ferried to freedom aboard amphibious landing craft.

The Los Baños Raid began early on the morning of February 23, 1945, and as one Army officer remembered, "The results were spectacular. Internees poured out and into the loading area. Troops started clearing the barracks . . . and carried out to the loading area over 130 people who were too weak or too sick to walk."[161] Swing monitored the progress of the near-flawless operation from a Piper Cub artillery liaison aircraft.

All internees were safely evacuated, and casualties among the American and Filipino troops were four killed and six wounded.

The Los Baños Raid is studied to this day. Airborne historian Maj. Gerard M. Devlin wrote in 1979, "Because of the highly accurate intelligence information, a perfect plan, and a faultless performance by the attacking troops, the Los Baños mission is still considered to be the finest example of a small-scale operation ever executed by American airborne troops. There is no doubt that it will remain a masterpiece of planning and execution and the blueprint for any future daring prisoner-rescue operation."[162]

Two months after the raid, Swing displayed tremendous personal courage during heavy action in the Philippines. His Distinguished Service Cross Citation reads in part, "He flew many dangerous flights in liaison airplanes at low altitudes. . . . Despite the protests of subordinates, he personally, and on foot, led tank destroyers forward through intense enemy machine-gun and mortar fire to place them in more advantageous positions. . . . General Swing strode fearlessly between tanks and machine guns, calling upon his troops to man their weapons and attack. Inspired by his fearlessness and heroic action, the troops attacked, silenced the Japanese fire, and seized and held the main enemy positions. . . ."

Swing went on to command I Corps, the Army War College, and the Sixth Army. He was promoted to lieutenant general in 1951 and retired three years later. From 1954 to 1960, he served in President Eisenhower's administration as commissioner of the US Bureau of Immigration and Naturalization. He died in 1984 at the age of ninety.

In August 1942, Paul Mueller was placed in command of the 81st Infantry Division at Camp Rucker, Alabama. A month later, he was promoted to major general. A combat veteran of World War I, Mueller led the 81st Division through training and combat in the Palau Islands in the autumn of 1944, including the capture of Anguar. Afterward, a detached regimental combat team of the 81st Division supported US Marine operations on nearby Peleliu. The 81st participated in mopping-up action on the Philippine island of Leyte and then demobilized in northern Japan in early 1946.

Mueller, who had graduated forty-fifth in the class of 1915, was later appointed deputy commander of the Third Army and chief of the army's

Career Management Division at the Pentagon. Apparently, no action was taken on a 1949 letter from General MacArthur recommending his promotion to lieutenant general. Mandatory retirement followed in 1953, and he died of a heart attack in 1964. A son, Paul Jr., graduated from West Point in 1950.

Edwin A. Zundel, a clean sleeve and member of the polo team at West Point, graduated twenty-ninth in the class of 1915. He served in France during World War I and took part in operations in the Solomon Islands and New Guinea as the artillery officer of the 41st Division in World War II. In 1948, he became chief of the Army Counter Intelligence Corps and later became inspector general of Far East Command and inspector general of United Nations Troops, Korea. He retired in 1953 with the rank of brigadier general and died in 1985 at the age of ninety-one.

Several members of the class of 1915 lost sons in World War II, including Maj. Gen. William Fraser Tompkins, who graduated sixteenth. In mid-1943, Tompkins was appointed director of the Special Planning Division of the War Department, which worked on developing a protocol for demobilization with the end of the war. In the summer of 1945, he was assigned as chief of staff, US Forces in the Pacific and later became commander of Army Service Command C in the Philippines.

By this time, he had lost two sons. Second Lieutenant George H. Tompkins, a night fighter pilot, died in France on September 11, 1944. His eldest son, Maj. William F. Tompkins Jr., commander of the 552nd Heavy Pontoon Battalion, was killed in action on March 10, 1945, as his command erected a pontoon bridge across the Rhine River just south of Remagen. A third son, Christopher, joined the US Marine Corps but was not permitted to serve overseas due to the loss of his brothers. Major General Tompkins died in 1969.

Two members of the class of 1915 were killed in action in the Pacific. Colonel John Ross Mendenhall lost his life aboard an aircraft due to enemy action on January 27, 1945. At the time, he commanded the 167th Infantry Regiment fighting the Japanese in New Guinea. A veteran of five major engagements during World War I, Mendenhall received the Croix de Guerre, the Purple Heart, and the Silver Star. He graduated 144th.

Major Frank McGee, who graduated 113th, was killed in the Philippines on August 7. Wounded in action during World War I, he had retired due to physical disability in 1922. He relocated to the Philippines and by 1926 had established himself as owner and manager of the Lauayon Plantation Company. When war broke out, he took command of the 107th Philippine Army Division.

At the end of 1945, Roscoe Woodruff wrote to Herman Beukema with the news of their classmate McGee's death. In turn, Beukema wrote in the *Assembly* newsletter, "From the time the Japs took over there, 'Maggie' and his guerrillas did magnificent work. He was given his final command soon after MacArthur's return to Leyte and was operating in northern Davao when the Japs got him."[163]

More than fifty members of the class of 1915 were active during World War II, holding combat commands, staff positions, and field posts around the globe. The end of hostilities coincided with a small thirtieth reunion at West Point during June week, and bad weather delayed the arrival of several members. Bradley delivered the commencement address. In Europe, twenty-six classmates enjoyed dinner at the Hotel Cap d'Antibes on the French Riviera.

As the exertions of war eased slightly, Eisenhower had plans of his own. He remembered:

> Shortly after the German surrender, it occurred to me that 1945 would mark the thirtieth anniversary of the graduation of my classmates and myself from West Point, and I planned a brief private celebration for those of us who were serving in Europe. I believed that we could fly to the United States, spend one day at West Point's graduation exercises, and be back on duty in Germany with a total absence of only three days. . . . I developed a high-pressure enthusiasm for the project and suggested that each of my 20 [sic] classmates in Europe should send a secret message to his wife asking her to meet him for a one-day reunion at West Point.

Within a few days, Eisenhower's best laid plans were derailed by orders from Marshall. Eisenhower recalled:

> Because circumstances prevented American units in Europe from returning to the United States to appear in the traditional parades of victorious troops, General Marshall wanted me to pick representative officers and enlisted men for return in groups of some fifty each,

for a short tour of our country. . . . These orders knocked my personal scheme out of the picture.[164]

Despite this disappointment, Eisenhower took quiet satisfaction in the defeat of Nazi Germany and the completion of the mission of the Allied Expeditionary Force. The soldiers of the class of 1915 had proven adept at waging war. Quite a different challenge—the waging of peace—lay ahead.

PART V

The Class the Stars Fell On

CHAPTER NINE

Power and Perspective

Flying in formation, more than thirty fighters and bombers greeted the transport carrying General of the Army Dwight D. Eisenhower home, and they escorted his plane to its touchdown at the national airdrome in Washington, D.C., at 11:11 a.m., June 18, 1945. Stepping off the plane with him was Lt. John Eisenhower, and there to greet them both were Mamie Eisenhower and General Marshall.

Hailed in European capitals as the triumphant supreme commander, Eisenhower was weary after three and a half years of war. "Oh, God, it's swell to be back," he sighed.[165] About two hours later, he addressed a joint session of Congress. The following day, he arrived in New York City and received a commemorative gold medal from Mayor Fiorello LaGuardia. A huge ticker tape parade followed, and four million New Yorkers turned out to welcome the hero as he rode through thirty-seven miles of the city's streets. That night, a dinner was held in his honor at the Waldorf-Astoria.

Then, at long last, it was home to Abilene. Along the way, Eisenhower's train stopped in Topeka, and he stepped off briefly to shake hands with a few of those who had gathered. As he climbed back into the railcar, he slipped and fell heavily on his troublesome knee, but the famous grin never left his face. At his boyhood home, his eighty-three-year-old mother and four brothers, Arthur, Edgar, Earl, and Milton, greeted him.

Seventy-five relatives, close and distant, gathered, and an entire floor of the Lamar Hotel was reserved for the reunion. The population of the prairie town swelled to more than twenty thousand, and Eisenhower spoke to the crowd of the great honor it had been to command so many men and women in the cause of freedom.[166]

The stay in the United States was brief, and Eisenhower returned to Europe as commander of the US occupation zone in Germany. He was responsible, directly or indirectly, for the welfare of millions, working to transport GIs back to the States as quickly as possible, to remove former Nazi sympathizers and members of the Party from positions of responsibility, and to provide food and shelter for throngs of displaced people.

In November, as General Marshall relinquished the post of army chief of staff, Eisenhower assumed the duties somewhat reluctantly. He was never happy in the role and had recommended Omar Bradley for the job. At the time, the army was in the process of downsizing from its peak strength of more than twelve million to slightly less than two million. He served as chief of staff for twenty-six months and grappled with the nuances of Washington politics and foreign relations as well.

Eisenhower's successor as commander of US forces in the European Theater and then US Forces of Occupation in Germany was Joseph McNarney. For seventeen months, McNarney dealt with a myriad of issues, including maintaining order and discipline among American troops and good relations with the peoples and governments where they were stationed; care for displaced persons; the apprehension, detention, and preparation for trial of suspected Nazi war criminals; and defensive military preparedness as the Cold War developed.

Amid the discharge of these tremendous responsibilities, McNarney was approached in 1946 by a delegation of rabbis trying to minister to the large Jewish population in the American zone of occupation in Germany. Many of these people were displaced or had been liberated from the horrific conditions in Nazi concentration camps. The rabbis had virtually no copies of the Talmud with which to conduct religious services and asked McNarney for help.

McNarney enlisted the assistance of two Jewish chaplains from the army and approved a project that brought a Talmud from New York to

Germany. "The plant that had previously been printing Nazi propaganda was now printing 500 sets of the Talmud—the only time in history that a national government published the Talmud," reported a Miami newspaper. Those displaced Jews who knew the story never forgot "the unprecedented humanism of General McNarney and the U.S. Army."[167]

During his 1966 interview with Marshall biographer Forrest C. Pogue, McNarney recalled a series of run-ins with the Soviets:

> Russian guards along the border would get tight and raid farms over on our side of the line. I would protest to Sokolovsky [Soviet Marshal Vasily Sokolovsky, head of the Soviet military administration in East Germany] but nothing would be done. Finally, I ordered the Constabulary to go after them. One night they caught the Russians coming out of a farmhouse and killed three or four. One of them must have been politically important. Sokolovsky demanded that I hang my people. I told him they were following my orders. He wrote two or three letters. I threw the fourth one in the waste basket.[168]

In March 1947, McNarney returned to the United States as his country's representative on the United Nations Military Staff Committee in New York. He moved on to lead Air Materiel Command at Wright-Patterson Air Force Base in Ohio, and then assumed his final active-duty post in September 1949, as chief of the Department of Defense Management Committee. He chaired an inter-service committee that tackled the enormous job of paring back the mushrooming defense budget. Again, McNarney was the right choice for the job, and he earned the enmity of some members of the military establishment in his role with what came to be known at the "McNarney Board."

McNarney retired on January 31, 1952, and accepted the position of president of the Consolidated Vultee Aircraft Corporation, which later became the Convair Division of defense contractor General Dynamics. On the twentieth anniversary of Convair in 1955, he reported that just over one in eight salary and wage earners in the San Diego area were employees of Convair. "In the next 20 years, they will face scientific and industrial challenges undreamed of in 1935 and only dimly discernible today," he told a gathering.[169]

In November 1958, President Eisenhower appointed a bipartisan group of "eminent Americans" to evaluate the US Mutual Security Program, a framework for providing military and economic assistance as needed to deter the threat of Communist expansion around the world. The group became known as the Draper Committee after its chairman, William Henry Draper Jr., a former army major general, ambassador to NATO, and investment banker. Eisenhower respected McNarney and asked his classmate to serve on the committee.

On February 1, 1972, McNarney died at Scripps Hospital in La Jolla, California, at the age of seventy-eight. Among the members of the West Point class of 1915, he stands out as an individual whose accomplishments were significant, yet neither prestige nor fame held lasting appeal to him. His forthright manner may have lacked emotion or a hint of sympathy at times, but he got the job done, either as Marshall's sole deputy chief of staff reorganizing the War Department, as the military governor of the American Occupation Zone in Germany, or in any other position of responsibility that he held.

When McNarney took the job at Consolidated Vultee, his classmates wondered how his matter-of-fact approach would play in civilian life. They also remembered, however, that he was one of their own. Following the thirtieth reunion in 1945, Leroy "Red" Irwin wrote in *Assembly*, "All in all, the reunion was a roaring success. Even the dour Joe McNarney was so softened that he became the principal in a bull session in barracks with a volubility that would have astonished some of his wartime co-workers."[170]

In a 1983 interview, Lt. Gen. Elwood R. Quesada, who had led IX Tactical Air Command in Europe during World War II and later became head of the Federal Aviation Administration, remarked, "Joe McNarney was the straightest of straight arrows, a real gentleman. If the world were fair, he would have been Air Force Chief of Staff, and he should have been."[171]

The death notice in the general's hometown newspaper noted that he was "known to Emporium people as friendly 'General Joe.'"[172]

In February 1948, Dwight Eisenhower retired from an active-duty military career that had spanned thirty-three years. In the spring, he accepted the presidency of Columbia University in New York. At the time, the suggestion that the world's most famous soldier would even entertain an invitation to venture into the world of academia seemed far-fetched. A rumor circulated widely that the trustees of Columbia had actually erred when one of their number suggested, "What about Eisenhower?" The thought was that the offer should be made to Dwight's brother Milton, a well-known educator and president of Kansas State College. The truth is that the trustees wanted Dwight Eisenhower.[173]

The new president relocated his office from an upper floor of the library that was accessible only by private elevator to the first floor of the building. He remembered in later years, "Students, the chief reason for the university's being, and for me the paramount appeal and attraction in campus life, were in danger of becoming numerical figures on forms and passing, unknown faces on campus."[174]

During this time, Eisenhower also began work on his memoir of World War II, the classic *Crusade in Europe*. Of its success, he wrote, "The book sold unbelievably well. In the fall of 1966—eighteen years later—I asked Doubleday for a roundup of the story and I was assured that the book had been a profitable venture on their part. At least 1,170,000 copies of *Crusade in Europe* were sold in the United States and there were contracts for twenty-two foreign-language editions. Even yet, orders come in every month for the book, which testifies not to its value as literature, but to the fact that people go on refighting the war."[175]

Meanwhile, Eisenhower served for three months as a consultant to James V. Forrestal, the first secretary of defense. Forrestal's newly created cabinet post unified command of the US military as a result of the National Security Act of 1947. In December 1950, Eisenhower was called to serve as the first supreme commander of the North Atlantic Treaty Organization (NATO), which had been formed in 1949 to counter the threat of Communist aggression in Europe and included twelve Western member nations pledged to mutual defense. He served as supreme commander for more than a year and a half.

All the while, speculation swirled as to Eisenhower's political affiliation and further as to whether he had any ambition to hold public office—specifically the presidency. By 1952, he could no longer deflect the questions and declared that he was a Republican. In rapid succession, his name appeared on the ballot in the New Hampshire presidential primary, which he won handily over Senator Robert Taft of Ohio. His political career gained momentum with the familiar slogan "I Like Ike," and twice, in 1952 and 1956, he was elected thirty-fourth president of the United States, defeating Democratic Senator Adlai Stevenson of Illinois both times with more than 440 electoral votes and more than 55 percent of the popular vote.

The world was changing, and during eight years in the White House President Eisenhower was confronted with a variety of issues. During his 1952 presidential campaign, he promised in a nationally televised speech to go to Korea, where United Nations troops, 90 percent of them American, had been at war since the June 25, 1950, invasion of South Korea by the Communist North.

"We could not stand forever on a static front," the president said later, "and continue to accept casualties without any visible results. Small attacks on small hills would not end this war." While continuing diplomatic efforts and demonstrating the resolve to escalate the war if necessary, he reenergized stalled negotiations. Seven months after Eisenhower took office, on July 27, 1953, an armistice ended the fighting.[176]

At home, Sen. Joseph McCarthy of Wisconsin gained national attention with his virulent attacks on members of government and organizations that he believed harbored active Communists and leftist political sympathies. Eisenhower chose not to confront McCarthy directly, arguing that such a response might give the vocal Republican even greater attention. During a 1952 campaign stop in Wisconsin, however, he allowed himself to be photographed shaking hands with McCarthy and decided not to deliver a speech criticizing his tactics while defending one of the senator's targets, Secretary of State George C. Marshall.

On July 21, 1953, Eisenhower wrote of McCarthy to his old friend Swede Hazlett, ". . . I believe in the positive approach. I believe that we should earnestly support the practice of American principles in trials and investigations—we should teach and preach decency and justice. . . . To give way in anger or irritation to an outburst intended to excoriate some individual, his motives and his methods, could do far more to destroy the position and authority of the attacker than it would do to damage the attacked."[177]

The tactic, which had been effective in the military, was much less successful in dealing with civilian political matters. Eisenhower had no direct control over McCarthy and his hurling of accusations, but a firmer stance might have curtailed the damage done to the reputations of many. Eisenhower regretted that he did not come more forcefully to Marshall's defense, and the affair damaged his friendship with former president Harry Truman.

During the Eisenhower administration, Congress passed the Civil Rights Act of 1957, the nation's first such significant legislation of its kind, and followed with the Civil Rights Act of 1960. Both were intended to end voter discrimination in segregated states. In the wake of the landmark Supreme Court ruling in the *Brown v. Topeka Board of Education* case, Governor Orval Faubus ordered the Arkansas National Guard to bar the entry of nine black students to Central High School in Little Rock. The president dispatched 1,200 troops of the 101st Airborne Division to the city to keep order and enforce the decision of the Supreme Court.

In October 1957, Eisenhower received a stirring letter. It read, "We, the parents of the nine colored children who have enrolled at Little Rock Central High School want you to know that your actions in safeguarding their rights have strengthened our faith in democracy."[178]

Another of Eisenhower's significant domestic accomplishments was the initiation of the immense Interstate Highway System that was envisioned with the Federal Aid Highway Act. On June 29, 1956, the president signed the bill into law while recovering from surgery related to an intestinal obstruction. He had seen the need for improvement in the nation's roadways as early as the Transcontinental Convoy of 1919 and had witnessed the efficiency of the autobahns in Germany. He believed that major highways were essential to national defense, to accommodate the growing number of automobiles on the roads, and to the growth of the tourism industry in the United States.

To lead the implementation of the Federal Aid Highway Act, Eisenhower called upon his West Point classmate John Stewart Bragdon as his special assistant for Public Works Planning. Bragdon, who had graduated fifth in the class of 1915, saw combat during World War I, served as an instructor at West Point during the 1920s, and held a series of engineering posts for the remainder of his career.

From 1944 to 1949, Bragdon was director of military construction for the army. He achieved the rank of major general, retired from the military in 1951, and worked in the civilian construction industry. From 1960 to 1961, he was a member of the Civil Aeronautics Board, and during the Kennedy administration he worked as a consultant to the US House Committee on Public Works. He died in 1964.

In relations with the Soviet Union, President Eisenhower pursued a policy of developing dialogue related to a burgeoning arms race while maintaining US resolve to defend freedom. In what came to be known both as the Cross of Iron Speech and the Chance for Peace Speech, delivered on April 16, 1953, he related that the high price of uncontrolled military spending would negatively impact the effort to feed and clothe the poor and to educate America's children. "It is humanity hanging from a cross of iron," he intoned.[179] During Eisenhower's second term, the Soviet launch of the Sputnik satellite in 1957 and the embarrassment of the 1960 U-2 spy plane incident that resulted in the Soviet withdrawal from a major summit meeting tested his administration.

Perhaps Eisenhower's most memorable speech was delivered on January 17, 1961, as he left office. The president's farewell address was prophetic and still resonates in recent history:

> In the councils of government, we must guard against the acquisition of unwarranted influence, whether sought or unsought, by the military-industrial complex. The potential for the disastrous rise of misplaced power exists and will persist. We must never let the weight of this combination endanger our liberties or democratic processes. We should take nothing for granted. Only an alert and knowledgeable citizenry can compel the proper meshing of the huge industrial and military machinery of defense with our peaceful methods and goals, so that security and liberty may prosper together. . . .[180]

On the evening of June 29, 1954, President and Mrs. Eisenhower hosted a dinner at the White House for members of the class of 1915 then residing in the Washington area. Among those attending were forty-four classmates and their wives, including Joseph Swing, Hubert Harmon, Leroy Irwin, Paul Mueller, and seven widows. During June Week 1955, Eisenhower attended the fortieth reunion of the class of 1915 and delivered the commencement address at graduation.

"As we approached Thayer monument a robin—subsidized no doubt by the Chairman of the Democratic National Committee—made a small deposit on the coat sleeve of the President of the United States," wrote John Wogan in *Assembly*. "Boye [Class President Frederick W. Boye, who had graduated 150th], marching alongside Ike, made a valiant effort to intercept the bird on the fly, but unfortunately, missed. A classmate whispered, 'They sing for the Democrats.'"[181]

Omar Bradley returned to the United States during the first week of June 1945 and reunited with his wife Mary for the first time in twenty-one months. There were victory parades in St. Louis and Philadelphia, and a few days later Moberly, Missouri, celebrated "General Omar Bradley Day" with a parade, speeches, and a fried chicken dinner at the Masonic Temple as the now-famous general attended the reunion of his 1910 high school graduating class.

A month earlier, as Bradley's hopes for a senior combat command in the Pacific faded, he had been summoned by Eisenhower to headquarters in Reims, France. Eisenhower dropped a bombshell, informing Bradley of General Marshall's pending retirement, his own reluctant but resolute acceptance of the army chief of staff post, and President Truman's specific request that Bradley take on the enormous task of heading the Veterans Administration amid the massive postwar demobilization. The Servicemen's Readjustment Act of 1944, better known as the GI Bill, was destined to reshape America.

When Bradley stepped into the breach, the VA was in disarray. The quality of medical care had been described by one associate of the new director as "medieval." More than $740 million a year was being paid in benefits to 1.5 million veterans or their dependents. One individual, age eighty-eight, was still receiving benefits as the dependent of a veteran of the War of 1812. By 1946, the number of veterans and dependents receiving some type of benefits or eligible to do so topped seventeen million.[182]

Bradley brought with him some capable members of his 12th Army Group staff who had served so well in Europe and tackled the problems of the VA head-on. He streamlined operations on a regional basis, did his best to remove the politics of the programs to focus on the veterans, expanded the available educational and job training opportunities, and grappled with an enormous insurance program with more than $135 billion of face value life coverage in the hands of eighteen million policyholders. His two years at the helm of the VA left their imprint on postwar American society, and the press reported that Bradley had reengineered "the medical service of the Veterans Administration from a national scandal to a model establishment."[183]

In November 1947, President Truman announced Bradley's appointment to succeed Eisenhower as army chief of staff. The job was often frustrating, a morass of issues including continued demobilization, the consolidation of the armed forces command structure, the maintenance of sufficient budgets to carry out the demands of a global power, the racial integration of the army, and particularly the enforcement of the Truman Doctrine of support for Greece and Turkey as a buttress against the spread of communism into the Balkans and the Middle East.

The dark days of inter-service rivalry grew even more contentious during Bradley's tenure as army chief of staff and boiled over during his two terms as the first chairman of the Joint Chiefs of Staff from 1949 to 1953. The air force and the navy squared off in bitter political battles for budget dollars and for preeminence in national defense at the dawn of the Atomic Age and as the primary deterrent to Soviet expansion around the world.

On September 23, 1950, Bradley, who thirty years earlier had worried that he would never advance above the rank of lieutenant colonel, was promoted to five-star General of the Army, the fifth and last officer to hold the grade. Along with the promotion came a pay increase to $17,000 a year.

Bradley presided over the Joint Chiefs during the Korean War and accompanied President Truman to the fateful meeting with General MacArthur at Wake Island in October 1950. He experienced firsthand the difficulties of dealing with MacArthur and the polarizing effect his presence in the Far East had on American public opinion. On April 11, 1951, Truman relieved MacArthur, replacing him with Gen. Matthew B. Ridgway. Bradley supported Truman's decision and weathered the criticism of the political right during the media furor that followed.

In Europe, Bradley was committed to the maintenance of a strong military presence to counter possible Soviet expansion. In the autumn of 1949, he was named chairman of the Military Committee of NATO, holding the position until the end of the following year. He remained as the US representative to the NATO Military Committee until his retirement from active service at the age of sixty on August 15, 1953. He had been a soldier for thirty-eight years.

In later years, Bradley and his "assistant" biographer, Clay Blair, were critical of Eisenhower's 1952 presidential campaign. Bradley recalled Eisenhower's attacks on Truman and his conduct of the Korean War and called his classmate's pledge to travel to Korea personally "pure show biz." Nevertheless, the bonds of army service remained strong.

After Eisenhower's landslide election win in 1952, Bradley sent a telegram that read, "Dear Ike. Congratulations on your victory. We shall be very happy to have you and Mamie back in Washington again. I am proud that this great honor has been bestowed upon a classmate from West Point by the American people, and it will be a privilege and honor to be serving under you again. Your job will probably be tougher than Overlord. Best regards and good luck. Omar Bradley."[184]

Although he had retired from day-to-day service, General of the Army Bradley was never completely away from his military roots. He frequently attended ceremonies and official functions as a representative of the government. Bradley was a close friend of Harry D. Henshel, the brother-in-law of Bulova Watch Company Chairman Arde Bulova and one of the company's largest shareholders. In 1954, he entered civilian employ for the first time since his boyhood, accepting a position as chairman of Bulova Research & Development Labs Inc., a subsidiary of the watch company responsible for the expansion of its defense product line. Arde Buolova died in 1958, and Bradley was elevated to chairman of the company.

Tragedy struck the Bradley and Beukema families on January 19, 1954, when twenty-nine-year-old Maj. Hal Beukema, the general's son-in-law, died when the F-86 Sabre fighter jet he was piloting plunged into the James River in Virginia. Bradley's daughter, Lee, was left with four children and later married a Washington attorney, Benjamin Dorsey. A fifth grandchild was born afterward. To be closer to their family, Omar and Mary returned to the nation's capital from California in 1957.

Major General James Van Fleet had every reason to be satisfied with the performance of the troops he commanded during World War II in Europe. His own combat leadership had validated years of quiet service and relative obscurity as he held true to his personal creed and maintained "The Will to Win." In September 1945, III Corps was at Camp Polk, Louisiana, waiting for orders to join the massing American forces intended for the invasion of Japan. Van Fleet arrived at Camp Polk on September 2 amid a raucous V-J Day celebration.

When III Corps was deactivated, Van Fleet went to New York to lead 2nd Service Command and then to serve as deputy commander of the First Army under Gen. Courtney Hodges. His son, Jimmy, was a cadet at West Point during this time, and when he was able Van Fleet attended football games and watched his son's standout performances with the Army swim team. During the postwar downsizing of the army, he held simultaneous posts as deputy commander and chief of staff of the First Army and later as commander of the military district of New York, New Jersey, and

Delaware. In December 1947, he returned to Germany to head operations, organization, and planning for the European Command. His stay was brief.

During World War II, a Communist political and paramilitary organization had been developing in Greece, and by 1946 a full-scale civil war had erupted between the armed Communists and forces loyal to the Greek government. The government forces were initially supported by the British; however, early in 1947 it became necessary for the United States to step in and enforce the letter and spirit of the Truman Doctrine, meant to protect Greece and Turkey from Soviet influence.

Eisenhower, then serving as army chief of staff, called Van Fleet to Washington. When he greeted his classmate, Eisenhower was tight-lipped about a new assignment and sent Van Fleet to meet with Secretary of State Marshall, who detailed a new and difficult assignment. Promoted to lieutenant general, Van Fleet was named director of the Joint US Military and Planning Group in Greece, essentially directing the effort to defeat the Communist insurgency.

Marshall asked, "Van Fleet, what can you do to help the Greeks beat the Communists?" Van Fleet replied that if the Greek government troops were determined to win, he could train and motivate them to become an effective fighting force.[185]

Van Fleet arrived in Athens in February 1948, and he spent several days visiting political leaders before gaining an audience with the king and queen. His initial assessment of the government troops was grim. Although morale was good, the troops suffered from a lack of quality leadership. "Greek commanding officers are intensely politically conscious," he wrote, "to the extent that they are reluctant to relieve obviously incompetent officers. . . . Minor indecisive clashes, characterized by a lack of offensive spirit, have had little effect as a deterrent upon the bandit aims."[186]

With support from the War Department in Washington, Van Fleet led the training and equipping of draftees and reinvigorated the Greek army. Within weeks of his arrival, offensive operations against the Communists yielded heartening results. When the Communists attempted their previously successful hit-and-run tactics in the Roumeli area, they were surprised to find themselves surrounded by government troops. During two weeks of fighting from April 15 to May 4, 1947, the Communists lost 409 killed and more than one thousand captured out of a force of two thousand guerrillas.

Although more than two years of difficult counter-insurgency warfare lay ahead, the Roumeli fight was a turning point. In the summer of 1949, government forces launched Operation Torch, a major offensive that effectively ended the capability of the Communists to stand and fight a major battle. While government forces lost about 150 killed and total casualties were slightly more than 400, the Communists lost 1,570 killed and 3,900 captured.

Van Fleet relayed news of the resounding victory to Washington. "Groups are so broken up that an organization on military lines hardly exists; no mining or harassing activities are engaged in and the omnipresent problems are survival from hunger and cold and escape from searching GNA [government] troops."[187]

In the spring of 1950, Greece held national legislative elections, and the relative handful of Communist guerrillas who remained at large were unable to disrupt the peaceful democratic process. During his Greek assignment, Van Fleet had demonstrated an awareness and understanding of the subtle differences between counter-insurgency warfare and traditional warfare between organized armies. He asserted to reporters that the methods and conditions under which counter-insurgency warfare was conducted were much more susceptible to the sentiment of the civilian population, climate, and terrain.

"We must be therefore keen on diligently studying guerrilla warfare and never assume that our lesson is learned and school is over," he advised.[188] Van Fleet returned to the United States and assumed a brief command of the Second Army at Fort Meade, Maryland. A bust of the general stands in the town square in Kastoria, Greece.

Van Fleet's stellar performance in the Balkans thrust him into the limelight when the time came for command change in Korea. Ridgway was somewhat reticent, aware that Van Fleet had made some unflattering comments concerning his conduct of the war after taking over for MacArthur and that Van Fleet was senior in terms of his graduation year from the Academy [Ridgway had graduated in 1917]. However, Ridgway was still a four-star general and Van Fleet would be compelled to take orders from him. The consensus was that Van Fleet could be counted on as a good soldier. Besides, Van Fleet was Truman's choice to command the Eighth Army.

Truman reportedly asked about Van Fleet's availability for Korea and was told that the general was already commanding an army. "What army?"

Truman asked. When he was told it was the Second, the president blurted, "Why, that's right up the road at Fort Meade; you can get someone to take that command!"[189]

Joint Chiefs Chairman Bradley was also sold. He wrote that Van Fleet had "worked miracles in Greece, completely routed the communist guerrillas, and insured the stability of the government."[190]

Van Fleet arrived in Korea on April 14, 1951, and a week later Communist forces launched a strong spring offensive. Under the weight of the assault, Van Fleet gave ground grudgingly and stubbornly defended the approaches to Seoul, the South Korean capital. When Ridgway flew to Van Fleet's headquarters and expressed concerns that some of the Washington brass feared his command would be cut off and annihilated, Van Fleet retorted, "Matt, this enemy doesn't know how to fight. They have no firepower behind them. They have no air power. We have all of that. We can just finish them off right here. I am very confident we'll hold."[191]

The Eighth Army did hold on the outskirts of Seoul, inflicting approximately seventy thousand casualties on the North Koreans and Chinese, even though the performance of South Korean troops in some areas was poor and the British Gloucestershire Battalion was shattered during the Battle of the Imjin River.

Van Fleet subsequently took the offensive, driving the Chinese and North Koreans back beyond their original line of departure and north of the 38th Parallel. The Communists suffered more than two hundred thousand casualties, and fighting was heavy in the Iron Triangle. By June, Ridgway considered a deeper advance into North Korea too risky and halted offensive operations. At first Van Fleet disagreed, but later he assented to the consolidation of Eighth Army lines.

The Eighth Army assumed a generally defensive posture as peace talks began in July. However, as the talks faltered, limited offensive operations resumed. Van Fleet was promoted to full general that summer as his troops seized objectives and casualties were high on both sides. Places such as Bloody Ridge, Heartbreak Ridge, and the Punchbowl became familiar names in homes across the United States.

Largely due to Van Fleet's force of personality and exceptional leadership, the Eighth Army remained an efficient fighting force; however, the concept of limited war was foreign to him. He chafed at the Truman and Eisenhower administrations as they sought an end to the war through diplomacy rather than victory on the battlefield. Supply problems further restricted operational efficiency. Van Fleet's suggestions that United Nations forces should mount a major offensive were rebuffed by both Ridgway and his successor, Mark Clark.

A staggering blow struck the Van Fleet family in the spring of 1952. Captain James A. Van Fleet Jr., an Air Force pilot assigned to the 13th Bomb Squadron at Kunsan, Korea, was lost along with two crewmen when his Martin B-26 Marauder light bomber failed to return from a mission on April 4, 1952. It was Jimmy Van Fleet's fourth combat mission of the war. Just a few weeks earlier, the general had seen his son for the last time when he stopped by headquarters on March 19, his father's sixtieth birthday. Jimmy's body was never recovered, and two years later he was declared dead.

Amid the sorrow following Jimmy's death and the frustrations of a combat commander instructed to remain on the defensive for an interminable period, Van Fleet contemplated the coming of his mandatory retirement. In late 1952, he was notified that his service was extended to March 31, 1953, at which time he was to be retired. General Maxwell Taylor succeeded him in command of the Eighth Army.

During his tour in Korea, Van Fleet won victories on the battlefield, helped to raise the professional standards of the South Korean Army, and was instrumental in the formation of a South Korean military academy. Although both Ridgway and Van Fleet tried publicly to maintain an air of decorum, their private relationship was sometimes rocky. Van Fleet confided to members of his family that he was pleased when Ridgway left Far East Command. Van Fleet also developed a warm but controversial relationship with South Korean strongman Syngman Rhee, who assumed near dictatorial authority in his country.

Before and after his retirement, Van Fleet was vocal in his opposition to the concept of limited war. After returning to the United States, he aroused a storm of debate, asserting that politicians in Washington had denied his command the opportunity to achieve complete victory in Korea. A fleeting hope that Eisenhower's election as president in the autumn of 1952 would signal that a commitment to military victory was dashed with the policy of a negotiated peace.

On their return to the States, Gen. and Mrs. Van Fleet enjoyed a grand parade through the city streets in San Francisco on February 25,

1953. Classmate Joseph Swing, commanding the Sixth Army, entertained the Van Fleets for two days at the Presidio, and other friends and classmates came by to visit. Later, Van Fleet had lunch and a private meeting with President Eisenhower and expressed his opinion that the war in Korea could be won. Testifying before the Senate Armed Services Committee, he contradicted the assurances of the Joint Chiefs that ammunition supplies had been plentiful in Korea. He described serious shortages and earned the ire of both Bradley and Army Chief of Staff Gen. Joseph Collins.[192]

Van Fleet settled into retirement in 1953 and wrote two provocative articles for *Life* magazine titled "The Truth about Korea, from a Man Free to Speak" and "The Truth about Korea: How We Can Win with What We Have." President Eisenhower's brother Milton persuaded him to join the board of the American-Korean Foundation, an organization that provided private aid to South Korea.

In the autumn, Van Fleet returned to West Point prior to the annual renewal of the Army-Navy football rivalry and delivered a rousing pep talk in the mess hall before 2,400 cadets. Removing his jacket, the general rolled up his sleeves and took off his tie, whipping up the audience. Finally, the dress shirt came off, revealing a white T-shirt emblazoned with the big Army "A." The assembled cadets roared their approval. The next day, Army upset a favored Navy team in Philadelphia, 20–7.

In 1954, Gen. Van Fleet accepted the president's request to serve as a special ambassador conducting a survey of US military assistance programs in the Far East. The following year, he returned to central Florida and the home he had left so many years earlier.

During the opening weeks of the Korean War, the troops of the US 24th Infantry Division fought heroic delaying actions against the North Korean onslaught. The division commander, Maj. Gen. William F. Dean, was in the thick of the fighting at Taejon on July 20–21, 1950. Dean was wounded, captured, and released in a prisoner exchange when the truce ended hostilities three years later.

Dean was awarded the Medal of Honor for his actions at Taejon, and much of the documentation provided for the honor came from his assistant division commander, fifty-seven-year-old Brig. Gen. Pearson Menoher, who remembered the division commander shouting, "My God, we must hold them. I don't want to have to fight for every mile of this ground again."[193]

After graduating forty-second in the class of 1915 and earning the coveted "A" in baseball, Menoher participated in the Punitive Expedition of 1916. As a young officer with the 9th Infantry Division, he remained in the United States during World War I. He served as the logistics officer and then chief of staff of XV Corps during World War II, taking part in the Normandy campaign, combat operations in Alsace and Lorraine, and the capture of the German cities of Munich and Nuremberg.

After Dean was captured at Taejon, Menoher briefly took command of the 24th Division. However, his own health rapidly deteriorated. He was retired from the army in 1952, and he resided in Southern Pines, North Carolina, near Fort Bragg. He died in 1957.

After World War II, Lt. Gen. George Stratemeyer led the Air Defense Command and Continental Air Command in the United States. In April 1949, he returned to Japan to take command of US Far East Air Forces. When the North Koreans invaded the south, Stratemeyer's airpower helped stem the Communist tide.

Stratemeyer received the Distinguished Service Cross for his actions during the critical period from mid-July to the end of September 1950. His citation reads in part:

> During the early days of the conflict, General Stratemeyer personally performed aerial reconnaissance of advanced airfields which were under attack by enemy aircraft and under fire by ground weapons, enabling him to plan immediately the most effective utilization of his combat air forces in the initial defensive phase. He directed the evacuation by air of American citizens from those advanced fields, continually subjecting himself to great danger. . . . Personally and at the risk of his life . . . he pressed forward on the ground by vehicle and on foot to the outermost advanced positions.

Stratemeyer suffered a serious heart attack in May 1951 and retired the next year. He died in Orlando, Florida, on August 9, 1969. In *Assembly*, a trio of classmates remembered his love for life and a round of golf. "He enjoyed saying things like, 'On a hot day, after eighteen holes, take a bottle of beer to the shower. The beer shouldn't be too cold. Just below room temperature. And don't guzzle it. Save some for when you're dressing.'"[194]

For Hubert "Doodle" Harmon, the years of World War II were fraught with frustration and sorrow. When the United States entered the war, Brig. Gen. Harmon commanded the Gulf Coast Training Center at Randolph Field, Texas. In November 1942, he was appointed commander of the Sixth Air Force in the Panama Canal Zone, and the following month he was promoted to major general. While the Canal Zone was vital to the movement of men and materiel between the Atlantic and Pacific, the German U-boat menace had waned and the prospect of attack by the Japanese was remote.

Harmon coveted a combat command, and in November 1943 he took charge of the 13th Air Force in the Solomon Islands and command of all air operations in the Solomons (COMAIRSOLS) on a rotating basis. By then, however, the battle for Guadalcanal had been won and the war was rapidly shifting to the southwest. Nevertheless, Harmon received the Distinguished Flying Cross twice during the period, and one of the citations reads, "He took part in many extremely hazardous flights into combat areas without escort in connection with planning operations for the destruction of the Japanese Air Force."

As operations in the Solomons ebbed, the 13th Air Force was reassigned to Gen. George Kenney's command in the Southwest Pacific. Harmon, however, was relieved of his duties after only six months in the Pacific Theater. While Harmon believed he had done "a damn good job" leading the 13th Air Force, Kenney apparently was not enamored with his performance and requested a change. In his postwar memoir, Kenney glossed over the situation, writing:

> General Arnold said he was sending Major General St. Clair Streett out to me, who could take command of the Thirteenth when it came under my control. . . . I asked him to let me have Streett right away. . . . Arnold agreed. Major General Hubert Harmon, who then commanded the Thirteenth, was to go back to the United States at the time of the transfer, as Hap had some job that he wanted to put him on.[195]

Harmon biographer Phillip Meilinger offers that Hubert "believed in his heart that he had succeeded, but lesser men who were jealous of his seniority and capabilities had pushed him aside. At this distance it is difficult to agree. . . . Harmon suffered from bad timing. His efficiency reports echo this assessment."[196]

In February 1945, Hubert's brother, Lt. Gen. Millard "Miff" Harmon, a prominent air commander in the Pacific Theater, was killed when his plane disappeared on a routine flight from Kwajalein to Hawaii, en route to Washington, D.C. An extensive air-sea search failed to turn up any trace of Miff or the aircraft. The brothers had been close, and Miff's death was a tremendous loss.

Harmon's experience, talent, and prior performance revealed excellent administrative capabilities, and in such positions he ultimately excelled. Arnold did in fact have an important assignment for Harmon, directing the Personnel Distribution Command with responsibilities for processing individuals deploying or returning from overseas duty, including wounded men who were convalescing and those who required additional training. In 1946, Harmon returned to Caribbean command, and in 1948 he was promoted to lieutenant general and named senior Air Force member of the Military and Naval Staff Committee of the United Nations in New York.

In February 1949, as the Joint Chiefs considered their defense plans in the event of war with the Soviet Union, Harmon was chosen to chair a committee to evaluate the capability of the Air Force to complete its strategic bombing mission. The Harmon Report concluded that the mission of delivering atomic bombs on Soviet targets could be accomplished but in itself would not defeat the Soviets.

Air Force Chief of Staff Gen. Hoyt Vandenberg was angered and wanted to make significant changes to the report. Some minor alterations were made, but Harmon stood by his guns and the report was submitted generally as it was written. Vandenberg remembered Harmon's stand and respected him as an officer of splendid character.

By December 1949, discussions surrounding the establishment of an Air Force Academy had gained sufficient momentum to warrant in-depth study. Vandenberg needed a proven administrator and organizer who could prioritize and execute a plan to deal with the many issues surrounding such a task. He chose Harmon, a man of unquestioned principles, as his special assistant for Air Force Academy matters. During the next five years, Harmon was consumed with issues ranging from curriculum to the location of the new academy to working with a Congress that moved at a glacial pace in approving the necessary legislation.

Finally, on April 1, 1954, President Eisenhower signed the bill officially creating the US Air Force Academy. By that time, Harmon had twice retired and been recalled to active duty. On August 15, 1954, he was named the first superintendent of the Air Force Academy, located temporarily at Lowry Air Force Base, Colorado, while plans were approved and construction carried out at the permanent site in Colorado Springs, which opened in the summer of 1958.

The establishment of the Air Force Academy was the crowning achievement of Harmon's military career, which spanned forty-one years. On July 31, 1956, he permanently retired, and the following year he died of lung cancer in the hospital at Lackland Air Force Base in San Antonio, Texas. On May 31, 1959, the administration building at the Academy was named Harmon Hall in his honor, and on the fiftieth anniversary of the Academy in 2004, Secretary of the Air Force Dr. James G. Roche formally proclaimed Gen. Hubert R. Harmon as the "Father of the Air Force Academy."

CHAPTER TEN

The Long Gray Line

Throughout his life, Dwight Eisenhower was passionate about golf. His favorite course was at Cherry Hills Country Club in suburban Denver. From 1948 until the end of his life, he was a member at Augusta National, home of the Masters Tournament, in Augusta, Georgia.

Eisenhower became quite familiar with the Augusta National course, particularly a loblolly pine 210 yards to the left of the tee and just off the fairway at the seventeenth hole. The president was said to have hit the tree with regularity, causing such great consternation that in 1956 he proposed during a meeting of the Augusta National governors that it should be cut down. Rather than overrule the president of the United States, Augusta National Chairman Clifford Roberts abruptly adjourned the meeting. The towering loblolly pine, known as the Eisenhower Tree, stood for another fifty-seven years before it was severely damaged by an ice storm in February 2014 and finally removed.

Eisenhower was also an avid fisherman, and one day after a walk around Augusta National, he proposed to Chairman Roberts that a dam should be built to create a spring-fed pond beside the eighth and ninth holes of the club's par-three course. Roberts approved, and Ike's Pond was built at the suggested location.

When the Eisenhowers left the White House, they settled on their nearly 190-acre farm in Gettysburg, Pennsylvania, a location that appealed to them because of its history and picturesque scenery, its proximity to New York and Washington, and their fond memories of the Camp Colt days. They had purchased the farm in 1950, but the intrusions of public service postponed the completion of extensive construction and renovation of the two-hundred-year-old farmhouse until 1955.[197]

At the age of fifty-eight, Eisenhower took up painting at the suggestion of his old friend and fellow politician Winston Churchill, and during his tenure as president of Columbia University, artist Thomas L. Stephens painted a portrait of Mamie and presented Dwight with a set of oils and brushes. As his affinity for painting grew, Eisenhower often sat down at his easel with regularity. A 1960 article in the *Saturday Evening Post* noted, "He paints simple, representational pictures. . . . He is impatient with art that is the product of introspection rather than observation." In 1967, he told a reporter from the *New York Times*, "There is nothing philosophical about my interest in painting. Rather, it is the best way in the world to relax. You put the surface of your mind on the canvas while the rest of your mind is making decisions."

During his last years, Eisenhower wrote several books, including the memoir of his presidency, *The White House Years, Volume I: Mandate for Change, 1953–1956* and *Volume II: Waging Peace, 1956–1961*. His other works include *At Ease: Stories I Tell to Friends*, in 1967, and *In Review: Pictures I've Kept, A Concise Pictorial "Autobiography"*, published in 1969. A compilation of selected addresses was released under the title *Peace with Justice*.

At long last, there was time, though fleeting, to relax for an extended period. Eisenhower enjoyed taking visitors on tours of the Gettysburg battlefield, cooking an occasional meal, tending livestock on the sprawling farm, and gardening. Still, at the age of seventy, he was never far from public life. The elder statesman of the Republican Party, he was consulted from time to time by political leaders and highly sought after as a public speaker. Presidents John F. Kennedy and Lyndon Johnson consulted him on matters of state. He attended the dedication of Dulles International Airport (named for his secretary of state, John Foster Dulles) outside of Washington, D.C., and in 1962 he visited President Truman in Independence, Missouri, to mend the rift that had developed over Joseph McCarthy during the 1952 presidential campaign.[198]

Financially, the Eisenhowers were comfortable with a $25,000-per-year presidential pension and retirement pay from the army. He had been required by law to resign his commission prior to assuming the presidency, and when his eight years in office concluded, Congress quickly voted to reinstate his five-star rank. A General of the Army was technically never relieved from active duty.

Health issues flared from time to time during Eisenhower's adult life, including Crohn's disease, ileitis, and heart disease, which precipitated several heart attacks, the first in 1955, and a mild stroke in 1957. In the spring of 1949, he did quit smoking, a habit that at its peak reached four packs a day.

In 1965, the class of 1915 celebrated its fiftieth reunion. Omar Bradley chaired the committee, and E. DeTreville "Det" Ellis helped coordinate the event for fifty-five classmates, thirty-eight wives, and fourteen widows. Guests attended a cocktail party at the Bear Mountain Inn, and the class photo was taken across the road from the superintendent's quarters. Those who wanted a copy were instructed to specify print No. 86 and pay $2. The festive class dinner took place in the West Point Army Mess.

Eisenhower participated in the groundbreaking ceremonies for a $110 million expansion of the Academy facilities, which would allow enrollment at West Point to increase from 2,500 to 4,417. *Time* magazine noted that during a walk across the campus, Eisenhower found the grounds unchanged "except for more equipment." During the walk, he happened to pass cadet Carl R. Stichweh, the quarterback who had led Army to an 11-8 win over Navy in the previous football season. Ever the fan, Eisenhower grinned and offered, "Good game, Rollie!"[199]

Later in the year, Eisenhower suffered two mild heart attacks. Digestive difficulties required the removal of his gall bladder in 1966, and between April and August 1968 the former president experienced four heart attacks and fourteen episodes of cardiac arrest. With the April heart attack, he entered Walter Reed Army Medical Center, where he would remain for the last year of his life. Mamie moved into quarters at the hospital.

Remarkably, Eisenhower maintained his memory and his interest in current events. His activity was limited to three forty-five-minute periods per day, but he received visitors regularly. His old friend Mark Clark remembered that Ike's favorite topic of conversation was the long-ago days at West Point.

On October 14, 1968, immediate family and members of the hospital staff gathered to celebrate Eisenhower's seventy-eighth birthday. Persuaded to move to the third floor window, the former president was greeted by a crowd of about two hundred well-wishers on the lawn below. The assembled army band and chorus broke into "Happy Birthday." He smiled broadly and waved. It was his first public appearance in six months.

Despite the risks due to his cardiac issues, Eisenhower underwent intestinal surgery in February 1969. During the weeks following the surgery, Eisenhower's tired and damaged heart declined considerably. On March 28, 1969, with Mamie and John at his side, he murmured, "I want to go. God take me."[200]

One of the most prominent soldiers and statesmen of the twentieth century had died. Tributes poured in. Eisenhower's body lay in state in the rotunda of the Capitol, and an estimated two thousand people per hour filed past to pay their respects. Honorary pallbearers included Omar Bradley and generals J. Lawton Collins and Wade Haislip, who had introduced Dwight Eisenhower to a young Mamie Doud years earlier.

Eisenhower had finalized plans for his state funeral in 1966, and following the service on the afternoon of March 31, the casket was taken to Union Station and placed aboard a train for the journey to Abilene and a second funeral on the steps of the Dwight D. Eisenhower Library. During the Abilene ceremonies on April 2, a strong wind blew in from the Kansas prairie, carrying the flag from the casket. For the remainder of the service, two soldiers held the flag in place. At the conclusion of the service, General of the Army and Thirty-Fourth President of the United States Dwight D. Eisenhower was laid to rest in the Place of Meditation on the library grounds. Mamie was interred beside him in 1979.

Mary Bradley died of leukemia in December 1965, and for several months the seventy-three-year-old Omar was despondent. All that changed the following summer. Omar Bradley had met Esther "Kitty" Buhler in 1950, when she interviewed him for a newspaper article on the island of Okinawa. More than fifteen years later, during a series of interviews related to the general's life story, a romance kindled. The two were married on September 12, 1966. Omar was seventy-three, and Kitty, twice divorced, was forty-four.

Kitty's zest for life captivated Gen. Bradley, and she encouraged him to remain active. The couple entertained frequently, including the occasional visit from one of the general's West Point classmates. General Bradley exercised, visited schools and military organizations, and spoke regularly at public gatherings.

A well-known screenwriter, Kitty's credits included the television shows *Dragnet* and *My Three Sons*. She had connections in Hollywood and New York. In 1967, the Bradleys took on a freelance assignment, traveling to Vietnam and writing about their impressions of the war in Southeast Asia for *Look* magazine. The following year, the couple relocated from Washington, D.C., to a home in Beverly Hills, where the general became well acquainted with the elite of the film industry.

Kitty was instrumental in the use of General Bradley's wartime memoir, *A Soldier's Story*, as source material for the Oscar-winning 1970 film *Patton*, starring George C. Scott in the title role and Karl Malden as Gen. Bradley. Omar and Kitty also made a lucrative deal that made them technical advisers during production.

General Bradley remained chairman of the Bulova Watch Company until 1973 and served on the boards of Food Fair Stores, a large grocery chain, and Metro-Goldwyn-Mayer (MGM). A month after leaving Bulova, the general suffered a life-threatening pulmonary embolism and spent days in the hospital in Los Angeles. During his stay, multiple blood clots formed and for a time his prospects seemed dim, but he pulled through.

In March 1975, Bradley was stricken with a blood clot on his brain and again nearly died. Kitty feared that the eighty-three-year-old general, confined to a wheelchair, might withdraw from life, and she was determined to keep him as busy as possible. As they were able, they traveled to West Point reunions and attended social functions.

In June, the Bradleys were unable to attend the sixtieth reunion of the class of 1915, but they joined in via telephone during the last dinner gathering. They were present at the sixty-fifth, however, along with ten other graduates, each of whom was approaching his ninetieth birthday.

When Bradley's health declined and medical attention became more continual, the couple relocated to Fort Bliss, Texas, which provided special accommodations for Bradley at the base hospital as needed. As his doctors permitted, he journeyed to Europe and the Middle East.[201] Bradley's mind remained sharp, and in 1979 he began working with noted author Clay Blair on another memoir, *A General's Life*. In January 1981, he was honored as grand marshal of the inaugural parade for President Ronald Reagan.

On April 8, 1981, the eighty-eight-year-old Bradley traveled with Kitty to New York to receive the Gold Medal Award from the National Institute of Social Sciences. Minutes after receiving the award, the general was wheeled into an elevator at the 21 Club. He slumped in his wheelchair and died of a blood clot on the brain.

Six days later, a horse-drawn caisson carried Gen. Bradley's body to its resting place in Arlington National Cemetery. Actor Bob Hope was among the celebrities and political leaders who walked in the procession. At the graveside, the old infantry song "Dog Face Soldier" was played with enthusiasm. It was a fitting remembrance for the old soldier whose concern for his troops had earned him the nickname of the "GI's General."

The New York Times reported that the congregation prayed in one theme, "'Time like an ever rolling stone bears all its sons away.' Then the Army Chorus sounded the second theme in the form of the 'West Point Hymn,' sung for the tactician and teacher who graduated with the class of 1915."[202]

Shortly after the general's death, army veteran Ellis O. Butler shared his memory of a chance encounter with Bradley in Boston after the war, with the El Paso Times:

> We had our fill of what we considered to be arrogant, overbearing high brass, eager to impress us with their own self-importance. But Omar Bradley was different—plain, soft-spoken, considerate, yet a brilliant strategist, and a leader we respected and admired. The combat GIs considered him one of us. . . .
>
> Suddenly I looked up and saw coming down the avenue towards me, an Army passenger car, bearing the flag and stars designating it to be the car of a general officer. And riding in the car, to my surprise and delight—General Omar Bradley! He was accompanied by several bemedalled aides and seemed as bored and out of place as I myself was feeling. Without thinking, I grinned and waved to him, forgetting completely that what I should be doing was saluting him. When General Bradley saw me, to him just another one of a million soldiers, he suddenly grinned, too, pointed to my Spearhead Armored Division Patch, and waved back to me![203]

On May 3, 1983, a bronze likeness of General Dwight D. Eisenhower, standing nine feet tall on a pedestal of red granite, was dedicated on the plain at West Point. Facing northwest, the likeness of Eisenhower was cast by Robert L. Dean Jr., a member of the Class of 1953. Present at the dedication ceremony were three members of the class of 1915: James Van Fleet, George J. Richards, and Jake Meneely.

Richards, a Pennsylvanian, graduated sixth and entered the Corps of Engineers. He participated in the Punitive Expedition, served as an instructor at the Academy, and held various posts in military districts across the United States. In 1941, he was named chief of the budget division and budget officer of the War Department, holding this key administrative position throughout World War II. He later served in a similar capacity with the Department of Defense and became the first comptroller of the army, managing wartime budgets totaling more than $160 billion. He retired in 1953 with the rank of major general and died in October 1984 at the age of ninety-three.[204]

Meneely, who had retired more than twenty years earlier, accepted an invitation to return to the army during World War II and commanded the Watervliet Arsenal in New York. With the rank of lieutenant colonel, he retired again in 1945. His son, John K. Meneely Jr., a Yale-educated physician and expert skier, had deployed to Italy during the war with the now famous 10th Mountain Division.

The younger Meneely witnessed the horrors of combat during the bloody fighting in the mountains of northern Italy and returned home to his family and private practice in Connecticut a changed man. Haunted by his wartime experiences, particularly the death of his best friend a week before hostilities ceased, he tried to cope with post-traumatic stress disorder (PTSD), turning to alcohol and barbiturates. One evening in 1963, he drove to his office, locked the door from the inside, and committed suicide, as much a casualty of war as any soldier who died in battle.

In Middletown, Connecticut, in 2013, Meneely's Jr.'s daughters, Grammy-nominated composer Sarah Meneely-Kyder and poet Nancy Fitz-Hugh Meneely, premiered their dramatic oratorio *Letter from Italy, 1944*, based on their father's correspondence from the frontline during World War II. The production is a tribute to John Meneely Jr.'s service and sacrifice, calling attention to the ageless emotional struggles faced by countless soldiers returning from war. Lieutenant Colonel Jake Meneely died in 1985 at the age of ninety-four.

For James Van Fleet, the completion of his fact-finding mission to the Far East meant some time to relax at his Florida ranch. He became more involved with the family businesses, including real estate development, citrus growing, and cattle ranching. He remained quite active, although a cancerous prostate gland was surgically removed in late 1954. He continued to write articles that praised a strong stance against the spread of communism and criticized the Washington bureaucracy for a perceived emphasis on NATO and Europe at the expense of military preparedness in Asia.

In 1956, Van Fleet traveled to Fort Benning to address a gathering of students in the Advanced Infantry Officers' Course. He told the audience that following his graduation from the same course in 1928, he had been deemed "not suited for further military education." He then noted wryly that the remainder of his army career had somewhat proven that assessment incorrect. He remarked, "Do your duty, stay with your soldiers, sharpen your fighting skills. If you are deserving, promotions will eventually come."[205]

A southern Democrat, Van Fleet nevertheless supported his classmate Eisenhower for president, organizing "Democrats for Eisenhower" during the 1956 campaign. Years later, he recalled saying, "I love that man. I would do anything for him, anything he asked."[206]

Van Fleet traveled widely, visiting Nationalist China, numerous countries in the Middle East, and the Mediterranean, and he returned to Greece to a hero's welcome. He was instrumental in the formation of the Korea Society, fostering good relations between the United States and South Korea, and became its first president in 1957. In 1960, a statue of the general was unveiled at the Korean Military Academy.

The following year, Van Fleet was asked by President John F. Kennedy to return to active duty for a brief period, and he served as a special consultant to Secretary of the Army Elvis Stahr. He assessed the capabilities of the army's Special Forces and the reserve units then on active duty. During seven months of touring bases and observing training, he was in his element among the soldiers on the rifle range and in the field. Completing his report, in which he praised the Special Forces and the spirit of the Reserve units he visited and warned that the demands of the Cold War were quite different from those of World War II, Van Fleet submitted his report in the spring of 1962 and returned to civilian life.

Throughout his retirement, Van Fleet remained close to his West Point classmates and was an active supporter of the Academy. He was honored by the University of Florida for his service there and was recognized during the 1973 football game between Florida and instate rival Florida State. In his eighties, the general remained active and lived quietly on his beloved ranch. He considered writing his memoirs; however, several attempts made little progress beyond some notes and an outline of content. The general did grant a series of interviews with an army officer, which were recorded in the spring of 1973.

In January 1984, Helen Van Fleet died of heart failure just as the immediate family returned from a two-week Caribbean cruise. In November, the general married sixty-five-year-old Virginia Skinner-Higgins Wells, whom he had known through the Korea Society. Tragically, she died in April 1986. At the end of the year, Gen. Van Fleet penned a heartfelt letter:

> My dearest friends and classmates of 1915, USMA: We all know that our Class was much more than just "the Class the stars fell upon." We were one fully united and that included every loving wife. I remember my Helen who stated to me that in the early days, and always to her very last. Yes, we are one happy Class. Det tells me that only three of our graduates are left—Vernon Evans, Det Ellis and Van Fleet. We still have with us many of our classmates' dear widows. . . . God bless them all. Still bright in my memories are some of the early meetings, when even Ike, along with Dad Herrick, the goat of the Class, would sit at the piano and lead us all in our WP songs. Happy days they were, and will remain so to the very end. Thank all of you for the lovely days my Helen & I enjoyed at all the meetings we attended. With the Greatest possible appreciation, and love, Van.[207]

In early 1991 Van Fleet wrote, "I am well and here on the ranch keeping an eye on my wild turkeys, deer and gators. Most of my groves were lost in last winter's freeze, and I don't intend on replanting anytime soon. Haven't made any trips lately, as, at 98, traveling is just too difficult. My grandson, James A Van Fleet III, is here with me from CO Springs and we keep fairly busy without ever leaving my desk. Best wishes as always to '15."[208]

On March 19, 1992, Freedom Park in the small town of Polk City, Florida, swelled with 1,500 visitors. The occasion was General Van Fleet's one hundredth birthday. Among those attending the ceremonies were twenty-three current West Point cadets. Several officers of his old 8th Infantry command were there. The 24th Infantry Division band played during the ceremonies, and the Golden Knights, the army's precision parachute team, dropped in for the observance. University of Florida football coach Steve Spurrier presented the general with a Florida Hall of Fame watch. The South Korean military attaché, Maj. Gen. Kwang Duk Han, attended, and congratulatory letters from President George Bush and Joint Chiefs Chairman Gen. Colin Powell were read.[209]

Cadet James Ward commented, "Everything that we aspire to be, he's already done. It's the epitome of the Long Gray Line."[210]

Since the mid-1980s, the general had suffered a series of strokes. To get around, he became more and more dependent on a wheelchair. In and out of hospitals during the last six months of his life, the general passed away in his sleep on September 23, 1992. Following the funeral in the chapel at Fort Myer, Virginia, Gen. James Van Fleet was buried in Arlington National Cemetery.

Major General Joseph McChristian, Van Fleet's son-in-law, delivered the eulogy, remarking, "With great self-confidence, contagious enthusiasm and common sense, he instilled in his football players, and in his soldiers, American and foreign, the Will to Win."[211]

Through the decades, several secretaries and scribes kept the members of the class of 1915 informed, writing updates and newsletter columns and maintaining the common thread of information as the officers were scattered across the globe in war and peace. The last of these was Det Ellis, whose service during World War II included fourteen months in various posts in England and two years in the office of the Quartermaster General as deputy director for contract adjustment, supervising all contracts and arranging for their termination after V-J Day. In 1946, he was transferred to Germany, and during the Berlin Airlift two years later he served as commanding officer of the European Quartermaster Depot. After thirty-five years of active duty, Ellis retired from the army in 1950.

Five years later, Ellis began devoting considerable time to the correspondence of the class, writing its newsletter and forwarding copies for inclusion in *Assembly* and working to make arrangements for reunions. As the ranks of the class thinned, he became a resource for widows and other survivors dealing with matters ranging from pensions to Social Security and military protocol. In May 1985, he traveled to West Point to attend the seventieth class reunion in company with the widows and adult children of several classmates. In October 1990, at the age of one hundred, he became the oldest living graduate of the United States Military Academy, and with the death of James Van Fleet he was the last surviving member of the class of 1915.

On March 12, 1991, scores of family members and friends stopped by Det Ellis's home in Chevy Chase, Maryland, to wish him a happy 101st birthday. His daily routine included making his own breakfast and compiling letters from family members and friends of his classmates to glean tidbits of information for the newsletter.

"For his classmates, especially, Colonel Ellis had an enduring admiration," wrote Philip A. Farris in a tribute that appeared in *Assembly*. "An example of this respect was shown in his determination to attend the funeral of General of the Army Omar Bradley. He drove 18 hours straight through alone from Florida to Washington, D.C., at the age of 91 to pay his personal respects to an honored classmate."[212]

Two years later, Ellis reported in the newsletter, "Your scribe recently had the pleasure of attending a Thanksgiving dinner with family, including all 6 of his great-grandchildren, ages 5 to 20. Your scribe still walks outdoors 2½ miles each day."[213]

Colonel Ellis died on January 22, 1995, at the age of 104. Following a service in the chapel at Fort Myer, he was buried at Arlington National Cemetery, where so many of his classmates and comrades had already gone to their rest. Many of his papers and other items were donated to the Eisenhower Presidential Library.

The last member of the West Point class of 1915 passed into history nearly eighty years after that long-ago graduation on the plain. Young and vibrant, those men of pride and promise could scarcely have comprehended the momentous events of the future, events in which they had been caught up and compelled to play varying roles, and which they came to influence like no other collective body of military or political men in human history.

The passage of time provides opportunity for discussion and evaluation. Some may say that Eisenhower, Bradley, McNarney, Van Fleet, and the others were simply living in extraordinary times, chasing Pancho Villa, fighting in the trenches of World War I, commanding legions on land and in the air during World War II, engaging the enemy in Korea at the inception of the Cold War, and ultimately ascending to the highest of postwar military and civilian offices.

Perhaps there is some truth in this assessment. After all, these were men, intensely human, imperfect, and flawed. Some of them disappointed. Some died young. Others faded from view. But 59 out of 164 wore stars.

So much more sublime it is to affirm that mere men are capable of rising beyond the ordinary, the mundane, and the routine when times and circumstances require it. The classic conundrum of whether the times make the man—in this case the men—or vice versa will forever be the subject of debate. Such is the nature of history, reflecting the fates of men and nations.

Comparisons have been made between the class of 1915 and the Class of 1846, which produced twenty generals, North and South, who fought in the Civil War. The Class of 1976 has yielded at least thirty-three active and retired general officers from among 855 graduates. These are distinguished men in their own right; however, never before or since has another group of US Military Academy graduates achieved with such breadth and on such a grand scale as have the graduates of 1915.

One conclusion is inescapable. The soldiers of the Class the Stars Fell On are worthy of remembering, with a legacy true to the West Point motto of "Duty, Honor, Country"—not only in theory, but also in the magnificence of their deeds.

ENDNOTES

1. The Eisenhower Foundation (Abilene, KS), www.eisenhowerfoundation.net.

2. Relman Morin, *Dwight D. Eisenhower: A Gauge of Greatness* (New York: Associated Press, 1969), 20–22.

3. The Kansas Historical Society (Topeka, KS), www.kansasmemory.org.

4. Carlo D'Este, *Eisenhower: A Soldier's Life* (New York: Henry Holt, 2002), 55–58.

5. Alden Hatch, *General Ike: A Biography of Dwight D. Eisenhower* (Chicago: Consolidated Book Publishers, 1944), 25–27.

6. Omar Bradley and Clay Blair, *A General's Life* (New York: Simon and Schuster, 1983), 23-26.

7. Ibid., 28.

8. Ibid., 28–29.

9. Peter Lyon, *Eisenhower: Portrait of the Hero* (Boston-Toronto: Little, Brown and Company, 1974), 42–43.

10. Merle Miller, *Ike the Soldier: As They Knew Him* (New York: G. P. Putnam's Sons, 1987).

11. Paul F. Braim, *The Will to Win* (Annapolis: Naval Institute Press, 2001), 5–6.

12. Ibid., 10.

13. Courtesy of the Cameron County Historical Society.

14. Ibid.

15. Ibid.

16. Phillip S. Meilinger, *Hubert R. Harmon: Airman, Officer, Father of the Air Force Academy* (Golden, CO: Fulcrum Group, 2009), 14.

17. *New York Times*, March 3, 1906.

18. George Kleine Collection, Library of Congress.

19. "Army Buys New Airplanes," National Museum of the United States Air Force, April 2009, www.nationalmuseum.af.mil/factsheets/factsheet.asp?id=668.

20. Kenneth S. Davis, *Soldier of Democracy: A Biography of Dwight Eisenhower* (Garden City, N.Y.: Doubleday, 1946), 129–130.

21. Miller, *Ike the Soldier*, 27.

22. Robert Charlwood Richardson, *An Intimate Picture of the National Military Academy and of the Life of the Cadet* (New York: G. P. Putnam's Sons, 1917), 32–24.

23. Robert C. Carroll, "West Point, a Century Ago, 1911–1920: An Amazing Decade," *Military Collector & Historian, Journal of the Company of Military Historians*, Vol. 65, No. 2 (Summer 2013).

24. Robert Charlwood Richardson, *West Point: An Intimate Picture of the National Military Academy and of the Life of the Cadet*, 33.

25. Col. Christopher D. Reed, "'The Old Army' 1898–1941: A Blueprint for the Future?" (US Army War College, Carlisle Barracks, PA), 2012.

26. *New York Times*, August 4, 1911.

27. Dwight D. Eisenhower, *At Ease: Stories I Tell to Friends* (Garden City, NY: Doubleday, 1967), 5.

28. Richardson, *West Point*, 59–60.

29. Ibid., 79.

30. Ibid., 60.

31. Ibid., 87.

32. Eisenhower, *At Ease*, 6.

33. Ibid., 8.

34. D'Este, *Eisenhower*, 66.

35. Eisenhower, *At Ease*, 6.

36. Miller, *Ike the Soldier*, 18–20.

37. "From Plebe to President," *Collier's*, June 10, 1955.

38. Eisenhower, *At Ease*, 18.

39. Bradley and Blair, *A General's Life*, 33–34.

40. Ibid., 31.

41. Braim, *The Will to Win*, 12.

42. *Howitzer* yearbook, 1915, 191.

43. usfa.edu/df/dfh/docs/Harmon52.pdf.

44. Miller, *Ike the Soldier*, 31.

45. Ibid.

46. Greg Botelho, "Roller-coaster life of Indian icon, sports' first star," CNN.com, July 14, 2004.

47. Miller, *Ike the Soldier*, 34.

48. D'Este, *Eisenhower*, 68.

49. Bradley and Blair, *A General's Life*, 31–33.

50. Ibid., 34.

51. Tom Coyne, the Associated Press, October 26, 2013.

52. Braim, *The Will to Win*, 16.

53. Ibid., 17.

54. Miller, *Ike the Soldier*, 31.

55. Dwight D. Eisenhower, *In Review: Pictures I've Kept, A concise Pictorial "Autobiography"* (Garden City, N.Y.: Doubleday, 1969), 17.

56. *New York Times*, May 3, 1915.

57. *New York Sun*, June 6, 1915.

58. bellsouthpwp.net/r/u/ruiz_b/luisraulesteves/luis_raul_esteves.htm.

59. Miller, *Ike the Soldier*, 45.

60. Eisenhower, *In Review*, 18.

61. Eisenhower, *In Review*, 18.

62. Miller, *Ike the Soldier*, 42–43.

63. Eisenhower, *In Review*, 26.

64. Bradley and Blair, *A General's Life*, 38–39.

65. Ibid., 44–45.

66. Ibid., 46.

67. Ibid., 43.

68. *Fiftieth Annual Report of the Association of Graduates of the United States Military Academy at West Point, New York, June 10, 1919*, 53–55.

69. www.worldwar1.com/dbc/ow_7.htm.

70. Braim, *The Will to Win*, 34–35.

71. Angela Serratore, "Past Imperfect: The Football Star and the Wrath of His Would-Be Bride," *Smithsonian*, September 4, 2013.

72. General Joseph C. McNarney, interview by Forrest C. Pogue, U. S. Grant Hotel (San Diego, CA), February 2, 1966. Notes 110N, Copy 2, courtesy of the George C. Marshall Foundation (Lexington, VA).

73. N. R. Grist, "Pandemic Influenza 1918," *British Medical Journal*, December 22–29, 1979, 1632–1633.

74. "Principal Facts Concerning The First Transcontinental Army Motor Transport Expedition, Washington to San Francisco, July 7 to September 6, 1919," Dwight D. Eisenhower Presidential Library, Museum, and Boyhood Home, Abilene, Kansas.

75. Lyon, *Eisenhower*, 58–59.

76. Eisenhower, *At Ease*, 185–187.

77. Ibid., 200–201.

78. Ibid., 208–209.

79. John Wukovits, *Eisenhower* (New York: Palgrave Macmillan, 2006), 41–43.

80. Eisenhower, *At Ease*, 214.

81. Wukovits, *Eisenhower*, 46.

82. Ibid., 44.

83. *Sixty-Ninth Annual Report of the Association of Graduates of the United States Military Academy at West Point, New York, June 13, 1938*, 273–278.

84. Bradley and Blair, *A General's Story*, 47.

85. Ibid., 55–56.

86. Ibid., 63.

87. Ibid., 83.

88. Ibid., 94.

89. Braim, *The Will to Win*, 47.

90. Dewitt S. Copp, *Frank M. Andrews: Marshall's Airman* (Washington: Air Force History and Museums Program, 2003).

91. McNarney, interview by Pogue, February 2, 1966.

92. Duane Colt Denfield, "Essay No. 9764," Historylink.org.

93. *Fifty-first Annual Report of the Association of Graduates of the United States Military Academy at West Point, New York, June 10, 1920*, 50–51.

94. Duane Colt Denfield, "Major Alexander P. Cronkhite is Shot and Killed during Training Exercise at Fort Lewis on October 25, 1918," *Historylink. org*, March 17, 2011.

95. Department of the Army, Office of the Judge Advocate General, courtesy of Marilee Meyer, West Point Association of Graduates.

96. *Seventy-First Annual Report of the Association of Graduates of the United States Military Academy at West Point, New York, June 10, 1940,* 72–75.

97. *Fiftieth Annual Report of the Association of Graduates of the United States Military Academy at West Point, New York, June 10, 1919,* 202.

98. *Fifty-Eighth Annual Report of the Association of Graduates of the United States Military Academy at West Point, New York, June 13, 1927,* 107–108.

99. *Seventy-First Annual Report of the Association of Graduates of the United States Military Academy at West Point, New York, June 10, 1940,* 294.

100. Eisenhower, *In Review,* 40.

101. Ibid., 42.

102. Wukovits, *Eisenhower,* 62.

103. D'Este, *Eisenhower,* 282.

104. Miller, *Ike the Soldier,* 359.

105. Ibid., 362.

106. Eisenhower, *In Review,* 45–46.

107. D'Este, *Eisenhower,* 307.

108. Bradley and Blair, *A General's Life,* 96-97.

109. Ibid., 97.

110. Ibid., 110.

111. Ibid., 113.

112. McNarney, interview by Pogue, February 2, 1966.

113. Ibid.

114. "Attack Upon Pearl Harbor by Japanese Armed Forces," 77th Congress, Senate Document No. 159, January 23, 1942, 20–21.

115. Forrest C. Pogue and George C. Marshall, *Ordeal and Hope: 1939–1942* (New York: Viking Press, 1965), 289.

116. McNarney, interview by Pogue, February 2, 1966.

117. Pogue and Marshall, *Ordeal and Hope,* 292.

118. McNarney, interview by Pogue, February 2, 1966.

119. Ibid.

120. Ibid.

121. Gen. Henry S. Aurand, transcript of interview with Major William O. Morrison, Abilene, Kansas, April 21, 1974, 2.

122. Association of Graduates of the United States Military Academy, *Assembly*, Winter 1962, 74–75.

123. Ibid., 6.

124. Ibid., 7.

125. Ibid.

126. Stephen E. Ambrose, *D-Day, June 6, 1944: The Climactic Battle of World War II* (New York: Simon & Schuster, 1994), 132.

127. Braim, *The Will to Win*, 62–67.

128. *Assembly*, September 1975, 119.

129. *Assembly*, January 1949, 18.

130. Peggy Hocker Small, freepages.military.rootsweb.ancestry.com/~cacunithistories/65th_Arty_Muster.html.

131. Edward M. Coffman, "My Room Mate . . . Is Dwight Eisenhower . . . ," *American Heritage*, Volume 24, Issue 3 (April 1973).

132. Eisenhower, *At Ease*, 263.

133. *Assembly*, July 1956, 84.

134. Dwight Eisenhower, *Crusade in Europe* (Garden City, NY: Doubleday, 1948), 156–157.

135. Bradley and Blair, *A General's Life*, 136.

136. Ibid., 150.

137. Ibid., 156–157.

138. D'Este, *Eisenhower*, 439.

139. Bradley and Blair, *A General's Life*, 207.

140. Miller, *Ike the Soldier*, 566.

141. Ibid., 567.

142. Eisenhower, *In Review*, 59.

143. Miller, *Ike the Soldier*, 603.

144. *Time*, June 19, 1944.

145. Miller, *Ike the Soldier*, 603.

146. *Time*, June 19, 1944.

147. *Assembly*, (October 1949, 43–44.

148. Bradley and Blair, *A General's Life*, 223–224.

149. Eisenhower, *Crusade in Europe*, 249.

150. Ibid., 250.

151. United States Army, www.army.mil/d-day/message.html.

152. Bradley and Blair, *A General's Life*, 249–251.

153. Ambrose, *D-Day*, 278–279.

154. Braim, *The Will to Win*, 89.

155. Bradley and Blair, *A General's Life*, 263.

156. Braim, *The Will to Win*, 93–94.

157. Michael E. Haskew, "Last Stand in Leipzig," *World War II Quarterly*, Fall 2013, 30.

158. Eisenhower, *Crusade in Europe*, 426.

159. D'Este, *Eisenhower*, 704.

160. *Assembly*, January 1950, 48.

161. Gene Eric Salecker, "The Los Baños Raid," *WWII History*, January 2013, 2–10.

162. Ibid., 10.

163. *Assembly*, January 1946, 20.

164. Eisenhower, *Crusade in Europe*, 432.

165. Miller, *Ike the Soldier*, 781.

166. Kenneth Davis, *Soldier of Democracy: A Biography of Dwight Eisenhower* (Garden City, N.Y.: Doubleday, 1946), 545–549.

167. Bob Diamond, "Gen. Joseph McNarney and the Talmud," *The Aventura News*, South Miami, Florida, September 15, 2011.

168. McNarney, interview by Pogue, Interview, February 2, 1966.

169. Richard F. Pourade, *City of the Dream* (La Jolla, CA: Copley Press, 1977), www.sandiegohistory.org.

170. *Assembly*, October 1947, 20.

171. pabook.libraries.psu.edu/palitmap/bios/McNarney_Joseph.html.

172. *Cameron County Press*, February 9, 1972.

173. Lyon, *Eisenhower*, 395.

174. Wukovits, *Eisenhower*, 170.

175. Eisenhower, *At Ease*, 329.

176. Dwight D. Eisenhower Presidential Library, Museum, and Boyhood Home (Abilene, KS).

177. Eisenhower to Swede Hazlett, July 21, 1953, Dwight D. Eisenhower Presidential Library, Museum, and Boyhood Home (Abilene, KS).

178. Lisa Grunwald and Stephen J. Adler, eds., *Letters of the Century: America 1900–1999* (New York: The Dial Press, 1999), 403–404.

179. Wukovits, *Eisenhower*, 174.

180. Eisenhower, *In Review*, 234.

181. *Assembly*, July 1955, 37.

182. Bradley and Blair, *A General's Life*, 447.

183. "Omar Nelson Bradley: General of the Army," Arlington National Cemetery, www.arlingtoncemetery.net/omarnels.htm.

184. Bradley and Blair, *A General's Life*, 657.

185. Braim, *The Will to Win*, 156–157.

186. Ibid., 170.

187. Ibid., 219.

188. Ibid., 222.

189. Ibid., 239.

190. Bradley and Blair, *A General's Story*, 475.

191. Braim, *The Will to Win*, 249.

192. Ibid., 217–225.

193. *The Taro Leaf*, April 1951, 2–3.

194. *Assembly*, Winter 1971, 115–116.

195. George C. Kenney, *General Kenney Reports* (New York: Duell, Sloane and Pearce, 1949), 340.

196. Meilinger, *Hubert R. Harmon*, 136–137.

197. *Assembly*, November 1990, 14–15.

198. Lyon, *Eisenhower*, 888.

199. *Time*, June 11, 1965.

200. Wukovits, *Eisenhower*, 177.

201. Bradley and Blair, *A General's Life*, 667–670.

202. Francis X. Clines, *New York Times*, April 15, 1981.

203. Ellis O. Butler, "A GI's Late Salute to General Bradley," *El Paso Times*, 1981, www.3ad.com/history/wwll/memoirs.pages/butler.htm.

204. *The Morning Call*, October 2, 1984.

205. Braim, *The Will to Win*, 345.

206. Ibid., 345.

207. *Assembly*, December 1986, 57.

208. *Assembly*, January 1991, 46.

209. Braim, T*he Will to Win*, 365–366.

210. *Assembly*, July 1992, 11.

211. Braim, *The Will to Win*, 371.

212. *Assembly*, May 1991, 4–7.

213. *Assembly*, March 1993, 63.

SELECTED BIBLIOGRAPHY

Bradley, Omar N. and Clay Blair, *A General's Life*. New York: Simon and Schuster, 1983.

Braim, Paul F., *The Will to Win*. Annapolis, Maryland: Naval Institute Press, 2001.

Davis, Kenneth S., *Soldier of Democracy: A Biography of Dwight Eisenhower*. Garden City, New York: Doubleday & Company, Inc., 1946.

D'Este, Carlo, *Eisenhower: A Soldier's Life*. New York: Henry Holt and Company, LLC, 2002.

Eisenhower, David, *Eisenhower: At War, 1943–1945*. New York: Random House, 1986.

Eisenhower, Dwight D., *At Ease: Stories I Tell to Friends*. Garden City, New York: Doubleday & Company, Inc., 1967.

Eisenhower, Dwight D., *Crusade in Europe*. Garden City, New York: Doubleday & Company, Inc., 1948.

Eisenhower, Dwight D., *In Review: Pictures I've Kept, A Concise Pictorial "Autobiography"*. Garden City, New York: Doubleday & Company, Inc., 1969.

Eisenhower, Dwight D., *Letters to Mamie*. Garden City, New York: Doubleday & Company, Inc., 1978.

Grunwald, Lisa and Stephen J. Adler, editors, *Letters of the Century: America 1900–1999*. New York: The Dial Press, Random House, 1999.

Hatch, Alden, *General Ike: A Biography of Dwight D. Eisenhower*. Chicago: Consolidated Book Publishers, Henry Holt and Company, Inc., 1944.

Lyon, Peter, *Eisenhower: Portrait of the Hero*. Boston and Toronto: Little, Brown and Company, 1974.

Meilinger, Phillip S., *Hubert R. Harmon: Airman, Officer, Father of the Air Force Academy*. Golden, Colorado: Fulcrum Group, 2009.

Miller, Merle, *Ike the Soldier: As They Knew Him*. New York: G. P. Putnam's Sons, 1987.

Morin, Relman, *Dwight D. Eisenhower: A Gauge of Greatness*. The Associated Press, 1969.

Uldrich, Jack, *Soldier, Statesman, Peacemaker, Leadership Lessons from George C. Marshall.* New York: American Management Association, 2005.

Wukovits, John, *Eisenhower.* New York: Palgrave Macmillan, 2006.

———, compiled under direction of the Joint Committee on Printing, *Memorial Services in the Congress of the United States and Tributes in Eulogy of Dwight David Eisenhower, Late a President of the United States.* Washington, D.C.: United States Government Printing Office, 1970.

INDEX